Better Angels

– IAN BIRKS –

An environmentally friendly book printed and bound in England by
www.printondemand-worldwide.com

Mixed Sources
Product group from well-managed
forests, and other controlled sources
www.fsc.org Cert no. TT-COC-002641
© 1996 Forest Stewardship Council

FSC

PEFC
PEFC/16-33-415

PEFC Certified
This product is
from sustainably
managed forests
and controlled
sources
www.pefc.org

This book is made entirely of chain-of-custody materials

Ian Birks

http://www.fast-print.net/bookshop

BETTER ANGELS
Copyright © Ian Birks 2015

A catalogue record for this book is available from the British Library

ISBN 978-178456-197-0

First published 2015 by
FASTPRINT PUBLISHING
Peterborough, England.

Contents

FOREWORD

Dr Diana Hulbert BSc MBBS FRCS FCEM

Diana is a Consultant in Emergency Medicine with a special interest in vulnerable patients in the Emergency Department.

I have known the Birks family for nearly 20 years. Our children have grown up together and we have shared the joys and challenges of parenthood. As a family they are a formidable team who stick together through thick and thin. They love, support and tease each other through everything.

My working life as an EM Consultant is rewarding, challenging and occasionally devastating. I cannot imagine doing anything else. The dignity and fortitude with which patients and their families deal with exceptional circumstances amazes me.

I wish there were a world where people would not walk through the doors of the ED in pain, frightened, confused and needing solace. That is a naïve wish, so that is why there are teams of dedicated healthcare professionals, like the one I am a proud part of, who are willing and able to step up to help others.

One of my nightmares is when my working and personal lives collide. I was not involved in George's treatment but I have treated a number of cases of meningitis and I lived every step with Siobhan and Ian, George's Parents.

This book captures what it was like for George and his family in a way that feels real and visceral. It is an honest account of a life-threatening illness and illustrates what it is like to suffer, cope, recover and survive.

It reminds us that there are Better Angels in the world who make the world better for all of us.

WELL DONE IAN, SIOBHAN, GEORGE AND ALL YOUR SUPPORT TEAM

DXX

PROLOGUE

The droplet-borne bacteria[1] settled onto the warm, moist lining at the back of George's throat. It is a tiny yet sophisticated organism, with a singular efficiency. It voraciously hummed its mantra, *'in, split, rip, secrete'* in a cruel parody of George's favourite Fat Boy Slim song *'Eat Sleep Rave Repeat'*. Once in George's bloodstream, it was whisked to all parts of his body to wreak havoc in so many ways. In the next two hours, endotoxins secreted by the bacterium would shock his immune system into meltdown. A torrent of cytokines would be released, causing massive dilation of his blood vessels, capillaries to leak fluid, and blood pressure to plummet. Tissues starved of oxygen would start to die. His heart would not have enough to pump and misfire. George's struggle had begun, but he did not know it yet.

---

[1] The most common microorganisms in bacterial meningitis are S pneumoniae, N meningitidis, and L monocytogenes. From http://emedicine.medscape.com/article

PART 1: INVASION

We have found ourselves rich in goods, but ragged in spirit; reaching with magnificent precision for the moon but falling into raucous discord on earth. We are caught in war, wanting peace. We are torn by division, wanting unity. We see around us empty lives, wanting fulfilment ... To a crisis of the spirit, we need an answer of the spirit. To find that answer, we must look within ourselves. When we listen to '**the better angels of our nature**', we find that they celebrate the simple things, the basic things – such as goodness, decency, love, kindness.

US Presidential Address[2]

20th January 1969

---

[2] Full transcript is given by http://bartleby.com/124/pres58.html

Chapter 1

24th April 2013. The Day of Infection

07:30

"GEEEOOORRRGE – stop bibbling about and FLAMING GET A MOVE ON, WILL YOU! Why do I always have to be on your case to get out of the door on time? You are fourteen, you should take responsibility – so step up, don't just stand there staring at me." Ian's rant had wound up to full momentum, crossing the line from chivvying along to seriously pissed off. His frustration made him assassinate George with why he was always late, rather than helping George get out on time.

"You have Athletics Club today – right? So where is your gym bag? Don't tell me you've left it at school again? Go get it – come on!"

OMG, Dad's off on one again. Focus, George – what's he yelling about? I look hard at Dad, trying to take it in, but it's really confusing when he shouts. It's just a wall of noise. I don't know what I'm supposed to be doing, but I must be doing it wrong again. Gym bag – right, now where did I leave it? Have I got Athletics Club today – must check? I root around in the floordrobe in my room – Mum thinks that word is so funny. Bugger – one trainer, that's so unfair. Half-found won't stop Dad's hissy fit. Ha! Found you, Mr. Gym Kit, that was lucky – and the other trainer, even better. I scoot down the stairs, which is fast for me but not fast enough for Dad, clearly. The jarring of the stairs makes my legs feel really stiff and sore – like I've been playing football. I hate football and haven't played for at least a year. I must tell Mum later.

Ian watched George descend the stairs towards him, gym bag in hand. He hesitated to bawl him out for his lack of urgency when they were already late. The time it took to search for words that did not involve *'for fuck's sake, George'*, nor delivering them at temple-throbbing volume, was just enough to release the valve of his frustration. With nothing to say, Ian just looked at his youngest son, aged a young fourteen. Blonde hair sticking up at the back from his double crown, shoulders like an aspirin bottle, lacking the muscle covering that full-on adolescence would bring, his shirt untucked over nondescript grey school trousers hanging from pencil hips. George had the huge blue eyes of his mother and the same slightly worried expression when not smiling. Ian felt guilty at his flash of anger. Being angry with George was like kicking a puppy, as he made an earnest effort to do his best even if sometimes he came up short. He operated to a different version of time to the rest of the universe, with double the minutes in every hour. That universe also had none of the complexity of multiple instructions and kept him mostly insulated from the harsh realities of deadlines, deliverables and dependencies. Ian knew that his big frame and assertiveness allowed him to bully George without trying to. He had to accommodate George's eccentricities, not pick at them. He had to try harder, he chided himself, and meet George more than halfway. The patience and understanding did not come easily.

08:00

Once George was off on the school run with Siobhan, Ian left for work as normal. No trips overseas this week – which was unusual, but welcome. At the first hold-up on the M25, he scanned his weekend emails – no dramas, which meant that the tension in his neck from hectoring George lessened slightly. He was straight into work mode, focused on the day ahead and gave no further thought to his exchange with his youngest son. His caffeine-energised brain tripped through what might be for supper (he liked to plan ahead), *why that plum would not GET OFF HIS BACK BUMPER?* and the best way to pitch a strategy to his uninterested boss in the States.

Middle son Fred, in Lower Sixth, checked that his reflection was looking good in the glass wall of the bus stop. All good. He listened to 'Thunderstruck' by AC/DC on his Google Nexus 4 while he waited for his beloved Number One-Eleven red double-decker. He also loved his phone, acquired a few weeks back through a dodgy deal with Dad. Both knew full well that Dad was a soft touch and that Fred was a crook with his *have I got a deal for you* schemes. But they enjoyed the back-and-forth, playing up Fred's cat-got the-cream smile and Dad's mock outrage at being ripped off.

Ben, the eldest and in Upper Sixth, was already on the train to Wimbledon and looking fierce. English Literature had always been his favourite subject, but not lately. The 'wake up and smell the coffee' style of his teacher had broken his confidence. He got the tough love thing to help prepare for the graft and precision needed for top marks, but it was not working for him, *yet*. Although now operating from within his shell, Ben was determined as ever to show her what he could do, and it was written all over his face. Like his father, thoughts of home, nutty George and a mundane morning would not enter his head for the rest of the day – why should they?

08:45

Siobhan dropped George at school as normal, watching him in her rear-view mirror as he ambled off down the path to his form room. She thought he had been a bit quiet over breakfast and more so in the car, with none of his DJ-ing through the radio channels to find something that was not old people's music. She struggled to pinpoint what his quietness could mean. To her, George was more complex than her two older sons. Complex in the sense of 'less predictable', with a narrower range of behaviours, some of them completely from left-field and so more surprising at times. Mostly the surprises were welcome ones that coloured George's quirkiness, but sometimes she wished that reading him took less effort so that she got it right more often.

Whilst driving on autopilot, her thoughts meandered from George to the day ahead. The 'old people' comment from George sparked the image of Mollie looking up at her from the story book on her desk the day before. Although she mustn't have class favourites, Mollie made her break her professional rule. Mollie was not only adorable with blonde curls, button face and dimpled smile, but she had such an earnest, direct manner that you could tell exactly what she was thinking and feeling. So there was nowhere to hide when Mollie had focused her quizzical gaze on Siobhan.

"Mrs. Birks, are you old?"

Siobhan had cringed, only too aware where this might be heading, but she knew that there was a thought in Mollie's six-year old head that would come out.

"That's an interesting question, Mollie, why do you ask?"

"Well, you've got grey hair."

"You're right, Mollie and thank you for mentioning it." The nuance of gentle sarcasm and gritted-teeth smile was lost on Mollie, whose confusion remained all over her face.

"But you move about a lot and giggle a lot, but old ladies don't do that."

Siobhan chuckled inwardly, remembering how she had burst out laughing and scooped Mollie into a hug. Poor Mollie had been even more confused – she still had not got her question answered and was bound to bring it up again.

09:00

That was horrible. I spit the coating of dribble and vomit into the toilet bowl. My mouth feels acidy and gritty and my head spins as I stand up too quickly in the cramped cubicle. I rest my sweaty forehead against the cool wall to make the spinning stop.

First lesson bell – I haven't got long.

I haven't felt this pants in ages – my guts ache with a post-chunder rawness that feels like I'm dying inside. My own thought seems overly dramatic to me. Maybe this is more than a sore head, as everywhere aches as though I'm dying in the middle of me? This is hell, I don't want to be here. I must tell the School Nurse.

10:00

It had been a good morning for Siobhan so far. The usual, nothing special, but pepped up by thirty little six-year olds desperate to impress her in Games. The view in front of her, however, was far from usual. Siobhan saw a forest of muddy trainers and socked legs, all stuck to the ceiling and jigging about with pent-up energy. Over the swooshing of her blood pulsing in her ears, she could hear the whole class giggling and cheering. She felt her face warming as it turned red with the blood pooling in her head. She knew she was mad to be doing this.

The kids in her charge loved it. They were swept up in the sheer excitement of rushing against the clock and seeing Mrs. Birks do a headstand. The noise they were making was a great release from the normal effort of concentration expected in their lessons.

Siobhan unwrapped herself from her headstand.

"Class 2S, you were brilliant! I said if ALL of you could get changed in less than four minutes then I would do a headstand. Well, there you go. It's important that we keep our promises, otherwise where would we all end up, I ask you?"

Mrs. O'Sullivan, her Teaching Assistant, was chuckling to herself at the back of the classroom, out of sight of the children. She, too, was amazed that Siobhan had done it, but she could see Siobhan had the skill to bring them all back down from the ceiling. This was a great bit of fun which the kids would remember and hopefully not tell their parents. Siobhan saw her at the back.

"I don't know why you're laughing, Mrs. O'Sullivan. When Class 2S get changed in less than two minutes, I seem to remember you promised to do a back flip on the playing fields in front of the Headmistress's window."

They all cheered and turned for Mrs. O'Sullivan's reaction. She had just enough to time to replace the withering look and tongue poke for Siobhan with a benevolent smile of agreement.

Esther, the school secretary, stuck her head around the classroom door, curious about the racket going on, but also to catch Siobhan.

"Mrs. Birks, when you have a mo', can you pop into the office please? I have a message for you."

12:30

It's such a relief to see Mum. She cuddles me – I don't mind as it's only me, Mum and the School Nurse. I smell of sick and I'm sticky with sweat. Poor Mum, that can't have been very nice for her. She bundles me up in the car and we head home. I can finally rest my head, gritting my teeth for every pothole and speed bump. I'll sleep when I get home, that's what I need.

16:15

"It's me, can you talk?"

"Sure, wha...?"

Before Ian could say any more, Siobhan dived in, with the minimum of words loaded with the maximum of information to share her mounting worry, delivered with a face-slap conviction that could not be ignored.

"George isn't right – he's floppy and not responding to me. It's not just a sicky bug."

"What makes you say that?" asked Ian.

"He has these dots on his chest that stay even when you press them – the CLASSIC symptom.[3] I've got to get him seen to."

Siobhan was right – it was a classic symptom that everyone grasps as a lifeline, but it was more a stereotype. It must occur enough to be recognisable, but unreliable for every situation.

---

[3] If you are seriously worried about someone who is ill, don't wait for a rash to appear – get medical help. But if they are already ill and get a new rash or spots, use the Tumbler Test. Press a clear glass tumbler firmly against the rash. If you can see the marks clearly through the glass seek urgent medical help immediately.
http://www.meningitis.org/symptoms

"Okay, okay, you're way ahead of me on this. Look – your worry will not go away unless we act on your instinct. Can you get him to the GP, or even A&E?"Siobhan had already decided and spoken to the GP. Her husband's words just dispelled her one remaining percent of doubt that she was being an overwrought and hysterical mother, although she felt panic rising in her in case her decisive call proved to be right.

"I can get him to the GP in thirty minutes. Please get here, we need you. I'll call, bye."

The line went dead and Ian stared at the display, feeling thrown sideways. The typical male logical response of problem and solution tried to kick in. But with no information and no solution, he felt impotent. At least he could get to where he was needed. He shut down his laptop, asked his PA to cancel his commitments for the rest of the day and headed for the exit early enough to raise a jobsworth's eyebrow. He walked calmly from the building, stopping on the stairs to chat to a colleague about an infuriating client who seemed hell-bent on finding a deal-breaker to fixate on. He did not know that the crescendo of *'in, split, rip, secrete'* was building and if he had, just maybe he would have left the car park in a squeal of spinning tyres.

17:20

It takes all my remaining strength to get out of the car and stand on the pavement outside the surgery. I rest my weight onto the waist-high wall – I can't stand up again without Mum lifting me.

As we go into the doctor's, the muscles in my arms and legs are too heavy. As I sit down I can feel my heart pounding away with a sprinter's power – but I'm sitting, for

Christ's sake. My head hurts like hell and even Mum stroking my temple makes it worse. I just need to keep still, lay my head in Mum's lap. Each breath washes through me with waves sloshing back and forth. I daren't cough in case I jar my head and spray lung fume everywhere. Let it stop, let me burn up, leave me be, leave me alone please ... I beg you.

George leaned over in his seat in the waiting room and laid his head on his mother's lap. Siobhan squirmed, trying to avoid the snippy looks. At any other time, attempted hugging of a teenager or any public show of affection would be fobbed off with a 'you're sooo weird'.

Siobhan re-read the poster on the surgery wall listing the symptoms of meningitis.[4] She felt like Charlotte, an old friend from university, who would never let an exotic affliction pass her by without Googling the full set of symptoms needed to join the stoic sufferers' club. George ticked every box. Ironically, the perfection of the match made Siobhan convinced that her shifted perception was playing her. Her thoughts were interrupted by the receptionist calling them through.

"George Birks please – for Dr. Catherine in Consulting Room 4."

17:20

When George's name was called by the receptionist, Siobhan and George lurched across the short hallway in a dysfunctional three-legged race as she held him up.

---

[4] Download resources and posters from MRF Website

"Hi Mrs. Birks, hello George. I'm Catherine, please come in. I can see George is a bit unsteady; shall we sit him down so I can take a look?"

Catherine was used to the churn of general practice, and cared for many chronically-ill patients every day. But a fourteen-year-old about to keel over was different – the urgently-ill were relatively rare, and demanded her focus.

Siobhan had never met Catherine before, but the doctor's open, engaging face and bright honey-flecked eyes above an easy smile put her at ease. Siobhan could not help but warm to her, like blue hands to a yellow candle. But it was not the face of grandfatherly gravitas that a doctor should have. Siobhan guessed the too-young, too-lightweight, too-girly first impression would have been an issue for some, but it was clear she knew her stuff and her sharpness of mind would show itself. It took two minutes to for Catherine to display the gravitas that some take twenty years to make effortless.

Catherine asked George how he was feeling. After two mumbled replies that she could not catch, she asked him if his head hurt and to hold up fingers one-to-ten depending on how bad the pain was.

I'm sorry. I'll try to say it again. I know what I want to say but I have a chilli-paralysed tongue in my mouth and can't get the words out for you. What is wrong with me? I'm in meltdown here, my face is cold and I ache in all my joints.

You say what? Rate my pain on a scale of 1 to 10? I can do that. I spread all ten fingers in my lap instead of speaking – it's easier. My eyes ask her to please give me something to stop the searing pain in my head.

That scale is pants; it's too detailed. Either 1 or 2 is not worth bothering with, a 5 – ish means gimme some Nurofen, or else it's a 25 and hurts like hell. That is where I am right now, so give me the strongest stuff you have. You do not want to fanny about with this. Mum's ringtone is the way to go. It starts with …

ring ring in a normal voice, then

Ring Ring Ring all crabby and urgent, then

RING RING RING RING in a shouty arsey voice, then

RIIINNG, RIIINNG, RIIIII … WHAAAAAAAAA and his head explodes. That's what my head feels like. Please just give me something for it and let me sleep.

With George sitting in front of her, Catherine looked shocked at what she could see. He was in a bad way; his balance was shot, his responses were slow and lacked coherence, and his skin was grey. She could tell by instinct how sick patients were by how still they stayed. Any rupture in the abdomen, appendicitis or contractions all make the torso immobile. With meningitis, often the head and neck are rigid, partly to reduce any pain from movement but also because the neck muscles become stiff in response to the impending disaster.

Next was the tidal wave of worry coming from his mother and those haunted eyes she would remember. The last jolt dispelling any remaining doubt, setting off alarm bells and threatening to overwhelm her rational thought, was the ten tiny red spots on George's chest that would not go away. Fortunately for George, he drew a doctor like Catherine, sufficiently strong-minded to act on her instinct and not wait for blood tests. With a breeziness that Siobhan could see through, Catherine said, "Mrs. Birks, would you and George mind sitting here whilst I just pop out for a moment – I'll be two minutes."

Her casual tone was a thin pretence. Once outside the closed door of Consulting Room Four, Catherine did two things. First was a call for an ambulance on a 'blues and twos' basis. She did not mean to bark her order to the dispatcher, but it had the effect she wanted. Sue, the practice nurse, heard sharp words and spun towards them, just as Catherine barked at her too.

"Sue, stop what you're doing. I need you to follow my instructions now." Sue was skewered by the intensity in Catherine's eyes and responded immediately. "Get me 2.5g of cefotaxime[5] as an intravenous injection. Single syringe to administer straight away through a cannula[6]. Bring it to Consulting Room Four – come straight in. Listen out for the sirens and bring the ambulance crew straight to me. Please get Dr. Shah to come now and fit the cannula for me, as I can't do it without his supervision."

Catherine returned within thirty seconds, not the two minutes she had promised. One minute later Dr. Shah joined them and fitted the cannula to George's arm, giving sterile access to his veins – he would need it for what was to come. The injection was rammed straight in with no word of explanation to Siobhan or George. Within four minutes, the lighthouse sweep of blue lights coloured the surgery wall.

---

[5] Dose from http://www.drugs.com/dosage/cefotaxime

[6] A cannula is a tube that can be inserted into the body, often for the delivery or removal of fluid or for the gathering of data. A venous cannula is inserted into a vein, primarily for the administration of intravenous fluids, for obtaining blood samples and for administering medicines.

"Mrs. Birks, that ambulance you can hear is for George to go to Kingston A&E now. You can go in the ambulance or follow by car – decide please."

"I'll go in the ambulance, I can't leave him," replied Siobhan, grateful for the first simple choice that day and swept along by the tide of authority. Her VW Golf would be abandoned outside the practice for two days. The only attention it would get was a couple of parking tickets.

The paramedics busied themselves over George, wrapping him in a blanket and fitting an oxygen mask before strapping him into a wheelchair. With Siobhan trailing behind, George was wheeled through the waiting room and a throng of shocked onlookers to the waiting ambulance.

17:40

Partway through his journey, Ian called Siobhan from his hands-free in the car. She fumbled to retrieve her phone from the bottom of her bag as she walked behind George's wheelchair. She sat briefly on the surgery wall, watching them put George on the ambulance tail lift. Not even a hello this time.

"I'm in the car park of the GP surgery. They're loading George into the ambulance to take him to Kingston A&E. Where are you?"

"Just by Heathrow, so... maybe another forty minutes. I'll come to A&E and find you."

"I just can't believe it ... it's all happened so fast. He's had an antibiotic injection and they think it is meningitis. He was so grey and was losing consciousness when they took him ..."

"Kingston is where George needs to be. He will be okay, babe. They'll isolate the bug and blast it with the equivalent of Domestos. He is strong and fit otherwise so it's not like he is a frail one-year-old or anything."

The confidence of his words fooled no-one as he tried to reassure them both with the little knowledge he had. Siobhan aha-ed in a non-committal way, knowing the words were well-intentioned. She wanted to shout at him that his attempt at reassurance wasn't any good. It did not take away her panic, nor give the hope she needed.

"Okay, come and find me when you get here," she replied in a robotic voice detached by distance and held-back emotion.

As the ambulance left the practice Car Park, Catherine watched them leave through the office blinds. The vertical slat she held in her shaking left hand set up a standing wave along its length, rattling its neighbours into a half-hearted applause.

As she turned back to her desk, she saw Sue's face peering expectantly through the arrow slit window of her office door. She waved the receptionist in.

"You OK? I saw the ambulance get away."

"Oh Sue, I'm sorry for snapping at you. Did it look like I was panicking?"

"No worries, we got done what we needed to," Sue replied warmly, shooing away any potential scratchiness. She liked and respected Catherine enough not to dwell on it.

"I just hope I'm wrong," confessed Catherine, surprising Sue.

"You mean...?"

"That it's not meningitis after all, so all I get is a bollocking for wasting scant NHS resources. That's much easier to deal with than being right," said Catherine, finishing Sue's sentence before she had even started. Sue was shocked.

"I've never seen meningitis before – is that what you think it is?"

"I do but it's hard to be sure. Meningitis is notoriously difficult to diagnose. In kids it can look like any other self-limiting infection. By time the signs are clear, it's too late. Do you know that half of patients presenting with what proved to be meningitis were sent home by their GP?"[7] Catherine paused, dragging up a chilling thought. "I remember a lecture on medical liability. It's strange it comes back to me now. At the time I dismissed the chap as a suit from the NHS Litigation Authority (NHS LA). He said meningitis and septicaemia are always Top 3 as important causes of litigation."[8]

Sue watched her deflate at her desk with George's electronic patient record open in front of her. Catherine held her face in her hands on propped elbows, then took a deep breath whilst rubbing her temples, trying to shift the tension.

"What do I put in his notes?" Catherine wondered, then answered her own question. "It's like part-completing his Death Certificate in advance with '*I promise to pay the reaper*'."

---

[7] Thompson, M.J. et al, *Clinical recognition of meningococcal disease in children and adolescents*. Lancet, 2006. 367 (9508): p. 397-403

[8] The NHS LA had paid out £285 million in damages and costs over the ten-year period from 2003–2013 relating to 281 meningitis claims. Jan 2014: Meningitis Research Foundation response to JCVI interim statement on Bexsero.

Sue did not have an answer for her, just a reassuring squeeze of Catherine's shoulder as she left the room.

18:00

Upon arrival, George went straight into the Emergency Room. Siobhan was taken by a different route to the Parents' Room in the A&E Department. She glanced at her reflection in the glass walkway as she strode along. The whizz lines of her movement were scratched by her straggly hair, her trailing handbag, the unbuttoned collar and her billowing cardigan. Normally Siobhan had the grace of a ballerina and her clothes accentuated her athletic figure in elegant motion. But not now. Instead, her clothes clung to her in a failed effort to keep up. Her tight expression carried a grimness which would have scared her class at school, and her eyes became the only feature that passers-by would recall. All through her life, Siobhan had been told to *'cheer up, it might never happen'* whenever she was not smiling. Well, it *had* happened.

18:50

Siobhan was imprisoned in the Parents' Room. There was another couple in there and they looked as terrified as she did. No-one spoke, all bound up in their own unfolding calamities.

A nurse and a registrar sat with Siobhan to keep her company. The tall blonde registrar meant well and was doing her best, but her efforts were having the opposite effect as her abject pity and resigned air gave Siobhan dreadful hints as to the seriousness of George's infection. The time in the Parents' Room was long enough for her to reflect on the devastating speed with which George had become desperately ill. She knew from the absence of anything positive from the medics the he had not yet reached the bottom of the pit of despair.

The registrar took Siobhan through to the Emergency Room to see George. He was dipping in and out of consciousness, but he did respond to Siobhan. Around him the trauma team moved with a desperate urgency in a blur of commands and passed syringes, swabs and monitors. Siobhan noticed the consultant standing at the head of George's bed, thoroughly bored as though waiting for a bus. He checked his watch, picked his nails, hummed a little. All the while, he was pushing fluid into George at an alarming rate. His bizarre nonchalance masked the critical activity under way to give George enough fluid volume for his heart to keep working.

19:00

Siobhan was still shaking from saying goodbye to George. He was barely conscious when she kissed him, mumbling words into his ear that Mum and Dad would be there for him when he woke up, that they loved him and not to be scared, it would be okay. Such abandonment tore at her, ripping apart all her instincts as a mother to care for her child. It was the most harrowing thing she had ever had to do, and she knew it would stay with her forever. She wanted them to wait for Ian to arrive so he could see George before he was put into a medically-induced coma. *It might be the last time he would see George conscious.* But they could not. George's spiralling deterioration was moving too fast.

19:10

Once Siobhan was out of the way, the anaesthetist could get on with the unpleasant task of intubating George to artificially open his constricted throat. It was never easy in children anyway, as their airways are narrower, but with meningitis the neck muscles stiffen, reducing the flexibility to tilt the head backward naturally. It took nearly half an hour, but Siobhan was spared from knowing.

19:20

In desperation, Siobhan had texted Diana thirty minutes earlier to see if she was able to talk. The text arrived as Diana left Southampton A&E after a heavy twelve-hour shift. As an A&E consultant, Diana was never out of contact and responded within minutes.

They had met twenty years ago, attending the same NCT classes for their firstborn children. At the time, Siobhan had found it disconcerting that a highly proficient doctor would attend classes led by a dreamy West Coast hippy to find out what childbirth was going to be like. Their bond of shared experience had flourished into a treasured friendship that had strengthened as their families grew up together. Siobhan needed that friendship now more than at any other time in her life. She had always said that one of the great things about Diana was her honesty. No spoonful of sugar. Ask a question and you get a straight answer. Lesser people try this, but shy away from picking up the shrapnel of their words. Siobhan did not feel brave, but she wanted that honesty now.

If Diana had not been a doctor then she would have been an actress, diva, celebrity and party girl all rolled into one. She was simply an interesting person that you wanted to be with. Her mischievous energy and flamboyant sense of fun drew people to her. But above all, it was her warmth that was the biggest draw. She simply liked people, and her ability to communicate made her a truly talented doctor.

To make consultant in her thirties in A&E, one of the most demanding specialties and still male-dominated even to this day, was a more tangible measure of her talent. It takes a rare set of qualities to deal with what comes through the emergency room doors, in whatever state, at any time. To then be the person whom all eyes turn to for leadership when decisions of consequence matter was one thing in itself, but it was the compassion and understanding to reassure a distraught mother that set Diana apart.

"Hi Siobhan, I got your text – is it okay for you to speak now? Good. Then tell me what's happened." There was none of her frivolity today. Diana went straight to work, knowing it had to be bad for Siobhan to contact her in the way she had.

"Oh Diana, thank you so much for calling me back so soon. It's George – he's in A&E at Kingston, they think it's meningitis."[9]

Diana kept her voice neutral, as any expression of urgency or surprise could potentially send Siobhan into a tailspin. She knew full well how dangerous that infection could be. It was notoriously difficult to diagnose, as there were never enough signals to be sure. By time there were, the window for intervention had been squandered.

"How long has it been and do they know what type of meningitis?"

Diana knew that the elapsed time was critical and she glanced at the time – 20:10. She guessed George would have come home from school with symptoms and thankfully not spent an uninterrupted night of sleep for the

---

[9] Meningitis is inflammation of the lining around the brain and spinal cord – the meninges. Septicaemia is blood poisoning caused by the same germs and is the more life-threatening form of the disease. From http://www.meningitis.org/symptoms

pathogen to swamp his defences. If he was in A&E, then he would already have had intravenous antibiotics, effectively treating blind with a powerful broad spectrum agent that would kill pretty much anything in a shotgun approach.

Siobhan answered her question mechanically to make sure she gave Diana the right facts. "He came home from school at lunchtime and I took him to the GP at four, then straight here in an ambulance. I don't think they have blood test results yet, but they're saying Meningococcal septicaemia and Type B."

Diana's unspoken thought screamed that Type B[10] was the worst possible. George was now into a nightmare scenario where time and severity would become an uncontrollable lottery. All the essential interventions had been made, so there was not much else that the Kingston team could do beyond managing his fluid balance to take the pressure off his heart and the implications of a body in shock, and ensure he remained oxygenated. From now on, the fight was down to George. The true extent of the damage already wrought would only become apparent in the next two to three days.

Diana prayed that George could evade the severest damage; some visible and manageable – such as lesions or scarring or some loss of function – but others life-changing, such as deafness, blindness, brain damage and amputation. The range of possibilities was wide and impossible to gauge. Instinctively, Diana knew Siobhan needed her reassurance now.

---

[10] There are several strains or 'groups' of meningococcal bacteria (A,B,C,W135,Y and Z). Most meningococcal disease in the UK has been due to MenB and MenC. From http://www.meningitis.org/disease-info/types-causes.

"Your GP did exactly the right thing getting you into hospital so soon. You are where you need to be and George has already had injectable antibiotics – yes?"

"Yes, that's right. He is going to be transferred by the Retrieval Team to PICU[11] in St George's. He's already in an induced coma. They've told me it's really serious but what does that mean?"

Diana felt for Siobhan as any mother would. Her experience told her that uncertainty was the hardest thing for anyone to deal with, so platitudes and probabilities were a minefield of latched-onto promises that she could not make. Unaware of the expectations set in Kingston, the only focus she could give Siobhan was for the next twelve hours.

"Siobhan, George has a fight on his hands. The doctors in Kingston have already done everything they can to give him the best chance possible. All we can do is focus on the next twelve hours – there nothing for you to do but worry, so let's accept that. The doctors will get on with treating it," Diana tried to reassure her. "I'm afraid you will not get the answers you need for some time yet. The doctors will need to see stability before they can really assess the situation. The induced coma is so that they can keep things stable and do the procedures and tests they need to without disturbing him."

The calm, matter-of-fact delivery was reassuring in itself, giving Siobhan a ten-minute breather from the unrelenting tension of the Emergency Room. She felt better for the brief connection with Diana, to hear the warmth of her voice. Siobhan had not learnt anything new, but then she had not expected to – that had not been the point of her call.

---

[11] Paediatric Intensive Care Unit

Diana took on board Siobhan's thanks, but doubting what help she had actually been. She closed the call down with the only help she could be, as a friend and being there.

"Promise me, call me at any time. Promise – agreed? I'll also put a call in to the team at Kingston, just so I know exactly what is going on. You are a brilliant mum and you've done exactly the right things to help George – be strong and you and Ian look after each other."

The line went dead. Siobhan went back to the Parents' Room to stew some more.

19:40

When Ian finally arrived, he was shown straight through Reception to the Emergency Unit. He was expecting to see a sedated George in a booth with a nurse in attendance, brow-mopping or some such, maybe a drip stand and the odd monitor pinging away. He knew Siobhan would be completely strung out from what she had already had to deal with during the day, so he had played out in his head how he would shoulder the burden, carrying them both with calmness and strength.

Some hope.

Instead, he was surprised to be taken directly to the Parents' Room to see Siobhan. He had never seen her like this. She had the terrified look of a caged animal and he felt her shaking as she clung to him. As he unwound her desperate hold in order to speak to her, Siobhan rushed into an explanation.

"Where have you been? We couldn't wait any longer. They've put him under and we are going to St George's in the next twenty minutes." They sank onto seats, holding hands, and went slowly through the events of the last two hours, Siobhan bringing Ian up to speed. They were interrupted by the registrar.

"I'm sorry to interrupt you, Siobhan. Hi Mr. Birks. I've got these antibiotics for you both to take. It's standard protocol that we give antibiotics to all members of the immediate family, in the same household, for any meningitis cases[12]. The Public Health Authority will also contact your sons' schools directly from the information you've given me."

"What about Ben and Fred?" asked Siobhan. "They're at home."

"It's okay if they take their antibiotics tomorrow. If you ask them to go into their GP Practice, I'll arrange for the medication to be there for them."

"Will they be okay tonight?" Siobhan asked anxiously.

"Yes, they'll be fine. When you speak to them, just ask them to keep an eye on each other and if there are any symptoms at all, then to come straight here."

"Thank you."

---

[12] The bacteria that cause meningococcal disease are common and live naturally at the back of the nose and throat. Human beings are the only place where meningococcal bacteria can live. At any one time, one in ten of us carries the bacteria for weeks or months without ever knowing that they are there, and for most of us this is harmless because, fortunately, most of us have natural resistance. They are passed from person to person through prolonged close contact: coughing, sneezing, breathing each other's breath or kissing someone who is carrying the germ[8]. The bacteria are so fragile that they cannot survive for more than a few moments outside the human body. For this reason, they are not very contagious; they cannot be carried on things like cups, toys, furniture or clothing. From MRF website

The registrar moved on to her second task. "We will be taking your son to St. George's in the next twenty minutes. If you come with me, you can see him before he goes." She tried to prepare them, adding, "It's very busy in there. Lots of people all trying to pack everything up ready to transfer him. We won't stay for too long as we'll be in the way, I'm afraid. If you'll follow me, please."

They were whisked into the Emergency Room to see George as the Retrieval Team had arrived. The words jarred, and Ian wondered why the urgency? The Retrieval Team sounded more like something you do with carcasses, ditched pilots or captured terrorists, not their fourteen-year-old son.

Ian and Siobhan were shocked to a standstill by the chaos before them. Their senses were affronted simultaneously and only fragments were freeze-framed; the monochrome sheen illuminating George's pale upturned face, like a drowning man gasping in the beam of a searchlight. Their vision was filled by the scrum surrounding George, with individuals whirring in and out, leaving George barely glimpsed between bodies. The cacophony of loud voices, repeated orders, multiple conversations and bleeping machines left them disorientated.

It was their first sight of George in a coma. He lay flat on his back, stock still on a gurney, arms slack by his sides and left leg kinked sideways. He had no pillow so his head tilted back, pushing his lower jaw defiantly upwards. The oxygen mask swamped his face. Multiple pipes snaked into his arms and stabbed into his neck. All his clothes had been cut off and scraps littered the floor, along with empty fluid bags, syringe wrappers and other detritus from the battle being fought above. He had only his boxers on and the bright pink and navy stripes clashed horribly with the grey, underworld colour of his skin. His eyes were resolutely closed and he did not look like George any more – as though his essence had retreated inwards out of reach from pain, prodding and poking.

Milling around George were close to twenty people – two full multi-disciplinary A&E teams across all ranks of doctors and nurses, one resident at Kingston and the other with the Retrieval Unit in the process of handover. The specialist ambulance was in effect a mobile Intensive Care Unit that allowed serious cases to be sucked into the specialist centre at St George's that serves all of south London suburbia.

With the shock came impotency. Ian's overloaded mind maxed out with a whirl of questions and confusion. '*What can I do beyond standing here, eyes wide asking dumb questions? How can I help? What happens next? Will he be ok? Why does he look so cold? Christ – is he already dead? Please God no – if so, surely they would have stopped all this activity? Please just wake up, George, Siobhan must be in bits, where is she?*' He stood like a shattered tree stump as the torrent of people swept around him doing positive things. His upper arm was gripped by a short fierce Australian nurse who dragged his useless bulk out of the way. Her fingers dug into the slack skin, stinging him like a wasp bite. Her nasal voice buzzed around his head with staccato words that he just could not take in.

"You are the father, right? Well, listen up. Your boy is real sick. He's had morphine so he has no pain and he's now in a medically-induced coma,[13] so don't expect any kind of response. We have to get him to Intensive Care straight away in my ambulance." The nurse thought she was being helpful by being direct and forceful with him, but instead

---

[13] Morphine is an opioid pain medication. An opioid is sometimes called a narcotic. Morphine can slow or stop your breathing. It may be habit-forming, even at regular doses. Morphine is used to treat moderate to severe pain and also maintain a medically-induced coma.

simply set him adrift, making him feel more inadequate. "There is no easy way to say this ... this is really serious, I have seen kids like this who have not made it. You need to get your head in the right place and prepare yourself for a tough time ahead. We will be leaving with him in the next ten minutes, so follow on over to St George's and come straight to PICU. You clear? You know where you're going?"

Ian nodded untruthfully. He could drive a car and he could find St George's, but beyond that he had no idea where he would end up – but that was not what she meant. He was still processing the sight of his seriously ill son and the wrenching gasp from normality to life-threatening in the space of an afternoon.

20:15

George was transferred with Siobhan in the ambulance to St George's in Tooting, South London, straight into the Paediatric Intensive Care Unit. Ian followed along by car, keeping up initially, but unable to follow the ambulance though red lights. He got lost, but arrived before them. He had no idea how that happened.

03:00

Later that night, Catherine lay awake with thoughts that meandered through a self-analytical vignette of the day. She told Sue the next day that she had slept badly, finally exhausting her mind in a spin of *'what-ifs'* for that poor, poor boy.

Wed 24th April : Siobhan's Diary

1015 call from School Nurse — high temp,
        vomiting at school

1230 picked up George from school

1610 saw rash on chest

1720 to GP — injection, ambulance,
        Kingston A&E

1915 intubated

1945 Ian arrived

2015 transferred to St George's. In isolation
        room — on ventilator. Stayed in Cedar Room
        overnight.

Chapter 2

January 2013 – three months before Infection Day

The screensaver on Siobhan's phone was a George selfie, put there some time ago but unchanged as Siobhan did not know how to. His face beamed back at her, distorted by the camera angle as though reflected by the back of a spoon.

If judging him unkindly, Siobhan could have said that George's head is too large for his body. Predictably, you can rely on elder brothers to be harsh, so it became a useful put-down. Unwittingly, George made it worse by dipping his head slightly to make a point in a professorial manner, as though looking over half-moon glasses.

George has a wide face, huge blue eyes and a pug nose. It is a trustworthy and earnest face with an openness that allows an untruth nowhere to hide. They say, though, that the best way to hide something is to leave it in plain view. When you know him well, George can make his open face a mask to hide behind, but to tell a lie, a real lie? How could you possibly even think such a thing of that face?

Siobhan knew that George's blue eyes could dial in three settings, a bit like modes on his beloved Nikon – SPARKLE for mischief, smiling, fun and '*I like you*', WORRIED so that you too look over your shoulder for the impending scary thing, and OFF for bored, detached, staring teenagerdom and '*go away, if you're not already sure*'.

Siobhan also had a short text conversation saved on her ancient phone.

'How was school?'

'Ok – just off bus'

'Where r u now?'

'Kingston'

'What u doin?'

'Just chugging along'.

She kept it as that was where 'Chugs' came from. The simplest and least-contrived nicknames invariably work best, and 'Chugs' did that for George. It had a face of cheerfulness and chunkiness. It conjured many qualities; a steady relentlessness which was George all over, even in the face of a ticking clock, or well-intentioned advice or even a kick up the backside. It was endearing; a boat that chugs will not tip, a car that chugs won't crash, a train that chugs nods you off to sleep. If you read his school reports over the years, but more between the lines of what the teacher wanted to say but didn't dare, the clues were there: *hard-working* (but sometimes in the wrong direction), *follows instructions well* (but perhaps too literally), *tries his best* (but not scaling the heights), *kind and thoughtful* (when he should be getting on with his work).

Nicknames develop, with nuances that you make your own. Maybe George grew into his, like a school blazer bought in anticipation two sizes too big, or perhaps it grew onto George like scales with the accumulated Post-It notes of use, layer by layer bringing depth and authenticity? Both applied to George, though no-one noticed the snugness of the fit happening in front of them. With each body blow that was to come, 'Chugs' came to encompass independence and resilience, stoicism to get through crushing challenges that would splinter others and a determination to come out the other side unmarked and full of hope.

Chugs does not scream, wail or cry.
Chugs is not a victim, nor wallows in self-pity.
Chugs gets on with it.
Chugs is there for you and holds your hand.
Chugs fills your heart and makes you smile.
It was a brand and attitude all his own.

I love a good list. Here are my all-time fave Top 10 songs. There are a few quirky ones on there. I don't bother with cool stuff. It's too much like hard work to keep up. So I do the things I like or pick ones just because they make me smile. 'Dangerous Love' always makes me laugh as Mum loves dancing around the kitchen to it really loud with me and Fred.

1. *'All of Me' by John Legend*
2. *'Dangerous' Love by Fuse ODG*
3. *'Wake Me Up' by Avicii*
4. *'Pompeii' by Bastille*
5. *'Turn Me On' by David Guetta ft. Nicki Minaj*
6. *'Superheroes' by The Script*
7. *'Wrapped Up' by Olly Murs ft. Travie McCoy*
8. *'Skinny Love' by Birdy*
9. *'Payphone' by Maroon 5 ft. Wiz Khalifa*
10. *'Don't Stop Me Now' by Queen*

Jen and I know all the words to 'Don't Stop Me Now'. We have been best mates for years – from about three years old, I think. Mum tells me Jen got into a strop with me over Pass-the-Parcel at my third birthday party. Apparently I thought the parcel was my present so naturally I should get it all the time and would not let it out of my hands. Sounds like a far better game to me, a bit like rugby maybe. My brothers really piss me off when they call us boyfriend and girlfriend, as she is not my girlfriend. We just get on really well and we help each other. Jen hates the twittery girls who go around in packs, and tells them so, which can't help much. I get bored at lunchtime as all the boys play football and I hate football. We both like quirky stuff and we laugh a lot.

So when Jen's mum died in Year Four, Jen was sad and didn't want to be fussed over by loads of people at school. She would get angry and tell people to get lost, even the teachers. But not me. She didn't mean it and it wasn't like her. The class teacher would always ask me to be with Jen — it seemed to help. I'm not sure why it did or what I did, but Jen would calm down. I held her hand and told her it would all be ok. She looked down at my fingers and told me they are like a red-eyed tree frog's as my fingertip pads are huge. It made her smile despite it all.

George had met Jen in Kingston but was vague about mentioning it. Not lying exactly, as though he had something to hide, just conveniently avoiding mentioning it so his brothers wouldn't take the piss. There was nothing to hide, of course, just two friends hanging out with no parents constantly prying over their shoulders. For Jen, that meant her whole family looking out for her, intrusive even if well-meant. For George, he just wanted to be himself, with no expectations to live up to or lists to tick off.

"So how was the skiing holiday then?" asked Jen, to make conversation, as George rarely did. It was one of his favourite subjects, along with Nikons, *Top Gear* and *The Big Bang Theory*.

From the very first moment, George loved skiing. His 'chugness' meant that his technique was more of a cascade down the mountain with parents in desperate pursuit bawling at him to be careful. Skiing brought out a different side to his character. Usually George would always stop to gaze at clouds, examine an insect or smell the breeze. Not so with skiing – he was always on a mission and that mission was danger.

"S'awright. I got my Bronze Award. That's much earlier than Fred, and Ben has only got Trois Etoiles and so that proves I'm a better skier than him. Bazinger."

Jen watched him act out the pantomime of toppling a line of girls on a nursery slope by skiing over their skis so they went down like dominos. They giggled together at *Tottie Takedown*. As George ran out of steam, Jen picked up the conversation again.

"What d'ya want to do?"

"Dunno – you got any ideas?"

"Nah."

"…"

"I've got this play to learn for school – could you read a part with me?"

"What, a chapter?"

"No, you div – a part, a character."

"OK. I'm no good at acting, but I'll help if I can."

"I knew you would. Thanks George." Jenny smiled at him, grateful for his gentle support. Her smile did not last long.

"I'll be Annie and you can be the Butler."

"But you're not a ginger."

"That doesn't matter, I'll be wearing a wig."

"Is it in your bag?"

"LOOK, forget the ginger hair, just read this bit – there, where I'm pointing."

They spent the next forty minutes together, lost in the world of *Annie.*

On a bitter January day, Catherine had been asked to attend a CME[14] session on Vaccination. These sessions were essentially training days that all GPs had to do. The intent was to keep knowledge fresh and skills honed, but for some it degenerated into a badge-collecting exercise to hit the required number of hours. For a thorough GP like Catherine, they were normally desperately dull as she searched for grains of new knowledge in the chaff of stuff she knew already. Luckily, the important seed of fresh knowledge was sown in her mind – before she even became aware of the branch of insight that the seed would become and before she had even met George.

She was a reluctant attendee, feeling guilty at abandoning her colleagues at the practice at such a busy time. January and February usually top the monthly rankings for mortalities in the over-80s from pneumonia, strokes and falls. But as her senior partner had reminded her, vaccinations were vital income for the practice, so she was crystal clear where her priorities ought to lie.

Despite the grim day which matched her truculent mood, the session on Vaccination piqued her interest, so much so that she noted down links to papers that she wanted to read. She knew that a successful vaccine existed for MenC but was unaware of coverage for MenB. This was new! This was a major step forward, as MenB is the most dangerous and hard to diagnose, particularly at the time when intervention matters most to prevent progression.

---

[14] Continuous Medical Education

The facilitator cited a hot-off-the-press article stating that it is now approved but not available on the NHS.

Novartis receives EU approval[15] for Bexsero®, first vaccine to prevent the leading cause of life-threatening meningitis across Europe

• Bexsero is indicated to help protect all age groups against meningococcal serogroup B (MenB) disease, including infants who are the most vulnerable.

• MenB disease is associated with a high human toll for families and communities, as it can be fatal or may cause serious, life-long disabilities in survivors.

• Novartis is working with health authorities to provide access to Bexsero as soon as possible.

"What use is that? What does 'as soon as possible' mean?" thought Catherine to herself. To licence a medicine for private use only is an automatic restriction to a tiny fraction of the population who could afford to pay for it or knew about it. Catherine channelled her irritation into a pithy question.

"Surely this is another example of the schizophrenia of the NHS? At medical school I was told that the UK had led the fight against meningitis with the introduction of the MenC vaccine, virtually eliminating the infection within just a couple of years[16]. We know the NHS has the experience of running pioneering public health interventions and a great track record of implementing superb vaccination programmes nationally when it chooses to. So why create a mess like this?"

The other delegates sat up in their seats for the first really interesting thing to happen all day. The lecturer dealt with the pin-pulled grenade with aplomb.

---

[15] Novartis PLC Press Release January 22nd 2013
[16] Jan 2014: Meningitis Research Foundation response to JCVI interim statement on Bexsero

"Let's put the politics to one side for now," he said, and defused her anger by agreeing with her. "The value-for-money debate will take months to play out. I agree that the *'not cost-effective at any price'* view will be a major stumbling block. In the meantime, with a relentless inevitability there will be 600 cases and 60 deaths per year while the scientists, health economists, accountants and politicians argue."[17]

Catherine slumped back, defeated by inertia. But the seed of retrievable knowledge had been sown.

---

[17] JCVI. JCVI interim position statement on use of Bexsero meningococcal B vaccine in the UK. 2013 (cited 2013 August)

Chapter 3

February 2013 – two months before Infection Day

All the trouble in the world is due to the fact that man cannot sit still in a room.

Blaise Pascal 1623-1662

Mrs. Webster, our English teacher, began the lesson by telling us about the new subject for this term – the First World War Poets. I'm not a big fan of poetry – why can't they just right what they mean in words you can understand, why right it as a riddle? Is it right or write? I can never remember, sod it.

"Who can tell me why Wilfred Owen was so influential?" began Mrs. Webster.

Arms shot skywards and a few heads at the back dipped to make themselves less noticeable. She hesitated in her selection.

"He writes from his personal experience in battle and in hospital recovering from shell shock."

"Thank you, Mark. A good answer, but next time wait for me to ask rather than shouting out, please. That's part of what I was looking for. Can you give me any examples of his nightmarish vision of trench warfare?" She pointed at Emily, who was polite but timid.

"The drowning of a soldier in a sea of mustard gas – but I'm not sure if that really happened or if it was a hallucination?"

"That's the thing about hallucinations, Emily, they are just as real to the person that has them. But in the example you give from *Dulce et Decorum Est*, that did happen to

Wilfred and it's his witness account that is so powerful. Any other examples – perhaps about shell shock?"

"*Batter of guns and shatter of flying muscles.*"

"That's excellent, James." She recognised the line from *Mental Cases* and probed to check his interpretation. "You mean that the soldiers relive their harrowing experiences day after day? Good, and on that theme of reliving – here is a famous quote from *Mental Cases* that you should all write down in your notebooks: '*Dawn breaks open like a wound that bleeds afresh.*' When we talk of shell shock here, we are using the words they used in 1917. What words would we use today?"

George put up his hand, he knew this one. "Post Traumatic Stress Disorder, or PTSD for short."

After my contribution Mrs. Webster doesn't pick on me again. My attention wanders, not that it's boring – if anything, PTSD sounds really interesting. I feel as though there is a lot going on in my head. It's hard to explain and I keep trying but I never seem to find the right words for Mum and Dad. Things are fizzing, confusing and I get a bit lost. It's like when I have too many windows on my laptop open at the same time and it gets overloaded and freezes. The same happens to me:

> *Tab1 is trying to listen to Mrs. Webster giving a list of instructions for a class exercise. I MUST write this down or I will forget it. Where is my pencil case?*

> > *Tab 2 is thinking why I can't explain things well to Mum and Dad.*

> > > *Tab 3 is Chang next to me poking me with his ruler to get my attention to mess about.*

Tab 4 is an image of those poor soldiers with hands over their ears trying to make the shelling noises go away. I can understand that. I'm not saying it is the same with Mrs. Webster shouting, but it still fills my head.

Tab 5 is my locker keys. I haven't seen them for ages and my PE kit is in my locker – well, it has to be there as I've looked everywhere else.

Mrs. Webster cracked on, unaware of George's distraction. "Ok, Class, please open your laptops and get on with what I have asked you to do. I want to see your best work and you have the rest of the lesson until 10.15 to get it done."

Tab 6 is YouTube with the part-watched episode of Top Gear *that I was watching in Registration. I really want to see it. That Bugati Veyron is awesome!*

Tab 7 is a flashback to my bus journey this morning. He was on the bus again. I was so worried that He was watching me that I missed my stop.

Tab 8 is the detention I got for being late. Where did Mr. Smith say I had to go? OMG, I'll get into more trouble if I miss it. It must be in the JCR after school. Mum will go nuts if I am late home again.

> *Tab 9 is ten unread emails waving*
> *their hands at me for my attention.*

All nine tabs are unruly children who have just burst into the room, clamouring at me for attention. Some shout, some cry, others just grab at me and others sparkle as the most attractive. My brain is frozen and in a panic of overload, I act on instinct, impulsively choosing the most comfortable – Top Gear. I feel trapped in a washing machine that spits me out when the rapid spin has finished, whether it is the right time or not. I open the YouTube tab and just have the pictures on with no volume. It gets all my attention so I don't have to face the spinning indecision and pressure. The others tabs don't go away, they just sit in the background, giving me an uneasy feeling which drains my confidence.

Mrs. Webster loomed over George's shoulder. He didn't see her.

"George, how are you getting on? You looked anxious when I was giving instructions, so I just want to check if you need my help? George, did you hear what I just said? George, let me see what you have done on your screen please."

As Mrs. Webster swiveled George's screen towards her, he jumped in his seat with surprise. Mrs. Webster thought he was play-acting as nearby classmates tittered. This sent an immediate shot of irritation through her at his silliness and immaturity. Her thoughts of *'Pl-eease, just get on with it, it's not difficult, just grow up'* itched to be said out loud, but she dared not. The image of the Bugati blasting across the screen with pyrotechnics blowing up trees in the background in true Top Gear style was lost on Mrs. Webster as she looked on in disbelief. It was her turn to have too many windows open, and this time her brain lost it.

Tab 1: Why don't you just do what I tell you!

Tab 2: I don't believe it. That's the third time this week I've caught you on your laptop in MY lessons watching rubbish.

Tab 3: There is no way I can catch up with the curriculum now. The rest of the class is in uproar, laughing at George's stupid behaviour.

"George, turn that rubbish off NOW! Collect your things and go and stand in the corridor until the end of the lesson. I will speak to you later."

I hate it when she shouts, sneaking up on me like that. If she just asked me slowly and reasonably then I could focus on what she wants and answer her. All eyes are upon me as I am now the centre of attention, with everyone laughing. I don't want this. I just want to be left alone. I can't let everyone see how crushed I am, so I scrabble for a way out of this confidence-shattering mess. I stand up, square my shoulders, stare at Mrs. Webster so she knows I have listened, smile – that usually works – and walk in very slow steps from the classroom so I don't bump into anything and make her even more mad.

I walk/run behind Mrs. Webster as she hotfoots it to the Headmaster's office. I can't imagine this is going to go well as she is furious with me. If she could whisk me off to an empty classroom, I bet she would give me a pasting – good job she won't, as she would be toast. I don't like empty corridors in case He is in the shadows. I still don't know where my locker keys are. What did she say homework was? Chang pisses me off – he never gets caught but I do.

Christ – what will the Headmaster say? I so need the bog right now, my tum doesn't feel right.

Mrs. Webster vented at George, still pissed off with him. "Right George – you sit there in the secretary's office until Mr. Morris is ready to see you. You'd better come up with a good explanation of why you behave so badly in my class and disrupt my lessons. It is so unlike you, George, particularly that childish march from my classroom. It's not clever, you know, and despite what your classmates think, it's not funny. When you are ready to apologise to me, you may come back to my lessons, but not before. So just sit there and think and do not do anything else."

I sit on the wooden chair next to the photocopier feeling dazed and sweaty. The secretaries look at me over their computer screens, three pairs of vulture eyes chipping at me. Thinking is the last thing I need to do more of. My brain is already fried with all the stuff buzzing about that whips up my confusion. This is all happening so fast and I've no idea how it came to this. I wonder at the choices I made and what I want to happen. I definitely do not want this – or what is about to happen to me. My unsettled tum lets out a small poot that unfortunately squeaks on the wooden chair, which acts like an amplifier. Sod it! I cringe and hunch my shoulders as though trying to suck it back in. I must look like Mr. Bean. Three pairs of eyebrows shoot up this time. I smile at them – I'm not sure smiling will work this time.

To hide my embarrassment, I stand up. The photocopier brand catches my eye.

Lexmark.

Tab 10 opens like iPlayer in my head. I can replay the exact words and images of the funniest clip you will ever see on You Tube.[18] It's a cat sitting next to a copier, trying to make it do its copying. The human voiceover says:

"Take the paper,

Take the flaming paper,

Look the paper tray is full and the rollers are going round!

So why don't you take the fucking paper?

Lexmark Easyshare shit!

Look, take the fucking paper, I've got to be somewhere."

The image ends with the cat losing control and falling off the copier. It sooo makes me laugh and I giggle to myself. I press the control panel to see if it really is Easy-to-Share. Nothing happens. I press it again and a light comes on – shit! I press it to make the light go off. It starts flashing and bleeping and then silence which lasts three blinks of astonishment before the noise starts again. Not from the dormant copier but the trio of vultures circling over me.

The senior secretary snapped at him, "George, what are you doing? You shouldn't be touching that – it is school property! If you've broken it, you are going to be in serious trouble. George, what have you done?"

At the end of the school day, George, Siobhan and Ian were summoned into the Headmaster's Office. All three felt like naughty school children. Oddly, only George looked guilt free. To call Mr. Morris agitated was an understatement. He was hissing, so spittle flecked the corners of his gulping mouth as he tried to articulate his

---

[18] Go see Cat and Copier at
http://www.youtube.com/watch?v=CSK1D3bZhRs

fury and indignation that a Year 9 boy would have the sheer audacity to contradict him in his own office.

"I am extremely disappointed in you, George. This is so out of character and not the standards we expect in this school. To play the clown in Mrs. Webster's lesson is just immature and you should know better." He was in a froth now, intending to intimidate George. "The most serious thing is the willful damage to school property. In MY office. I do not understand why you would do such a thing. What do you have to say for yourself, young man?"

"I didn't break the photocopier, I just pressed a button." George stared right back at Morris in direct rebuttal. Intimidation only works if the victim is scared – George clearly was not.

"Are you saying my assistant is lying?"

"I told you I did not break the copier." George's belligerence was unchecked, righteous in his honesty but unaware of the battle slipping away from him.

"Right, that is enough – we are not making progress here and I will not have such disrespect and insolence in my office. I suggest, Mr. and Mrs. Birks, that you take George home for the rest of the day to think about his behaviour. George, you need to understand that any more of this and you leave me no choice but to exclude you for three days."

He faced George but the words were an undisguised salvo at the parents. If they did a better job at instilling better manners, his life would be so much easier.

George, Siobhan and Ian left the office; George at his usual pace, which was just on the edge of saunter if you chose to see it like that. Ian and Siobhan could not have got out of there quick enough, to leave behind the shame and humiliation of the last few minutes. In the doorway Olivia, George's form teacher, caught Siobhan's eye. Siobhan offered a resigned smile that said *'He's my son, I love him, but please don't judge him, he's not at his best'*.

Olivia took a risk and whispered, "He'll be ok. He's just trying his wings, that's all."

At that moment Siobhan and Ian did not feel on George's side, which was uncomfortable. There was nothing they could condone, deny or ignore in what George had done. The only explanation could be untruths being told somewhere or just simply a one-off aberration in George's behaviour. They both hoped so and wanted answers from George themselves.

Olivia was the last to leave as the Birks scuttled out. She had been in the meeting but had had the good sense to keep quiet and blend into the background. *Morris was a prick.* She knew that her lack of experience meant Morris would not listen to her and definitely not brook any view different from his own.

Olivia knew for a fact that the copier was not broken, just frozen, simply needing a reset. George should not have touched it, but he was no vandal. She cared about George and did not see him as a criminal. She had seen him struggle with inappropriate behaviour before. It was as though he had a range of behaviour limited to just A-to-G and he selected the wrong one.

It was not the time to suggest to Morris that rather than a good talking-to, maybe George needed a good listening-to. Morris was still full of bluster and indignation, latched onto having his expectations met. *'All "me me me, as the only intelligent person in the room". Prick.'*

As she closed the Headmaster's office door, she asked herself, *'When would be a good time?'*

The immediate post-mortem of the cringe worthy interview with Morris got nowhere in the car home. George was a rabbit caught in headlights and there was too much shame bubbling. Ian and Siobhan only revisited the conversation later that evening, sensibly without George.

Ian chanced his arm with a conversation opener. "Hey Shiv, I saw this article about headspace[19] in a business magazine on the flight back from Zurich. There's even an App for it."

"Right — so what is it then?" Siobhan smiled slyly, sensing he was out on a limb and the opportunity to get him with a pithy a one-liner.

"OK babe, you asked, so are you sitting comfortably?" He skimmed and paraphrased the article, chunking his wonky interpretation together with clearer regurgitated text. "Mindfulness is an ancient Eastern technique that sharpens mental focus, boosts your mood, relieves stress and improves memory and concentration. Used by... US Marines, UK Government, even Gwyneth Paltrow! It's all about meditation for modern life but without all the Buddhist bit."

"Your words or the article?" Siobhan checked.

"Mine. I'll carry on..." Now reading to avoid her skeptical interruptions, he continued, "In a world where the sheer volume of mental chatter, both externally and internally, to which we are exposed, we can use meditation as way to cope. It sounds a great technique to switch off when you get home. It really hit a chord as it gives you that bit of time when the world stops spinning and you get a chance to catch up and step back on again."

---

[19] Headspace techniques taught by Andy Puddicome. From https://www.headspace.com/faqs/category/our-approach-to-meditation-and-mindfulness

It was pretty obvious to Siobhan where he was coming from. Teach George to use this quasi-meditation technique and – job done. "I can see it being effective for you at work. You have control over your circumstances and can think rationally. But other than you being grumpy and preoccupied at times, you are not the problem, it's George."

Ian looked earnestly back at her, waiting on her words, anticipating the possible verbal knee-capping. She edged back from her harsh dismissal and barbed quip, choosing instead to explain her insights. "It's not about George taking a step back and chillin' for ten minutes, it is far more fundamental than that. It's not about volume of chatter and filtering it – for George the chatter becomes a crescendo that is so overwhelming, he ceases to function rationally – what's left are some random behaviours to fill the vacuum. He knows they're not right. George being belligerent or badly behaved is something we've never, ever seen from him before. It doesn't just go away if he is able to relax. It stays with him all the time when he's in one of his anxious phases. It's a state of mind – from the moment he wakes up. We've seen this before in phases lasting several weeks, like his summer exams. But he does come out the other side. We need a way to help him when he is full-to-the-brim. To help him recognise it and to centre himself on who he is. I don't have any answers, other than to hang in there with him until he comes out the other side himself." Siobhan moved the conversation onto generalities. "That's the problem with teenage boys. The can be such towering masses of angst nobody notices. It's a bit of a cliché, but some teenagers reliably develop a sense of being isolated. You know, that whole adolescent thing, *no one understands me*, becoming disconnected, a bit lost. . I can see that a little in George, being a bit lost, I mean."

"What? Introspective and lacking in confidence – I can see that too," agreed Ian.

"I dunno, it feels like we're fishing here."

"No, let's stay with it, this might be useful, help us understand, maybe?"

"So – if you push an introvert into a corner? You get an animal response of belligerence, and confrontation as they have nowhere else to go, even if it is wholly out of character."

"Well, it sure was a shock to see George act that way. I never knew he had it in him."

"I just don't get the whole *Top Gear* thing. He has been told so many times and caught so many times. What explains that? Is he stupid, deliberately disobedient or just acting on impulse, not thinking through the consequences? What is so compelling for George that he repeatedly risks a teacher's wrath – *Top Gear*?"

"Well, kids today do live online in the way we never did. For them it is simpler than real life."

"You may be right."

"I tell you though. It's gonna take real work and effort on our part and a willingness on his to coach him out of his safe isolation into the real world with real people."

Chapter 4

But if you close your eyes,
Does it almost feel like
Nothing changed at all?
How am I gonna be an optimist about this?

Lyrics[20] from Pompeii by Bastille

Thurs 25th April, Siobhan's Diary (the day after Infection Day)

No change – desperate

Stayed in Cedar Room

On ventilator still

They say that for coma patients, of the five senses, hearing is the last one to go and the first one to return. This is why nurses speak to their patients so much – partly to maintain their connection to a human being, but also in the hope that they can be heard.

Siobhan had latched onto this and was compelled from first seeing George comatose to speak to George at every opportunity, sharing her thoughts with him. This was not going through the motions of words to fill the empty spaces, just tossing seeds onto fallow soil and hoping they would sprout. No, these were words that mattered to her; that she was compelled to say. That unfathomable connection of mother and son was real and alive for Siobhan, giving her the utter conviction that George would hear her subconscious feelings, even if not her actual words.

---

[20] Permission sought from BMG Rights Management (UK) Ltd. Full lyrics at metrolyrics.com

Siobhan closed her eyes to squeeze the tears back in and to help her concentrate on channeling her words to George. "Fight it George, we want you back, we love you so much."

She tenderly stroked George's brow and drifted away in reverie. She did not see the two-dimensional husk of her son, lying before her. In his body's place she saw the kaleidoscope of George with fragments swirling into a vibrant and complete whole. She saw the trusting baby, the busy toddler, the sparky child and the uncertain young teenager. She saw all his smiles, his hopes, his tears and all his love.

The warmth of his limp hand connected her memory to other hand-holdings. She smiled, knowing how rare it was for a fourteen-year-old to love holding her hand, even now. Their hands joined their wingtips as they were Spitfires swooping across the beach in Salcombe. She felt his sweaty nervous hands on his first day at school, puffed up in his big boy's scratchy uniform. Earlier still, she'd even loved, in a way, his gobby fig-roll encrusted fingers scrunched in her hair to make her squeal and buck as George, in the backpack, giggled. The smell of figs always reminded her of George as a baby, as fig rolls were the only thing close to a fruit he would eat.

Despite the noise of the busy ward with its bleeps, whirring, crying and chunter of activity, Siobhan was alone with her thoughts. Alone and abandoned without the real George there.

Georgina pinned the Red Badge of Doom to her dark blue tunic. As a senior nurse in PICU, she was used to taking responsibility for her patients, but the Badge of Doom took her out of her comfort zone. Instead of hands-on care of sick children, she had to take on a supervisory role over her peers, which was always a delicate balance. Georgina had Clare, Sophie, Beth, Rowena, Holly and Izzy as part of her team, all highly trained PICU nurses operating at the highest standards. Today meant the overseeing of eight very sick children in PICU, with George the sickest and so assigned the bay closest to the nursing station.

"George, what am I to do with you? I turn my back for one minute and you jumble up my tidy pipes!" Her mock-scolding added human warmth to the sterile, technical environment in PICU where machines outnumbered patients at least five-to-one. She was serious, though, about her tidy pipes, verging on the obsessive. To Georgina the pipes, tubes and wires arranged neatly and in sequence on the pillow behind George's head were her measure that she was in control and that her care was of the highest standard. This attention to detail on a minor issue signified everything else had been monitored and checked. Tidy pipes meant drugs administered, charts updated, machines checked, face stroked and her patient spoken to as she tidied them.

It was reassuring for Ian and Siobhan to watch Georgina in action. Her light-heartedness and ready smile helped to smooth their permanent scowls of worry. As parents, they very quickly recognised the compassion in Georgina and so had absolute confidence in her.

It was late on Thursday evening. The consultant paediatrician, Dr Jonathan, opened the door to the Parents' Lounge across the hallway from PICU and invited Siobhan and Ian to join him. The privacy meant there were truths to air that none of them wanted to hear. He had had a long day and was on duty for the rest of the weekend. The long hours and difficult cases came with the turf he had chosen as a specialist in the NHS. He thought he had kept his weariness from his demeanour, but Siobhan sensed instead a sadness at what he was about to say.

"Well, this is where we are. George has got through the last twelve hours as best we can hope. His sats – sorry, oxygen saturation levels – have got no worse but his breathing is taking whatever energy he has. His high heart rate tells us that. He is over the infection as such – in fact, the meningococcal bacteria were killed that first night by the powerful antibiotics he had. Our challenge is managing the devastation the infection has caused around his body. You can see he's swollen at the neck, hands and feet. His vessels are leaking so he has maybe five litres too much in his tissues. The fluid also pools in his lungs – we can see on the X-ray that one lung is flooded and of no use to him. If his oxygen levels deteriorate we'll have to hook him up to a different type of ventilator to help him out. There are many steps we can take to relieve the stress on his heart, although we are approaching the limit of safe dosages."

His next words stood between them like granite tombstones – immovable in time. It was a boast that as a father, Ian would never want to make.

"I need to tell you … right now, George is the sickest person in the hospital."

Jonathan paused, for his own benefit too. He was never sure what parents took in when he have them grave news. He suspected only a fraction registered.

"To repeat myself, we have a devastating set of challenges to manage. The only way I can think of to describe it … it's like walking along a roof-line, it could go either way. You need to prepare yourself that he may not make it – I have seen children in George's situation die, and those that survive suffer with life-changing events. We need to take each twelve hours at a time – each parcel of time is better for him as we can get more of his functions stabilised. We are doing everything we can for him. George has the best team looking after him and I am here all night and over the weekend."

He could now see that his words had made an impact. Ian looked dazed, processing the information inwardly, frozen as his world fell apart. You could see the hold that fear had on him by the clench of his jaw and tightness around the eyes, almost cringing from it. It was only now, for the first time, that he grasped with paralysing terror that they might lose George. Despite the previous warnings, which had slipped through his mind without sticking, the realisation only dawned now through the precise, direct words of Dr Jonathan. There was nowhere to hide in misplaced optimism or deluded probabilities. Where do you go when two policemen with sombere pitying expressions call at your door at three in the morning? They are only there for one reason, to bring you news you dread. Siobhan's eyes filled her face as they searched for hope, but her tears spilled over as she sobbed quietly. Dr Jonathan resigned himself to the impact of his words – it came with the turf.

This was not the time to fully share his experience and deep professional concern for George. He knew that the infection had been beaten that first night, but George was still at the stage where one in five patients die[21] from the shock of body-wide septicaemia. It was usually the heart that gave out from the strain as organs began to fail one by one from poor oxygen supply. The visible symptoms here and now were the tip of the iceberg where one in four

---

[21] In recent decades, about one in five cases of meningococcal septicaemia has been fatal, but quicker and better treatment are improving the chances of surviving. From http://www.meningitis.org/disease-info/types-causes/meningoccal-disease

patients suffered a life-changing disability[22]. He ran through a mental checklist that made him feel powerless despite his years of training – heart failure, irrecoverable kidney damage, amputation, hearing loss, blindness, psychological problems and post-traumatic stress disorder for some.

Siobhan and Ian would spend the next four weeks in an otherworldly place fearing for their child's life. The world they existed in was drab, tasteless, muted. Time either went very fast in anxious bewilderment or very slow in dormant anticipation of a test result, a positive word or a glimmer of recognition. Conversations felt unsatisfying, like late-night repeats, or else blurred by white noise of a badly-tuned TV channel. Their shared lifebelt was their burning hope of bringing George back. It began their waking thoughts, energised their demoralising visits and drove them forward. That hope was planted as an unnoticed kiss on George's warm face at the end of each day.

During the night George's sats dropped further. With one lung full of fluid and the other partly filled, the level of oxygen in his bloodstream was getting dangerously low. The intervention needed was a brutal one and George was put onto an oscillating ventilator.

Most ventilators work as a simple pump, inflating and deflating the lungs as you would a balloon. The trouble is that Mother Nature's design is far more refined in order to exploit the elasticity of the lungs, using energy wisely so as not to damage the connecting tubes by completely emptying and filling with each breath. The oscillating ventilator is a fearsome beast and is used as a last resort to get oxygen saturation levels above 70% for patients whose lung function is poor. It is a big bit of kit, the size of a

---

[22] Wright, C., R. Wordsworth, and L. Glennie, Counting the cost of meningococcal disease : scenarios of severe meningitis and septicaemia. Paediatric Drugs, 2013. 15(1): p.49-58

washing machine that sits in the corner, growling on a permanent spin cycle. Rather than pumping, it *shakes* air into the lungs, using a respiratory rate four times greater than normal and very small tidal volumes. This type of ventilator is thought to reduce ventilator-associated damage to the lungs[23]. Not only that, it shakes the entire body so that everything vibrates – eyelids, lips, jowls, bingo wings, toes. Imagine being strapped to a truck engine at full chat for hours on end. Fortunately for George, he was not awake to suffer this torture – but Ian and Siobhan felt every minute for him.

The oscillating ventilator became a barometer of progress that they became attuned to. Just seeing it being wheeled in set off a Pavlovian response of anxiousness that George's oxygen levels had dropped as his lungs were still full of fluid. Their mood plummeted with the realisation of how dependent they were on this brutal machine to keep George alive.

Fri 26th April, Siobhan's Diary

No change – 12 hours at a time. 50/50

One lung full of fluid

Put on oscillating ventilator – just horrible

Stayed in Cedar Room

When Georgina studied George, seemingly asleep and bare-chested, the full extent of the damage from the septicaemia became apparent. There were not many expanses of skin untouched. It was as though a clumsy

---

[23] From http://en.wikipedia.org/wiki/High_frequency_ventilation

painter had messed up opening a tin of deep purple paint and splattered his head and chest all over. If he then stepped back and swore, knocking the tin off the bench to splash his legs and stomped in the puddle, then that was what George's legs looked like.

The purple lesions[24] were deep and would gradually blacken. The skin itself was unbroken for now, but as the surface layers died, open wounds would develop. George's feet and shins were the worst and at this early stage, Georgina knew that the plastic surgeons were concerned that he might lose several toes, both heels and potentially need skin grafts on both shins.

Small nasty lesions threatened unsightly disfigurement – the tip of an ear dipped in black, the tip of his nose coloured in, a black beauty spot on his cheek, an inky fingertip. It all relied on the underlying blood flow, to nourish and cling onto these small appendages.

'Poor George,' Georgina sighed. *'He has a long way to go.'*

---

[24] Septicaemia also causes blood clots to form throughout the network of tiny blood vessels in skin and muscle tissue. Tissue that is starved of oxygen this way dies and becomes blackened. This can cause widespread scarring, and in extreme cases can lead to amputation. This can also happen within vital organs, like your kidneys, causing kidney failure in very severe cases. From http://www.meningitis.org/disease-info/types-causes/meningoccal-disease.

Chapter 5

When you are young enough to need advice, you are too stupid to ask for it

When wise enough to ask for advice, you no longer really need it.

Anon

Ian's parents, Jean and Dave, were waiting in the corridor outside PICU as Ian and Siobhan came through the double doors. They dismissed any hellos to dive into the latest update. Ian rattled through the events of the day, but well aware of the circling phrase planted in his head that he had to relay; *'George is the sickest person in the hospital right now'*. He was unsure he could say those words without crumbling completely. It was the last person you would expect who pitched him over the cliff-edge.

It was Dave. He is a solid bloke – in build, in manner and deed, described by an uncle with a knowing wink as 'still waters run deep'. Beneath the reserved and dependable surface was a thoughtful, considerate soul that was seldom glimpsed. So when Ian started to struggle with the telling and the fateful phrase, Dave knew. He just knew this was the hard stop – the pain point in the telling that tore at the fabric of hope and will and self-control. On impulse, Dave stepped forward and hugged his son. Dave had never been a demonstrative person, so the hug had a purity and meaning far beyond either of their expectations, even if they did look like two drunks holding each other up. They held onto each other as though Dave were the last remaining reference point in Ian's ability to cope. That solidity had been there for Ian all his life, not ever called upon in adulthood, but now becoming a girder of strength bolted to the floor. The grounding gave him the stable seconds to hide his face, gather himself and regain control.

They both stepped back, awkward at what had happened and unfamiliar with the intensity of feeling they had just shared. As one, they both cast eyes downwards, scanning around them, now more conscious of their surroundings.

As days processioned past the PICU observation windows, Siobhan and Ian came to rely on the emotional support of Jean and Dave and Siobhan's mum, Margaret. George's grandparents were resolute and they were there at any stumble, accepting that it was not usual role grandparents sign up for.

At the weekend, the bedrooms reserved for parents across the hall from PICU were already assigned to single mums. Dads got sent down the corridor. So Ian was shepherded off to Jungle Ward for the night. Not really sure what this meant, but grateful for somewhere to sleep not far from George, Ian followed the nurse along the corridor. With an armful of bed linen, he was shown onto an empty dark ward of a dozen beds.

"Here you go, take your pick and make yourself at home. The early morning wake-up call is free. The cleaner comes in at five-thirty. Night night."

"Thanks, goodnight," said Ian in an upbeat tone, trying to mirror the same cheeriness.

From the pool of light in the entry hall way, he looked around the quiet dark ward. During the day, the ward was used as a staging post for children recovering from day case procedures. At any other time it would have been filled with bustle and yip. The stillness at one in the morning felt uncomfortable, as though he had been the last to leave and got shut in by mistake. A cold slimy suggestion wormed into his consciousness that maybe the essence of others had not left yet or had been shut in too. Eeyore, Pooh, Piglet, Batman and Rhino looked balefully back at him, hoping he would join their lonely club. Their cartoon smiles, intended to be cheery and welcoming, leered at him instead, creating the same unease as painted clowns' faces. The outlines he could barely see in the distance had the same expressions, crowding in with more shadows than they should have had, and pleading with him to join them too.

"Get a grip man, 'fraid of the dark? Now, who do I want to be tonight? Pooh – you can forget it, you tubby dozy loser. I am a righter-of-wrongs and I feel like I am Batman tonight!" He glanced around just to make sure no-one heard him say that.

Saturday 27ᵗʰ April, Siobhan's Diary

Pizza fest

Visitors

By now, the doctors had known that George's kidneys had shut down. No-one had mentioned this specifically to Ian and Siobhan. They assumed blood filtration was routine for patients in Intensive Care, aware that George's kidneys were not working, but for now unconcerned. Given time, his kidney function would return, wouldn't it? They did not appreciate the long-term implications of chronic kidney failure, and this realisation was three weeks in the future. If they had asked the direct question, they would have been given a straight answer, but they had not asked, so the wait-and-see status quo was easier to accommodate all round.

Blood tests showed that George's urea and creatinine[25] levels were way beyond normal ranges and continued to rise inexorably. Although his catheter[26] drain bag filled superbly, it was just collecting the five litres of excess fluid that had been pumped into him. It was not 'good urine', as the body's wastes had not been removed and were accumulating in his bloodstream. His blood needed filtering whilst in PICU and there was a machine for that too. It resembled a small blue robot on stilts, the size of an airline carry-on bag, with dials, LED displays, pumps and plastic pipes all jumbled together on its face. It disobeyed Asimov's Second Rule of Robotics[27] in that it had a will of its own, deciding when it would work contentedly or set off a battery of bleeps when feeling unappreciated. It drove the nurses nuts as it ruled them, as desperate for their attention as a bawling infant. Each alarm initiated a round of top thumping, side whacking, pipe twiddling, position-changing, reset button stabbing and finally bursts of unladylike swearing. They even had a replacement blood filtration machine waiting in the wings, but it was a sister to the first one and *'a complete and utter fat-arsed moody cow bitch',* according to Georgina.

---

[25] Creatinine is a substance formed from the metabolism of creatine, commonly found in blood, urine, and muscle tissue. It is measured in blood and urine tests as an indicator of kidney function.

[26] A catheter is a thin, flexible tube which is inserted into the bladder, usually along the tube urine naturally passes through, or through a hole in your abdomen directly into the bladder. The catheter usually remains in the bladder, allowing urine to flow through it and into a drainage bag.

[27] A robot may not injure a human being or, through inaction, allow a human being to come to harm. A robot must obey orders given it by human beings except where such orders would conflict with the First Law. A robot must protect its own existence as long as such protection does not conflict with the First or Second Law.

"There's only so long you can stand and look at a person in a coma. Let's be real – they don't do much, do they?" asked Fred with typical frankness. He had asked all the technical questions he wanted. Ben had cracked a few jokes at George's expense. Siobhan had busied about straightening his hair, his pillows and Get Well cards. Even her cheerful one-way conversation with George was flagging.

For something to do, Ben stood up and made everyone look at him. "I know, George Top 10 Funnies – let's do it."

"So is that about George or things he has done?" asked Fred, wanting to be clear on the rules.

"I think Funnies that George has done or said would be more chummy, don't you?" said Ian, attempting to make a sensible comment – over which he promptly drove a bus by adding, "What do you reckon is Number 1, Ben? It has to be *who is Ann Summers*?"

They all laughed at Ben, who squirmed again with the embarrassment of being caught on a lingerie website by his annoying younger brother. Quick as ever, though, Ben had one of his own.

"Well, if that's how you want to play it, then Number 2 has to be *I'm looking for tits.*"

"Ha, good one," said Fred. "That was a classic. The best bit was those two students glaring at Dad. Seeing George do what Dad does with the long lens on his camera."

It was Ian's turn to be the stooge and they all drowned out his protests of innocence.

Siobhan called them to heel. "C'mon – shushhhh! Can you be a bit less 'boysie' please? It feels like I'm in an Inbetweeners episode."

Fred went next. "I remember George at the Water Pistol Party. It was just brilliant. When all the parents came for pick-ups, Diana started it by dropping a cup of water in David's lap to make it look like he'd pissed himself. All hell broke loose and I remember the kids standing around amazed at their parents throwing water at each other. And who was the worst? George with that flaming pump gun thing. He was a monster."

Everyone surrounding George's bed smiled at the happy memory of a George full of life. Their smiles dissolved and stuck on their teeth. It was the moment when the DJ changes records and you appreciate what quiet is, or when the conversation in a crowded pub lulls. They all had the same realisation at the same time – it was the memory you might say at a funeral. Siobhan moved first.

"It feels odd sitting around his bedside talking about him."

"Does it feel morbid to you?"

"Nah, not at all – it's all just a rehearsal so we can give him a hard time when he wakes up," said Ben, trying to keep the banter going.

"You lot are too rowdy. We are disturbing the others. Let's go and get some pizza."

Sun 28th April, Siobhan's Diary

Moved out of isolation unit

Big day of tests, x-ray, ECG, chest drain in

O2 all over the place – back on oscillator?

On continuous blood filtration as no urine

Georgina chatted away cheerfully. It was a sunny day, George was an audience that could not escape and all her patients were how she wanted them, pipes tidy and ready for handover to the next shift.

"Hi George – how's it going, mate? You were jumpy in the night. Any good dreams you want to share? What was her name?" She chuntered about, smoothed his hair – *'how does it get so scruffy in the night?'* – and plumped his pillows that acted as bumpers to hold him in. "We thought you'd have to go back on the oscillator – so I put the machine just where you could see it, to scare your buns off. Well, it worked – you must have been so scared, your oxygen levels stabilised. Good news is, we didn't need to plug you in."

Ian and Siobhan kept up a continuous coverage of visiting George, back and forth, sometimes overlapping in the car park to exchange parking tickets. They both developed the habit of clasping George's hands and especially his feet upon arrival, to check that they weren't cold and to stimulate blood flow with their own warmth. They did not want his toes to die.

Mon 29th April, Siobhan's Diary

Visitors

Transit team / Medical Centre / Kingston Hospital

called

Med student from UCL – must tell Fred

"Hey George, I think you're a bit of a celebrity," chirped Siobhan, injecting some energy in case she could get a spark of recognition. She carried on anyway with her one-way conversation and rattled through the list of messages for him. "Wow, matey – you've certainly made an impression with all these people asking after you. There's another message from the A&E team at Kingston, just wanting an update on your progress. Catherine called again – that's six now. I reckon she thinks you're a good looking guy. What do you think? Here's one from the Ambulance Crew – wanting to know if you are awake yet. I'll tell them you're a lazybones, being in bed all day."

The post-it notes in her hand were paltry evidence of the number of people caring for George, wanting him to wake up. She felt a mix of emotion, surprise and gratitude. She couldn't really explain it, just an upwelling of warmth to the many, many people who held George in their thoughts. You couldn't bottle it. It must do some good, mustn't it?

Tues 30th April, Siobhan's Diary

CT scan of brain – any bleeds or damage?

BP haywire and bright red in lift

Moved head for first time

When Ian arrived for the evening shift, he brought a camera.

"It feels a bit weird taking a photo of him –do you feel the same?" Siobhan hesitated, holding the camera by her side like a shoplifter, reluctant to draw attention to herself. They had been told by the medical staff to take pictures for when George was ready to talk about what happened to him – to give him the evidence he needed to process the trauma. Neither of them wanted to, but felt a duty to do what they could to help him.

"I think it's okay, really I do. It's not as if the photos will go anywhere. We may not even keep them. The point the doctor made is justification enough for me. George will ask what happened to him and we'll need to be able to explain it to him."

"Okay then. I'll make sure I get the machines in and the drug pumps and less of George looking so ghastly."

As the first flash went off George jerked massively.

"Wow – did you see that! George just did a huge twitch! Watch, he may do another..."

"Do you think he can sense the light, or know we are here?" Siobhan still hoped.

"Dunno, maybe ... there's this thing called hypnagogic jerks.[28] It's like when you're dreaming and you fall or trip in your dream and you do an almighty involuntary jerk. When you are asleep, the brain is uncoupled from your muscles by the reticular activating centre. A bit like the clutch in a car being in neutral so the engine isn't connected to the wheels. It's a safety mechanism so you don't do yourself damage when you dream. Sometimes a bit of linkage remains in place and you get these jerks."

"Where did all that come from? Is it for real or are you being a jerk and making it up?"

---

[28] A hypnagogic jerk is an involuntary muscle spasm that occurs as a person is drifting off to sleep. The muscle spasms may occur spontaneously or may be induced by sound, light or other external stimuli. Some people report hypnagogic jerks accompanied by hallucinations, dreams, the sensation of falling, or bright lights or loud noises coming from inside the head.

Ian ignored her, lifting his chin to continue his lecture. "I remembered it from college – you see, I listened rather than chatting at the back about lip gloss and Whitney Houston lyrics."

"Anything else you remember, like what patronising means?"

"Yeah, loads – but all useless stuff. 'Polyhexamethyleneadipamide'– that's nylon, that is. 'Kugelschreiber' – that's ball-point pen in German. 'Gondwanaland' – that's the name of the first southern super-continent. Want any more?"

"No thanks, nerdy."

Photos I

1: First day at School

This is the first day of a new school year. I have to say I look angelic, don't you think? It's unusual to get a picture of the three of us together where we're not messing about. Maybe Mum left the hangers in our school blazers and hooked us up to the apple tree.

2: Me and Jenny

This photo always makes me smile whenever I see it. Jen is great fun and a complete nutcase. She is one of my best friends.

3: Skiing

This is me and Ben on a ski lift in Valmorel. I'm a much better skier.

4: Me reading on beach

I reckon I'm about eight years old in this photo. I look like a cool surfer dude, sitting in my sand-hollow chair. That's my Birds of the Coast book I'm reading.

5: Me baking

Great British Bake Off here I come! These cakes are for our Diamond Jubilee street party, so must be July 2012. I look so young, but this is only eight months before my illness.

6: Snowball

This is me playing with Mum. I didn't actually throw the snowball – so it's just for the picture. Mum would've killed me if I had done, a real hissy fit.

7: Ben, Fred and George in Spain

We are in the mountains of Northern Spain. It was a roasting hot day and we were trying to cool down in pools and eddies of the fast-flowing river. We had a proper swim but the water was sooo cold. It would be great to kayak down there.

8: PICU on Day 2

I don't like to look at this photo much – I find it scary to look at now. Obviously I have no recollection, but it's clear I was in a bad way. I'm told I had five litres of extra fluid in me, which explains why I look so hench. On my left is a stack of eight drug pumps for my heart, to maintain my coma state, and more antibiotics and pain relief.

9: PICU on Day 2 close up

On my right is that annoying blood filtering machine – it was so temperamental and the alarm went off all the time. The tube in my mouth goes into my lungs so that the ventilator can work. The tube up my nose goes into my stomach for feeding. They were really annoying so I pulled both of these out at different times. The nurses were not pleased, and stuck them straight back in again.

10: ME!!!

Handsome dude – this is what I looked like before I was inflated! My dad reckons he's more handsome than me – as if!

11: In the hoist in PICU

This is when I was lifted out of bed in the PICU at St George's. I am smiling at the joy of getting up for the first time in four weeks. Looking back, the wounds on my legs look dreadful but they're so much better now.

12: Awake in PICU

This is my favourite stripy blanket, which Mum brought in for me as I always seemed so cold due to the morphine. So this is our family all together again.

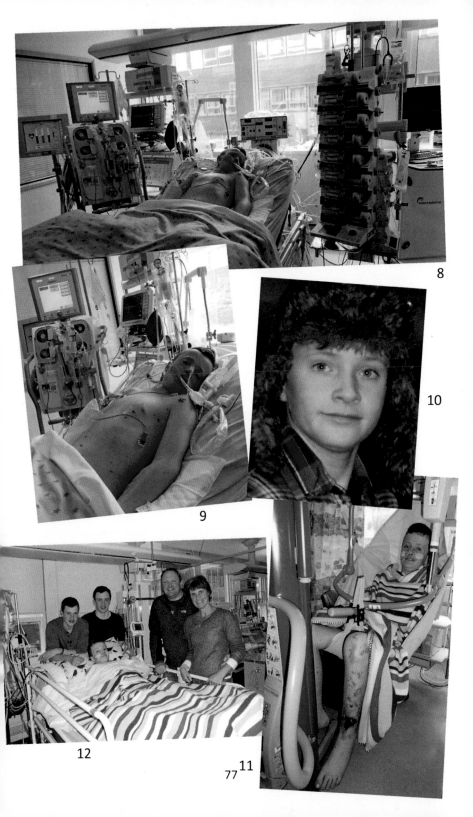

8

9

10

12

77 11

PART 2: RESTORATION

Chapter 6

Everyone is a moon, and has a dark side which he
never shows to anybody.

Mark Twain (Samuel Langborne Clemens) 1835-1910

*I enter at Level 2 – that's good, I think. This level is
better than the black abyss in the Basement where I have
been. I can see straight ahead, but with a restricted view
from my visor so the bright circle is ringed with fuzzy
darkness. This is so dazzlingly bright; maybe the brightness
can be turned down on the display?*

*I'm not sure if this is a Shoot'em Up or a Quest-type
game, so I'll just go with it for now. In the shimmer of white
light, I scan the empty car park and office buildings in front
of me for targets. I must find the No-See-Ums before they
can get a shot in. There is a small R2D2-like robot next to
me. She is on my team but – not being rude – she doesn't
look much use. She must have weapons I activate with
credits or fuel cells or something. I hear bleeping, which is
the countdown to the start. Here we go.*

*There is an almighty explosion of white light. I can't hear
it through my helmet, but I can feel the vibration in my
shoulders, bum and the backs of my thighs. It must be
behind me and I am falling… spinning … falling.*

Coming round from a coma was a gradual process for
George, as he had been in a drug-induced state for nearly
four weeks. For children, the analgesic of choice is
morphine as it is well-tolerated. It is excellent for pain relief
and although it causes respiratory suppression, it does so
less than the alternatives. In the early stages, a drug-
induced coma also helps the immune system to fight a viral,
bacterial or systemic fungal infection. By shutting down the

body's main functions, which consume the most energy and other vital resources, the immune system has a chance to tackle the infection with as much vigour as possible. Trouble comes, though, in the longer term, as morphine is also an opioid or narcotic which is addictive, turning George into an unwitting junkie. His body had grown to crave the euphoria the morphine gave him.

The doctors warned Siobhan and Ian that he would wake up gradually. 'Patchy' was the word they used – so sometimes lucid, some involuntary twitching and possible hallucinations, which could be unsettling for George as they were real to him. That last bit was English understatement at its ludicrous best. George was entertaining in his energy and inventiveness coming out of a coma, but thankfully he remembered only fragments.

My heart pulses gently in my ears. At least, I think it's mine, but it's very far away – or maybe someone else's? I don't want to open my eyes. I don't want to wake up. If I don't wake up then maybe He will go away. It's cold and black in the basement. I dread being on my own – with Him. I can't see who He is but I know He is there in the corner – waiting. If I keep still He won't see me. I don't want Him to know I am here too.

The blackness sweeps into my field of vision, narrowing the tunnel I can see through until it is a dull glow at the centre which fades and abruptly snips out. Just black and still ...

While Siobhan sat with him, she held George's hand as she always did. Absentmindedly she patted it, squeezed it, and even blew a raspberry in it. She held her breath.

"Was that...? Oh God!"

She felt a flutter of a squeeze back. Her heart leapt, hoping it was not her imagination. She stared without blinking at his eyelids, praying for them to move. Siobhan hauled Georgina in, breathlessly telling her what had happened.

With all the tenderness she could muster, Georgina explained, "Oh Siobhan, he's there, but not how you want him to be. He's dreaming in his own world, not yours yet. But do keep stimulating him, as they're starting to reduce his morphine. You will reach him soon."Georgina hugged her so she did not have to look at Siobhan's pleading eyes and crestfallen face.

Wed 1ˢᵗ May, Siobhan's Diary

Opened your eyes for doc

Lots of head moving, hand squeezing

Doctors view you waking up so wean off morphine

– made you a drug addict

Heart and kidney scans ok and no damage visible

Weird – how does that work? I can see colours behind my eyelids like scarves of light. It is night time – it must be, I'm lying down. He is still there. I want Him to go away – he just draws all the light to Him and makes me cold and dark. I am back. I have to tell you so you know. My eyes are gummed shut. My lips are stuck. I want to get up.

That's good! That's good! More cool water on my lips please. Yes, on my eyes too, get the glue off so I can open them.

I can hear voices now. I don't know the words or who made them.

Hang on – I recognise your sing-song voice, Mum.

I know you're there, Mum! I know you love me. I'm safe now you are here. Your hand is warm on my cheek. The rest of my skin is on fire. Jesus, it feels itchy. My fingers are burning and I daren't scratch. Why are my feet tied up and so numb?

See – I can nod my head like you asked me to, Mum.

Mum, don't cry. There's no need, I'm here. I'm back now. I'll hold your hand, Mum, make you feel better so you stop crying, just like I did for Jenny.

Sat 4th May, Siobhan's Diary

Pulled tubes out

Talking now

Multiple poos

Very fidgety, twitchy, saying bizarre things

George was in the middle of a conversation with himself as Siobhan looked on. She shivered as the otherworldliness of his words filled her with worry. Was this the morphine or a new George? She wanted the old one.

"Yeah, not too bad. Feel really hollow."

She tried to ask him if he needed anything.

"What you say? ... something to eat? ... favourite thing? Rum and onion fudge please ... No, I don't mean that – you know my favourite RUM and ONION … Big bag so I can share it … Really tired… gotta sleep…"

I open my eyes but only to slits so He wouldn't know. He is back lurking at the side of my vision. I don't like this; I really do not like this. I keep moving my head to try and get a good look at Him but he never stays still long enough. I close my eyes to ease my aching eye muscles and see if I can calm down a little. I can feel my own blood pulse in my temples, building the bubble of anxiety rising in my chest.

Please just go away.

Please just leave me alone.

I feel so vulnerable lying here. I'm not tied down or anything but the bed sides hold me in and all these pipes and wires stop me moving easily. My feet are still tied together – why is that? Who would do such a thing? It makes no sense to me.

SHIT, He's still there, I saw His shadow.

My heart is pounding now and my face is burning. My back feels prickly like I'm lying on biscuit crumbs. I have to get out of here. I have to do something now. I'll get these flaming pipes out, that's what I'll do. This nose pipe can go. I pull it and it does hurt, I keep pulling and it keeps coming. I cough and splutter and a nurse is next to me taking the tube from me – good girl, you can have it, I don't want it. What she say? More what? I can't hear you … speak to me … eyes closed…drifting …

Sun 5th May, Siobhan's Diary

Pulled tube out again

V restless

Fell out of bed in the night

Banged head and pupils different sizes

On heparin – bleed – so another CT scan

I have a cloak just like speccy Harry Potter's invisibility cloak. The problem is, mine isn't so cool, mine isn't make-believe and I can't choose when I wear it. It wraps around me, holding me in like I am bandaged and wounded and seals in the threshing of my insides. It restricts me and my ability to do anything other than hunker down and hope it goes away.

While I'm wearing it, I am not me. I am confused, panicky, distracted. I do not think straight. I jump at anything loud or sudden. Things that I am meant to do, get lost after the first sentence. The perfect storm for me is a coming-together of my overloaded brain and my anxiety cloak slipping around me – I hope it never happens as it would be really scary. I don't know how I would stop it or where it would stop. Would I be the same George afterwards?

Mon 6th May, Siobhan's Diary

Legs redressed – very painful

No sure if need skin grafts

1st time on facebook – no messages sent

Tues 7th May, Siobhan's Diary

First talk of dialysis

Possibly moving hospitals

"What's he looking at?"

Ian, Ben and Fred were travelling back from visiting George. Ian had noticed the passenger in the van alongside them staring across, fascinated by something.

The journey back through Wimbledon was a rare opportunity for a reflective conversation – that did not involve sport, food or laddish stuff. Ben was broadly positive in his view of George.

"I've not seen George in the last week so I really noticed a difference. He looked a fair bit better to me – less pale, not so swollen and at least there is a person there dreaming and twitching, rather than a comatose body. He must be fried with all those drugs though."

Ian agreed but did not respond – distracted by the traffic and Fred beaming in the rear view mirror.

"Look what I've found! Multipack of doughnuts. Result!" He had been scavenging through a bag of stuff to be brought home as it wasn't needed in the hospital. Fred practically inhaled Doughnut One, but it took his neck muscles to squeeze down the two bites of Doughnut Two. Doughnut Three was slowing him down, his puffed out cheeks proving the bottleneck. The bag got snatched through to the front seats so Ian and Ben could do their best to catch him up.

At the next set of lights, the van alongside them braked to a stop, giving the passenger a longer chance to stare at the three of them.

"Hmmm, we can't be looking good," said Ian.

"What's so bad about three blokes eating doughnuts?" crumbed Fred, with a doughnut stored in each cheek.

"It's not three blokes – its two dudes and a man-sized chipmunk in the back."

Chapter 7

If you are going through hell, keep going…

Winston Churchill

Wed 8th May, Siobhan's Diary

Sat up for first time

Sat 11th May, Siobhan's Diary

Sat in chair

Gillian – clinical psychologist

George's normal healthy covering – some might say chunkiness – was a fresh five-week-old memory. So the transformation to his current frailty was all the more startling. He had lost thirty percent of his body weight, down to 38kg, the average weight of an eleven-year-old[29]. His solid legs had wasted down to skinny Twiglets, shaky and scarcely able to hold his standing frame, let alone move. No more *'Sun's Out – Guns Out'* – his kayaking biceps had disappeared. Never-before-seen cheekbones carved the edges to his wide face, now completely dominated by eyes made vivid with the thrill of sitting up for the first time, albeit bolstered by pillows.

Without a specialist renal unit for children in St George's, the adult renal unit had been persuaded to take on George as a stop-gap. On Sunday Ian and Rowena, one of the PICU nurses, wheeled George to the Adult Renal Unit at St. George's on a voyage of discovery prior to the first

---

[29] From http://www.buzzle.com/articles/average-weight-for-children-by-age.html

session. It took an age through the maze of corridors and lifts. The team greeting them could not have been more helpful to reassure George with all the tubing, pumping and dials, but it did not take away the impact of the unit. George mentioned later that it felt like a down-at-heel garage, where people rather than cars come to be serviced. It made him quiet and thoughtful for the rest of the day.

The consultant renal specialist, Alasdair, sat Siobhan and Ian down to walk them through the treatment just given. All had gone well, George's levels and blood chemistry had been scrubbed back to normal – for a person with no kidney function.

"I need to be very straight with you both. I am used to dealing with adults, but I am not a specialist in the care of paediatric patients. There are long-term implications for growth and development where George needs that specialist care, so I have set a limit of three dialysis sessions here. He needs to move on from what we can do for him here to get the best care possible."

"We appreciate you being so honest – so what are our options?" Siobhan responded.

"The specialist Renal Units are in Great Ormond Street, Manchester, Birmingham, John Radcliffe in Oxford and Evelina London. You need to be in one of those. Unfortunately, there are only beds available in Manchester and Birmingham."

"We're not going there," said Siobhan emphatically – end of discussion.

"I agree with you," Alasdair replied unexpectedly. "If it were my family, I would refuse that too. There is no way you can make those distances work and retain some semblance of family life." He continued, "I will do all that I can to get you a bed in a unit nearer to home. I will sit on the phone until I get an answer, and we have some favours we can pull in. Just be patient with me and I will come back to you."

"Thank you," they both replied, pathetically grateful for Alasdair's determined help. They did not realise it, but the next two days would decide their fate for the next two years.

Mon 13th May. Siobhan's Diary

Moved to ward –HORRENDOUS

Filter stopped

Agency nurse – What dose are you on?

No doctor in 28 hours

Ian back to work

Ian and Siobhan had tucked George up for the night, making sure he was comfortable, had taken his meds and that someone was on the way to fix the blood filtration machine, which had stopped yet again. They waited outside the four-bed bay George was in, out of earshot but within eyeline. They were waiting for a doctor to show up. Ian had both barrels loaded and was ready to blow the head off anyone with a stethoscope round their neck.

"Look, just calm down, getting angry won't help." Siobhan tried to reason with him but just made it worse.

"I am calm, just furious, and this has to change," hissed Ian.

They were at the end of the worst 28-hour period since George became ill. Yesterday had been a horrendous day.

At lunchtime, George had been transferred from the high-dependency PICU to the general children's ward. If a plan had been hatched to move from the best possible care to the abject worst, then it could not have been better designed or executed. It started to go wrong as soon as the bed wheels stopped moving in the new ward.

Nothing happened. Once the porter had gone, no-one appeared to check them in. The blood filtration machine that had been wheeled down with George sat there – also doing nothing. The afternoon drifted by, with the odd fleeting glimpse of a nurse. The machine still sat there, unplugged both to the wall and to George. When a nurse did stop, she may as well have loaded the bullets herself, for her rushed cheeriness did not register the stone-faced parents.

"Hi, erm, George?" she said looking at the folder of his file rather than the notes inside. She did not have the time or inclination to read on, but directed her question at George. "What medicines are you on?"

"Read the fucking chart," muttered Ian to Siobhan, barely keeping a lid on it. He stepped in to rattle off the dosages and remind her that the last dose was now overdue. When the shift changed at 19:30, he did the same for the new nurse, and again the next morning for the next new face in an agency uniform. Siobhan changed George when he needed it, badgered the nurses into replacing his feed drip, and emptying his drainage bag when it was fit to burst. They did not see a doctor of any description for a full twenty-eight hours after leaving PICU.

By late afternoon, Ian went hunting for the matron or doctor or anyone he could unload on. The poor Matron that he found stood startled by the intimidating torrent she was blasted with.

"I just don't understand how you can go from round the clock care by two nurses to this – I can't believe it. We were 100% dependent for everything but now we're expected to be completely independent – it just does not work like that." Ian was close to losing it. "We have not seen a doctor in the last twenty eight hours – that's completely unacceptable. The blood filtration machine has worked for just three hours in that time and no-one knows how to work it!"

There was no swearing, but no let-up for her to defend herself – she could not. She did try but regretted it immediately, as it was a losing conversation she had had before.

"Mr. Birks, I have a ward of many ill children and your son is one of twenty-four. I get patients sent to my ward without any notice and a budgeted staff level that does not change. I already have the maximum number of agency nurses I am allowed."

The swear-fest in Ian's head stayed there, thankfully, but only just. Siobhan would not forgive him for behaving like an appalling vest-wearing thug. He chose his words carefully.

"Your staffing levels and budget problems are not helping my son. He is just out of Intensive Care and no-one has taken up the mantle of care for him. We've just put George to sleep for the night. We are not leaving until we have seen the doctor responsible for the ward. You need to bleep him now to tell him that and get him here. What I'm demanding is not unreasonable – you know very well how far below the minimum standard of care we have come to. It stops now – with a plan going forward that that we agree on tonight."

While they waited for the doctor to appear, Ian mulled over how they had got to this point. He felt sorry for the staff mostly – the Matron was a competent, caring professional who was as frustrated with the system as he was. The nurses did their best but surely the bare minimum was not why they became nurses? He wondered at what point the 'system' took on a life of its own, became the root cause and generated the excuses. Once employees are reduced to just coping with whatever comes through the door, then there is no catalyst to highlight the shortfalls. It must be so dispiriting when what can be done bears no relation to what is needed.

His thoughts were interrupted by the arrival of the senior registrar. As she walked towards him, she opened with an apology, admitting that she and her team had been elusive and that the care George had received was poor. Ian would have put it more strongly than *'not showing us at our best'*, but at least there was an acknowledgement the handover had been lacking. It was no excuse, but all parties only ever saw the general children's ward as a staging post, so George fell perfectly through the cracks. What had been going on behind the scenes, which Siobhan and Ian were unaware of, was the searching, cajoling, and wheedling to get George into a specialist centre able to cope with his kidney failure. Centres of excellence such as Birmingham Children's Hospital and others had all been offered up as options, albeit with hideous distances to travel.

This was a *Sliding Doors* moment, as it was for Gwyneth Paltrow in the 1998 movie. For her, the pivotal twist to the plot featured a brunette Paltrow and a blonde Paltrow alternating through two parallel universes based on whether she caught a train or not. In a 'what if?' moment of a phone's being answered or not, George's luck was about to change. The Renal Unit of Evelina Children's Hospital, just across Westminster Bridge from Big Ben, had a bed available and so became the front runner. The move was set for two days' time.

Tues 14th May, Siobhan's Diary

No feed, dressings changed, physio

Babies crying all night

Washed and cleaned by mum

Had matron in

Worst of NHS

Chapter 8

Wed 15th May, Siobhan's Diary

Consultant apologised

Off to Evelina – amazing place, everything

checked

Best of NHS

It was a bitterly cold day for George to breathe fresh air rather than the institutionalised version, for the first time in four weeks. It cooled his cheeks and made his eyes water, but he said it felt good.

The stress of the last four days made for a subdued journey in the ambulance. It was a watershed. Until now, St George's was known, and apart from its recent faults, they had brought George back from the brink and kept him alive. The PICU team had been superb and it was scary to leave their care. Ian and Siobhan knew nothing of the Evelina and felt the burden of responsibility for George, not just the immediate days ahead but for the fabric of his life to come.

In the back of the ambulance, Siobhan got chatting to Dave, an agency nurse who was along for the trip. He had only been doing an extra shift and had drawn the cushy job of riding shotgun – coincidentally, going to the Evelina where he normally worked. He rattled off a slew of names, including the infamous Sheila, but it made no impression on Siobhan – yet. His enthusiasm for the hospital was encouraging and brightened Siobhan a little, just enough to dispel her perpetual worried face.

The transfer to Evelina was a deliverance. Walking into the Evelina Children's Hospital that first time made them feel blessed. It was a step from the dark ages into a cathedral of light. 'A hospital that doesn't feel like a hospital', Evelina presented a bright and spacious environment designed to be engaging, fun and exciting for children – who, more than any other patient, might feel fearful about their stay. The clarity of design shone through – the patient, not the institution, was the focal point.

'The Evelina hospital is formed from two main elements, a standard three-storey box and a glassy volume nuzzling up to it with a curved and glazed roof form. The light-filled atrium forms the main communal area, housing a school, meeting area, radio studio, snack bar and wrap-around garden, all suspended at tree-canopy level. It is overlooked by every ward in the hospital, with healthy natural daylight finding its way to every bed through the expanse of glass. Achieving the vision for the atrium was key in Evelina's mission to create an open and welcoming environment for its vulnerable young patients.'

Mission statements were puff and nonsense to Siobhan and George. They judged what they could see and feel. They saw the striking building, true enough, but the smiles of the security staff and the welcome from the ward teams meant more, received as genuine and heartfelt. George was disconcerted to be treated like a celebrity, pampered even. For the first few hours on Beach ward, Bed 26, the questioning, noting, testing, examining was forensically thorough, edging towards draining and invasive. It was as though the collective knowledge of George's illness that had travelled with him from St George's was quarantined, scrubbed clean, disinfected and re-stated on clean sheets.

George met the team that would map his path through the challenges ahead, holding his hand, dragging him at times, but all the while with cheerfulness, utter professionalism and unquenchable warmth. For the first time they met Mel with her chirpy efficiency, Sheila with her sleeves rolled up and forcefulness, and Stewart the consultant, who would oversee George's care with the diligence of a father for his own family.

There was a lot to do. Most pressing was the fallout from no kidney function – George was carrying at least four kilos too much fluid. It was crucial to work out George's dry weight so that dialysis could be effective and to avoid stressing his heart. Blood chemistry ran in parallel, to pick up on the stop-gap dialysis and get salts, urea and creatinine all back in acceptable ranges.

Next was the visible damage. George's legs from the knee down were heavily bandaged – all of which would need to come off for the plastic surgeons to assess and begin treatment. George was a waif at 38 kilos, looking out with deep-set eyes from a thin pale face. He seemed lost in the blankets of his hospital bed, like a wizened old man watching the world bustle by.

Then there were the things they did not know about, but needed to. For every visible lesion, there was potentially another hidden one, affecting some of the fine tissues, eyesight tests to look for retinal damage, hearing tests, a full cardiovascular assessment to check for damage or irregularities, scans of the defunct kidneys to explore any remaining options, and MRI and CT scans of the brain to evaluate potential deep seated damage.

Diana's words, from that very first night in Kingston A&E, echoed in Siobhan's mind – *'you will not get the answers you need for some time yet'*. The true extent of George's illness was starting to rear its head. She felt overwhelmed, with a pervasive despair taking hold as she sat down next to George's bed to try and take it all in.

Neither she nor George had time to drift down. Over the next seven days they were scooped up, organised, shepherded, cajoled and prompted by the Evelina staff, orchestrated by Sheila and Stewart. Kay gave up her Sunday so that dialysis could continue every day to filter off excess fluid. Kay is like your favourite Auntie. She is one of the most experienced nurses on the Dialysis Unit and has seen it all. Each time, they coped with the sickness, the drop in blood pressure and the coldness.

For each dialysis session, George's hospital bed was wheeled into the Renal Unit. As he could not walk, he had to be lifted onto the scales to be weighed if the hoist was not available. When George first arrived, Tinu, one of the dialysis nurses, would scoop him up in a blanket to move him from his bed to the scales, with scolding from her colleagues – *"You will hurt your back, you can do that with little ones but not fourteen-year-olds."*

Whilst George was plugged in, Siobhan herself was given the full treatment too – coffee, supportive chats, sent off to get herself lunch, dispatched for a sleep in the Parents' Room. The battery of tests, treatments and dressings kept their daily schedule full and productive with no time for erosive contemplation.

When they were allowed to think through what had happened, even that was carefully corralled by Laura, the psychologist, who made her first appearance that week and would be ever-present over the next year. Laura has the kindest smile and her gentleness allows children to feel comfortable enough to tell her how they are feeling. She quickly built a trusting relationship with George.

Day by day the relentless program of care started to show progress.

I like Laura very much. She came and spoke to me for ages. She listened. She asked me how I became ill and what it felt like. She helped me understand what has happened to me.

One month ago, just after my fourteenth birthday, I had meningitis, which has left me with some scars and knackered kidneys. I have googled it and know what meningitis is but I don't want to know more – I find it upsetting. When I looked at the patient stories on the MRF website,[30] I only skimmed two or three before I had to stop. It made me go cold, those poor children. It could have happened to me and that was sooo scary. But more than anything, it really upset me seeing kids the same age as me with no hands or feet or even whole limbs missing.

My kidneys are rubbish. I wish they would just flaming wake up and just do something. They say that when the body is so ill, the kidneys are the first organ to stop functioning. Well, mine took one look and surrendered straight away with not a peep since. That's pathetic.

I am more than my meningitis and rubbish kidneys. When people ask what I was like before I was ill, I would have said loads of things; I love kayaking and sailing, Sheldon Cooper is the coolest person on the planet and my Nikon is THE best camera. One day I want to go to Africa on a safari. My cooking is getting really good now. My Pad Thai is awesome – I am not being big-headed, just saying a job well done. Dad and I make a good team, he is my sous-chef and does all the chopping which I have to say is helpful. The hardest bit is remembering all the ingredients. My top tips are not to burn the finely-chopped ingredients like garlic and chillis as it makes them bitter.

Nowadays, people do not really ask about me, just about how I am feeling. I am different to the day I got ill. I had never been sick before. I have never had my life so shepherded and controlled before – well, at least I never

---

[30] Go to http://www.meningitis.org/about-us. There are 400 first-hand stories in an online Book of Experience, in words and on video. It will make you cry.

noticed. So much has happened in such a short space of time that everything has changed. I am a lot quieter than I used to be. More watchful as I try to work out if I should say what I feel, or words to please other people. My life took a fundamental right turn to a destination I had never thought of. The map of my life has been turned through ninety degrees; I'm still moving forward but will end up somewhere else. I wish I knew where and that uncertainty is the scariest thing.

On day two at the Evelina, the registrar from the Plastic Surgery team came to assess George's legs for himself, comparing what he could see with the notes. To do that, he needed to remove George's dressings. A simple routine task - in his head. He introduced himself to mother and patient with a courtesy that his own mother would have been proud of. Crucially, he did not tell Ellen, the Ward Sister, what he was doing.

He started to fiddle with the bandages on George's legs to look at the deep wounds. George became increasingly nervous, as the bandages were stuck and scabbed to the tissues beneath so each movement pained him, causing a reactive twitch which made it worse.

Ellen came flying out of her office like a Jack Russell, full of pep and vim. She was at him in an instant.

"What do you think you are doing to my patient? No way are you taking those dressings off until he's had some paracetamol first, then they have to be soaked in Appeal. Come back in thirty minutes – we will soak the dressings for you."

The registrar did not argue and shuffled off meekly, grateful that no-one had heard nor seen his humiliation. He did not realise that a Nurses 1 versus Doctors Nil score line would be around every nurse station within minutes. Ellen had one last nip at his ankles.

"And next time, please come and tell me what you plan to do to my patients – so we can help you then. That tore him off a strip, don't you think?" Ellen added to Siobhan, pleased with her own wit. Siobhan did her best to keep the surprise from her face and hid the smirk beneath her hand in a self-conscious gesture. It was not fair to laugh at the well-intentioned registrar. If Ellen had just shown what taking responsibility for your patient meant, she liked it. More of that, please!

The dialysis team on Beach Ward were a very impressive bunch. Starting at the top, Stewart, the lead consultant, was vastly impressive and clearly an expert in his field. He got to know his patients well but also the parents, so that they were fully on board and supportive of the long-term care plan.

The nursing team – Carmen, Kay, Georgie, Tinu and Little Katie – as a whole were well-trained and thorough. They combined the core nursing skills with specialisms of plumbing to connect the machines, IT helpdesk to fix them when playing up, play leader, theatre critic, DJ – the list went on.

Most of all, they brought their personalities and warmth to work with them every day to boost the kids' morale, keep the Unit upbeat and get to know their patients over what proved to be, regrettably, long periods of time.

George got to know many of them. Tinu was a great example. She loved dancing and needed no encouragement to pump up the volume and boogie round the ward, shaking her booty. Little Katie was unbelievably cheerful and always at the centre of activities such as cinema on a Saturday, baking, organising trips and many, many more.

George knew most of the other kidney patients on the same schedule as him. At fifteen, Deni was one of the older patients on the Dialysis Unit and would soon transfer to the adult renal team. She was a small, self-contained individual. She was popular with the nurses and they had invested time to train her in sterile technique to get her own trolley ready. It helped them but gave Deni an element of self-sufficiency which the younger kids envied. Deni was either asleep (she was even better at sleeping than George) or occupied, with a serious face which would lighten up on her own terms. At Saturday's session, Deni was excited about the imminent birth of her baby brother.

Deni came bounding into the Unit the following Tuesday, desperate to tell her news. Over the weekend, her Mum had gone into labour. That was the hook.

Skillfully Deni reeled in everyone on the Unit, turn by turn of the spool in one long-running conversation with multiple players dipping in at different points, all expertly choreographed by Deni.

To Tinu and Georgie – *"Guess what? Mum has given birth."*

To Little Katie – *"Mum had twins. Wow it was amazing. She is going to call one of them Carmen."*

To Siobhan – *"Did you hear? Twins, it's fabulous, both girls."*

To Carmen – *"That's unbelievable, to have twin girls when expecting a baby boy."*

To Stewart – *"I don't know how they could possibly have missed that on the scans and ultrasound."*

The penny dropped first for Little Katie. "You little minx, she's played us all. It was a little boy all along, wasn't it?"Deni cackled, smug that she had completely suckered them all. Stewart harrumphed off, muttering about scans to himself, trying to preserve his consultant's dignity.

They never saw the registrar that Ellen had savaged again. He either moved to other responsibilities or was too scared to show up. Instead, George had Dr Inger caring for him on a hands-on basis as his plastic surgeon. She had followed George's progress from first admission, when the lesions on his legs were ugly and looked like they needed skin grafts. She was a quirky mix of old-school formality that did not sit well with her warmth as a person. A pent-up bundle of repressed emotion that meant you never get to what she really felt. She took time with a forensic examination of George's legs, toes, heels and extremities to assess the need for skin grafts. She took inordinate care over his dressings. Siobhan loved her school-teacher directness – a woman after her own heart.

"I have not spent 20 years to become a consultant and have all my good work undone by you not eating enough protein," Dr Inger told George. The barrage continued so that George was left in no shadow of doubt that protein was essential to skin repair and that he had to eat loads, starting right now.

"Good," thought Siobhan. *"That's what he needs – clear, simple and a boot up the backside."*

Siobhan liked Dr. Inger from the very beginning. Perhaps it was her unique dress sense that told you most about her. It was as though the rules of fashion were for the guidance of the wise and the obedience of fools. Some days Dr Inger could be sophisticated, with her hair in a French chignon, or starchy in a tweed two-piece, or sporty in a miniskirt. Her rebellious days, where fashion was thrown out of the window as the rules did not apply to her, were striking and fortunately rare. That was what Siobhan like most of all – her powerful independence that could not be moulded.

Over the next month, it became clearer to Dr Inger that skin grafts would not be needed. Fortunately the underlying blood flow was good and the 'outside-in' healing had taken well to reduce the very visible damage. The skin on George's shins was very thin and badly scarred, but it had repaired itself to spare him further discomfort.

Chapter 9

Life doesn't come with an instruction book. That's why
we have fathers.

H. Jackson Brown, Jr.

After two weeks' leave, Ian returned to work full-time.
The lack of engagement from his US boss meant his
Business Unit was leaderless and all issues came to him by
default anyway. Sitting at his desk in a rare quiet moment,
he struggled to concentrate. Rather than fight it, he went
with what was distracting him. He focused on the nagging
guilt in his mind. *Was there something he could have done
to protect George?* To find answers, he called a work
colleague, Angie, who he was sure would know.

"Hi Angie, it's Ian here."

"Hey Ian, good to hear your voice. I hear your son is
making great progress, which is so encouraging and I bet a
huge relief."

"Sure is – there's still a long way to go but he's a tough
kid and wants to get back to how he was. Angie, I'm calling
because I want to ask something of you..."

"Fire away, I'll do my best to help," said Angie without
hesitation, and she meant it.

"How about some background first – so at least I can
ask sensible questions. I knew there is a vaccine for
Meningitis C. It's very successful and been around for a long
time. But not the case for Men B?"

Angie, being a scientist at heart, could not resist delving
into first principles. "Well, Ian, it has been a notoriously
hard job to develop a MenB vaccine.[31] Unlike other bacteria

---

[31] From http://www.meningitis.org/menb

that cause meningitis and septicaemia, the sugar coat of MenB bacteria does not trigger an immune response, because it looks like developing human brain cells. This means that the immune system doesn't recognise it as a foreign invader, and this protects it from attack. So using the sugar coat just doesn't work for MenB vaccine development. The search for a MenB vaccine has had to focus on other elements of the surface of MenB bacteria but it has been very difficult to find elements which are both 'visible' to the immune system and present in every MenB strain. Even elements that are usually present are extremely variable, so the immune response against a vaccine made from one kind of MenB may not be capable of killing all the different MenB strains."

Ian cut through the science bit. "But it sounds like some progress has been made. It's like this, Angie – I was given your name by the Marketing Department as a person who would know about Bexsero – the experimental Men B vaccine from Novartis. We did some work on it last year and it was your client – right? You know we claim that as a company we have worked on all of the Top 50 best-selling drugs. Well, I assumed Bexsero would be up near the top of the list with other vaccines?"

"Well, you're half right and half wrong – let me explain. I agree that vaccines are normally good sellers as they should be used in the 'at-risk' population, which tends to be large depending on the condition. The trouble with Bexsero[32] is that it has only just been launched, but for private purchase only so that restricts it to 1% of its possible sales. It's also impossible to get hold of – have you heard or any awareness campaign or seen any reporting of its availability?"

---

[32] Novartis press release from
http://www.novartis.com/newsroom/media-releases/en/2013/1672036.shtml

"No, I haven't. That's really surprising. It's as though the launch came and went and no-one noticed, least of all yours truly," admitted Ian.

Despite working in the pharmaceutical industry, the launch of Bexsero had completely passed Ian by. His professional pride was dented; how could he not have known? As a father he felt guilty that he should have, and somehow made sure the risk was taken away from his son.

"You're not the only one, believe me," said Angie, unaware of the significance of her reassurance. "Bottom line is, the Government does not want the cost of vaccinating all kids when very few actually get meningitis. Recently, the JCVI recommended against adding Bexsero to the UK national immunisation programme as it is not considered to be cost-effective –"[33]

"Sorry Angie, what's the JCVI?" interrupted Ian.

"It stands for the Joint Committee on Vaccination and Immunisation. Basically, it sets policy and assesses cost-effectiveness. As you can imagine, it's a tough rationing call to make – to be dramatic about it, how many kids do you allow to ... I mean how many cases each year before voters deem it unacceptable."

Angie caught her tactless comment before voicing it, but Ian had already completed her thought for her. It deepened his pit of guilt and he wanted to know more of what he should have done, even if was a scarring exercise. If licensing had been a non-event, surely public awareness campaigns were the next step?

He thanked Angie for her insight and wrapped up the call, putting aside what he had learned to chew over later.

---

[33] From
http://www.ukmi.nhs.uk/applications/ndo/record_view_open.asp?new DrugID=5391

By ten o'clock the News was just repeats, so it burbled in the background unwatched. Siobhan was concentrating on edging a partly-finished quilt which was draped over her knees as a temporary duvet. Ian was sitting on the sofa next to her and doing... well, not doing anything really. He had learned long ago not to get caught idling on the sofa whilst Siobhan was busy. Of the many things on his mind, that was not one of them.

Siobhan sensed a palpable tension in the air, with a restlessness coming from the other end of the sofa. "You're quiet," she stated over the top of the quilt.

"Yeah, sorry," said Ian, present in body but with no lights on. She knew his mind was active, but not here, in the room with her.

"Anything happen at work today?" she persisted gently.

"Nahh, not really," – still just as vague.

"How is that new global deal coming along?"

"Early days, ink not yet dry on the contract."

"Jesus, I'm dying of boredom here. Why are you being such a drip? Shape up, matey – or I'm off to get someone more interesting."

Ian laughed, dragged out of his thoughts. The quilting-obsessed, rave-fuelled, wannabe-cougar of a wife of his in her fluffy slippers was funny.

"Ok tiger, I was talking to a colleague at work today. I found out there is a vaccine available for Meningitis B. It was licensed three months before George fell ill."

"So? You've lost me. I don't see the significance."

"Well, obviously George could have had it and his kidneys would still be working."

Ian was picking at the scab of guilt over his lack of awareness. He should have known – he more than most, working in the industry.

"I realise that, but back in January, unless you had a crystal ball, how would you have known? Do you know of any kids who have actually had this new vaccine?"

Her words came out harsher than she intended. The sarcasm gave an edge that wasn't needed, but he was irritating her with his screwy judgment. *"Oh no,"* she thought – he had gone all quiet again with that wounded look. *"He really is making this into something when it needn't be."* Before she backtracked, Ian continued, spilling the words, desperate to unload them and face up to his sentencing.

"It's not just the vaccine. I keep thinking back to that day – your calls, the Emergency Room, George lying there." He paused in the moment back then, re-paralysed with the same desperation. "What if I'd been working from home that day? I would have picked up George, not you. Do you realise what would have happened?"

"Well you weren't, so it's pointless going back over it," countered Siobhan, instinctively trying to jolt some objectivity into him. Her voice carried no sympathy to permit him to dig deeper – just common sense that he needed, to see things as clearly as she did. It failed. Instead he pulled open the deep open wound of recrimination he had sliced in his thoughts so often. He stared forward, face expressionless as he began what was to him an excoriating confession.

"But I know what I would have done. I would have jollied him along, put him to bed with Calpol. I can hear myself saying it, *'sleep is the best medicine'*. All so I could get on with calls without being disturbed. A few more hours would have meant the infection could have taken hold and wreaked more damage." His voice fractured, his eyes glistening in the telling. His words ached like nothing he had rehearsed. "I would not have cared enough or been patient enough. I would have failed him, Shiv – as his father, I would have failed him. I know with absolute conviction he would have died."

Siobhan was stunned. The person she loved most in the world was flailing at himself and she did not know what to say.

"You're judging yourself all wrong," she said, shaking her head to plead with him.

"Maybes don't matter. The outcome would have been George dying and that shatters me," he said softly, eyes downcast with the shame he felt.

"Listen to me." She lifted his head and held his face in her hands so he had no choice. "You weren't there. You did not see him. You would have done the right thing, I know you would. Just stop beating yourself up – or I'll start, and then it'll really hurt."

Her words, her faith in him and her respect helped. Having his face cupped, his eyes held by hers and her understanding, broke the dark glassiness of his reverie. He tried to respond with a smile but her hands slipped and squashed his lips, nose and cheeks into a single fleshy lump. Knowing she had pulled him back from the emotional cliff edge, she threw him a joker role to play.

"You know how it is for all parents. Your First Born gets a tiny scratch. It gets washed, TCP-ed, a Mickey Mouse plaster and a hug. Middle One gets told to go and get a plaster from the cupboard. Last Born gets asked – is it dripping? No? Then give it a rub and it will be fine in a minute."

He half smiled, opening the door a little, so she flipped the quilt over his knees too, making a warm cocoon. They held each other for a while, letting the stillness return.

"I'm just glad it was you at home that day. You cared enough to see he was sweaty with fever and to make him comfier with a fresh T-shirt. Your instincts were right when you saw the significance of the rash on his chest. You were brave enough to stick your neck out, making it the emergency it had to be."

She interrupted him, to help him fend off his corroding recrimination. Siobhan made her point for the second time. "It's exactly what you would have done had you been there."

"No, it's not. You saved George's life that day. You saved our son, no-one else. I know you did and I believe that." His jaw jutted, offering all-comers their best shot. "George knows it too – well, he will when he is able to appreciate what you did for him. I know it now. You are such a special person and I love you all the more for it."

By the end of May, George was still very unwell, but stable. Jean and Dave had travelled to South West France, staying there for a week to unwind and do some sightseeing. It was a chance to step off the emotional roller coaster of the last four weeks.

A visit to the walled city of Carcassonne had been on their 'must do' list. It lived up to the guide book enthusiasm of a fairytale castle set on a hilltop with turrets and crenelated walls as though drawn with a child's view of what a castle should look like. The cathedral, surrounded by the high walls of the castle, was a magical place, untouched over the centuries but mobbed nowadays by tourists.

Despite the crowds, there was still a respectful and subdued atmosphere inside the nave.

It was the hush that reminded Jean of the Intensive Care Unit. The stillness of a medieval knight lying prone with his arms at his sides, encased in his stone sarcophagus. She saw George in the same position and just as cold. Although not a religious person, Jean wanted to get rid of the chilling image she had created, and had the impulse to say a prayer for her grandson. With that, she paid her two Euros for a tea light and took it to the iron grating with hundreds of other lit candles.

She prayed, "Keep your fighting spirit, George – we so want you to get well and be happy. Amen."

Chapter 10

"So what do you fancy for lunch, Chugs?" asked Ian, finally lifting his nose from his iPad. He had already agreed with Sheila that if George was up for it, she was okay to let him out of the hospital in a wheelchair for an hour or two.

"Sushi, do you think?" George put on his most endearing smile, knowing full well that his Dad would have to leave the hospital and take a long walk to go and get it for him.

"OK, but the deal is, you come too."

"What do you mean?"

"Well, we wrap you in a blanket, bung you in a wheelchair and you get out of here for a while. Sheila is okay with it. What do you say?"

"Sure – let's do it."

"Jeez George, have you been eating all the pies?" Ben had never pushed anyone in a wheelchair before. It was really hard work – physically. He had to concentrate; aware of his responsibilities to his pushee. Every kerb could tip George out; every crack in the pavement was a rattle. Other people were an inconsiderate nightmare – they just won't get out of the way or let you through. Ben swore he was going to run down the next sodding tourist ambling along reading their emails and not looking where he was going.

But, as a one off, on a glorious life-affirming spring day, it was not so bad. In fact, the novelty value of the wheelchair was good fun, making George the centre of attention, which he responded well to, signalling Ben to greater speed and whizzy turns. The distant dance music drew them along the South Bank and added to the party atmosphere that had come upon them.

The street entertainers worked the crowd well, pulling up pretty girls and young kids to follow their dance routines. They pumped the volume to get the whole crowd jigging about, Gangnam-style.

"Hey, look at this. I can still throw some cool shapes even in a wheelchair!" George was loving it, not in the least self-conscious. Siobhan and Ian stole a look at each other of affirmation and hope. To see George's reaction was great, that he was not fazed by the wheelchair, but more that he was energised and responding. It was the first time they had seen a glimmer of his usual spark and they were overjoyed, but just hopeful that it would continue.

Yo! Sushi was a perfect choice. They parked George and his wheelchair at the end of the conveyor belt. They sampled the dishes until they had a pile of multi-coloured bowls which turned into an eye-watering bill for a jumped-up snack. Then again, Ian did not care as George was happy and enjoying himself.

"So George, remember this, fella. First trip out, beautiful sunshine and your favourite – sushi. It doesn't get better than this."

"It could if I didn't have this tube up my nose. Thanks Mum and Dad, for bringing me. Do you think we should head back now? I'm feeling done in."

As they trundled back to the ward, George was practically asleep. It was a contented sleep from an exciting and successful trip.

Their next trip out was on the pretext of George taking photos and practising with his new Nikon.

"C'mon George, take the flaming brakes off. You already have loads of pictures of Big Ben. That and flowers and birds and more flowers," Ben moaned, losing patience.

No response from George – he still had a picture to frame and was trying to make the blue sky fully saturated.

"We could make it a bit more interesting if you want? I'll hold out my hand to make it look like Big Ben's sitting on it, or I could pretend to lean on it, or I can pinch the top of it to make out I'm taking it home. What do you think?"

Still no response from George, so Ben gave up with a shrug. He went back to watching the tourists doing all the dumb things he had just suggested for George.

I've got used to people staring at me in my wheelchair. Kids are okay, they just stand and stare with no hiding it. Some people will look anywhere else but me. I make sure I eyeball the ones who stare unashamedly. They always look down, embarrassed, and so they should.

I am staggered sometimes at the dumb things people say. Is it being stupid, or simply not thinking, or do they just have no idea what really goes on?

"You poor thing, it must have been awful in Intensive Care!" – *I expect it was for Mum and Dad, but I was asleep all the time. Waking up was a bit funky as I think I became a bit of a druggie but I soon settled down.*

"It must be really boring on dialysis for 4-5 hours three days a week." – *sometimes it was but normally there was tons to do.*

"Will your kidneys start working again?" – *No, not like ever. They're knackered and no use to me now.*

"Are you better now?" – *like I've had a cold, sneezed a bit and now I am over it?*

"It must be great with the wheelchair, being able to sit down all the time!" – *I can tell you it it's not, you moron. I suppose sitting down is better compared to the agony of standing up when you have no skin left on your heels and toes.*

"I had meningitis when I was a kid and I'm fine now." – *not like this, you didn't.*

"Hey fella, cool shoes!" – *Yup, tell me about it, the Granny shoes with slick Velcro straps are gonna be the next big thing.*

"At least it's not for long." – *like an hour or two, you imagine? Try two months and then think before you open your pie-hole.*

"Careful, you nearly ran me over!" – *believe me, if I had meant to get you I would have done.*

"Are your feet really sore then?" – *OMG you complete and utter hat-stand. Imagine no skin on your feet and you might just understand. Do they not think before they open their mouths? I try so hard not to cut them down with a pithy back-at-yer. Should I be more understanding as they don't know? But I do find it hard.*

Amaya was another of the unheralded supporters that Ian and Siobhan came to rely on. She was assigned as the in-house social worker to help parents cope with the impacts of serious and long-term illness. Many of the families she dealt with were desperate for her help, having had family life disrupted and careers put on hold to deal with their sick children. For others, the level of desperation meant the family had fractured, needing more than simply support. When this happened, the interventionist side of social work reared its head, forcing Amaya and her colleagues to act in the best interests of the sick child. As you can imagine, she was not universally popular.

Amaya was a bubbly personality who loved her job, helping people as much as she could within the boundaries of the system. She introduced herself one day in late May by sticking her head around the blue curtains of Bed 26.

"Hi guys, I'm Amaya. I saw you coming up in the lift and I wanted to say hello and see if I can help in any way?" She went on, pushing through the murmured hi in reply and looks of *'who's she?'* bewilderment from Siobhan and George. "I am the social worker for Evelina and I want to check you're doing okay?"

"Right, good to see you, thanks for coming round," replied Siobhan warmly. "Well, we're doing a lot better now that we are here and George is more comfortable. I'm not really sure how you can help – what sort of things?"

"Let's start with Travel to begin with."

"I know! How do people cope? It costs so much just getting here. The best part of twenty quid per day parking, ten quid Congestion Charge and then bits and bobs like lunch and coffees – it all mounts up when you do it every day."

"Well, I've got forms for that!" said Amaya triumphantly, digging a sheaf from her bag.

They spent the next forty minutes going over Travel Claim Forms, Disability Allowance Claim Forms and the disability Blue Badge application, which carried an exemption from Congestion Charge and access to disabled bay parking. Amaya knew from experience that it was better to do the questions together rather than hand out forms which would be swallowed up by a handbag. She knew a stressed and worried mum would never find the unhassled free time to sit and concentrate on the detailed forms. Although it was in her nature to sweep people along with her enthusiasm, whether they wanted it or not, it worked and Siobhan was grateful for her help.

I feel the disappointment in our house when I am home from the Evelina, for the first time in early June. Mum and Dad had been so excited and really built the day up into something special. I suppose after nine weeks in hospital, a homecoming is a big deal. I think it took about two hours for the disappointment to settle on us. That is the time it takes me to get bored with the TV, to scan my Favourites on my iPad and for my bum to go to sleep sitting in the same place.

Nothing much has changed from the hospital, really – I don't sleep in my own bed as I can't get upstairs, I have loads of tablets to take and the feeding tube is still up my nose. I'm still in the wheelchair so I can't go anywhere, even if I had the strength to, which I don't. It's the same as the hospital, just in a different place. I don't know why we didn't realise that.

I am back at the Evelina tomorrow, for dialysis and to have my chest pipes cleaned. I am there every other day. Hopefully as I get stronger, I won't need to go there so much.

Towards the end of an unusually dull dialysis session, Ian fired off a question from left field.

"Say, George, if you could wish for something, what would it be?"

George looked back at his father beneath a furrowed brow to convey a level of concentration rather than confusion at this dumb-ass question.

"Is this an anything-goes-in-the-whole-wide-world-wish for us to talk about or an everyday-wish? I would love to go on a safari and have a Bugati Veyron, OR if I can have an everyday wish then a double choc muffin and a Froffee from AMT will have to do."

"How about a wish in the middle? So something you would really like to do, or someone you would like to meet, or place you want to visit? Just to set some ground rules; we can't go kidnapping anyone; stealing fast cars or robbing banks; long flights and intergalactic travel are also no-nos."

Jeez. He's now drawing me into a dumb-ass conversation. We talk of a number of things like meeting David Attenborough or going on BBC Springwatch, or spending a day with a wildlife photographer, or best of all, buying me the Nikon 7100 I want. I can't see that happening. Dad listens, nods and scribbles away in his journal. I think I bored him, as I'm not sure he is really listening now. We end the conversation when he goes back to his newspaper and I put the headphones on for the overhead TV.

What was all that about? Did I give him the answer he wanted?

He is an odd bloke sometimes.

I know what I would really wish for. No surprises – just for my kidneys to work. Bizarrely, I still piss a bit, but not that much and not very good stuff apparently. It still has all the gubbins in it that a pair of normal working kidneys would take out. A few weeks ago, I pissed buckets for a few days. Mum and Dad got all jumpy and thought it was a sign my kidneys may be working again but no such luck. I knew they were bolloxed so I didn't get my hopes up.

Chapter 11

Ian pulled smoothly away, leaving the swanky office decked in glass and chrome behind him in the rear view mirror. He clocked the dark semicircles under his eyes. He felt shattered, deep down, knowing that sixty-hour weeks and cold sweats of worry in the middle of the night had taken their toll, giving him a sleep deficit that was hard to catch up on. He noted-to-self that he must get an early night and take on less. Easier said than done – most colleagues and clients had been really sympathetic but after the initial two weeks away when folks were reluctant to call, any allowances given had ebbed away. The deadlines remained, along with the long hours to meet them. He felt the tension of the day seep away, replaced by fatigue. He did not notice that the wave of relaxation was more suited to putting down a bedside book at the end of the day than ninety miles per hour on the M4.

What happened in the next three minutes seemed like a conspiracy of events but was utterly predictable. Like every day in rush hour, the traffic was heavy and concertina'd for no apparent reason, demanding a level of concentration Ian lacked. His BMW 5-series was built for effortless autobahn driving but demanded no active engagement beyond driving a dodgem. The bright sun made him squint, making already hooded eyes practically closed.

Up front, the builders' van five hundred metres away in the fast lane obscured the chain of cars ahead. So when it braked heavily, Ian failed to notice the illuminated braked lights that were outshone by sunlight and kept going. The gap closed rapidly as the now-stationary van, packed with tools and rubble, became a magnetic hard wall that was going nowhere. Normally, in the final millisecond you would expect a stamp on the brakes and a smoking last-resort skid to lessen the impact. Ian's head-bobbing drowsiness meant that he was oblivious to his fate and thundered head-on into the van at forty miles per hour. Being the first ball in a Newton's cradle, Ian's car transferred its momentum into the van, which did actually move, but into two other cars in a chain reaction.

Bizarrely, his ears got it first, with the concussion of the impact, then simultaneously a phenomenal whack in the chest as the airbags exploded. The combined effect of flattened lungs, the cabin filled with white dust and the airbag propellant replacing all the oxygen, left Ian panicking to breath. He scrabbled out of the driver's door and doubled over in the central reservation, trying to suck in air and alleviate the pain in his sternum. His chest felt squashed flat and gasping wasn't going to inflate it. After a minute or two, he found whispered breaths, sucking in air gently without seeming to move his rib cage worked of a fashion and he was able to relax more. He shuffled through four lanes of stationary traffic, to the hard shoulder where a group of grim faced drivers waited for him, last to arrive but first to crash.

The builder turned to face Ian. This was not going to go well; his van was wrecked and his already-exhausting day had just got a whole lot worse. The understandable torrent of swearing and accusation never materialised, although he had every right to. Instead, he led the huddle, checking no-one was hurt and swapping details. He even had the good grace to ask after Ian's pained chest, although it must have been a huge effort of will not to jab it with a finger and bawl Ian out for being so dozy.

Ian called Siobhan from the hard shoulder to tell her what had happened, deliberately downplaying to crash to avoid worrying her. He spoke quickly so she had no chance to interrupt his parcel of information and leap to conclusions.

"Hi Shiv, it's me."

"What do you want?"

"Listen, I've had an accident but I'm okay." He kept speaking so the explanation could come in one slug. "Just a shunt, that's all. I'm on the hard shoulder of the M4, waiting for my car to be towed. The computer in the flaming thing has immobilised itself so it can't be driven." He glossed over the fact that it was undrivable and his chest hurt like hell. "When I get to the garage, I'll let you know more."

"Do you need me to come and get you?" Siobhan asked.

"I think so, just not sure yet."

"That's ok, I can do that later. You sure you're okay?"

"Yeah, I'm fine, just pissed off the car is bashed up."

"Well, you get it sorted and let me know. Text me or something." Siobhan put the phone down. *He told me he's okay so that's all I need to know, he's a big boy and can clean up his own mess.* She was surprised at her own calmness, knowing she would never have reacted like this six months ago. It was as though she was numbed to stuff that wasn't really important, having developed the intuition to focus on the critical and urgent. *That's what it was – a recalibration.* It's the kind of description Ian would have used. She went back to sorting out George's catch-up work from dialysis that morning and preparing supper.

She had read in some *Cosmo* article or something mostly forgotten that Health, Husband and Home were the trinity of a balanced life. Get one out of whack, like moving house, and life is demanding and all-consuming. Changing two, like moving house as a result of a divorce, and most people reach breaking point with the upheaval. All three – well, that's losing the plot completely for everyone. She counted her blessings that Husband was in balance, if a little dented.

As the last of the cars were towed away, Ian got dropped by the Police at the recovery garage to rendezvous with the tow truck, his mangled car and more paperwork.

The metal bench on the station platform allowed Ian to sit bolt upright and in doing, ease the pain in his chest. He tilted his head back and let out a shallow sigh, relieved that it could have been a whole lot worse. The blue sky was a stunning crisp blue around him – an artist would have said it looked unreal; the sky is never just one colour. He wished his life was one simple colour. Normally at this time of year, he would be relaxing under a holiday blue sky. He closed his eyes to stop his wandering thoughts. He picked out specific thoughts from the whirlpool mush in his head: *'forget the holiday, just be grateful you are still in one piece'*, shame at his lack of responsibility, guilt at the worry he would cause Siobhan and a nagging realisation that he was close to his own wheels falling off, not just his BMW's.

In contrast to Ian's disastrous day, George was having a hugely successful one.

Normally when I come in for dialysis, all the precious blue badge bays at the front of the Evelina are full so we have to go to the main car-park almost under Westminster Bridge. This means getting the wheelchair out of the boot, setting it up, strapping me in and wheeling me all through the hospital to get to the Evelina wing. I sit here like a bag of spuds, no use to Mum or Dad. Well, lately I have been walking from the car from the start. Mum calls it a BTN walk – a Better Than Nothing effort. So I walk as far as I can get, with Mum following along behind with the wheelchair and then I slump back into the wheelchair for the rest of the trip.

Well, today I made it. Yo George! I walk all the way from the car to the Evelina. It was exhausting and my heels particularly were very sore. As I come through the automatic doors, the security lady and her mate both stand up and clap and cheer. Everyone looks round as though they are mad. They hug me and tell me how tall I am.

Yes, George is in the building! It amazes me that they even notice or even realise what it means to me. Looking back I guess they had only ever known me arrive comatose in a bed or seen me every day pushed around in a wheelchair. I suppose they didn't even know I could walk.

Chapter 12

Sooner or later we all sit down to a banquet of consequences.

Robert Louis Stevenson

After ten weeks under the care of the Evelina, the time came for a review of progress with Dr Stewart – one of the lead consultants in the Renal Unit. Progress was good, they all knew that – but the unanswered questions clustered around the future.

Stewart walked Siobhan and Ian through the current situation, referring to George's thick file of notes as he went.

"In many ways, George is a model patient. He has settled well into the routine of dialysis, he is managing his fluid brilliantly and you are doing a great job keeping to his restricted diet. You will have seen a change in him – the fatigue, lack of energy, loss of appetite. I am afraid these are normal for dialysis patients and there's very little we can do to avoid them. If he isn't eating well, it makes it hard for his body to grow and gain weight – so we always have to pack the calories in."

Siobhan interrupted him. "How about his blood pressure? It hasn't been a good week – poor George had bad headaches and threw up after both sessions last week and on Saturday his blood pressure went through the floor and he almost fainted."

"That's a problem of our own making which we can do something about – it's called profiling," replied Stewart confidently. "We have to get him down to his dry weight each session by taking off fluid. If we do it at the wrong rate or too much towards the end, it unbalances his levels. It's a bit like a pilot flying to Edinburgh – a skilled one will ascend gradually, avoid the patches of turbulent clouds and descend gently. But if you blast off the take-off, pedal to the metal and then dive-bomb the landing – then the passengers will see their lunch again. I'll speak to Kay to see if she can work her magic to make it easier for George."

"Thank you, that's a help. I'm worried about the future for George, his schooling has dropped away and he seems so resigned, you know? What is your thinking about the transplant?" asked Siobhan.

Stewart understood the need for a future plan to latch onto, not just the routine but more a need for hope for the future. He got the easy bit out of the way first.

"You know what George has been through – it will take a long time for his body to recover, to get to a healthy weight and his strength back for a major operation. For that reason alone, we are looking at a transplant at least nine months into the future – so perhaps spring next year. Finding the donor – fingers crossed from the family – and with all the tests and paperwork takes a fair while anyway. We can look at an option for home dialysis if you wish. I think you are ideal candidates for it."

Ian chipped in to tease out the tougher part of Siobhan's question before Stewart had got to it, if he had ever intended to. "The timing makes sense, and yes we should explore home dialysis if you think it would work for us. Even with that, though, George has already missed a chunk of Year Nine, and with GCSEs starting in September, he's going to miss much more. I feel for him trying to catch up stuff and fill gaps. Then there is the transplant in April potentially, right before exam time ... "

Stewart nodded in agreement, put his glasses down, all physical cues for Ian to stop speaking and listen. "Ian, I hear what you're saying. I am a doctor, not a teacher, so my priorities are to get George well – the schooling has to fit in around that in my mind. The team at the Hospital School is superb, George is an intelligent boy, and together we can keep things ticking along." Stewart changed direction with a question where he wanted them to arrive at the right answer. "Who says you have to follow the timetable and expectations for everyone else? They don't have the life-changing challenges George has. We can change the rules for him. You don't have to do GCSEs all in one go, you can even do one in three months if you have to. And on the other side of the transplant," he went on, warming to his theme, "there is no reason he can't lead a normal life. With good fortune, his new kidney will last him 15-20 years, and well into his thirties. All the important things for a full and happy life – college, relationships, home, family, career, all of those remain open to him."

Siobhan and Ian acknowledged Stewart's good sense, but it was a shift they needed to wrap their thinking around. The appointment trickled on to its natural end, and they promised to reconvene at the next monthly review and hang some other issues on the broad framework Stewart had outlined.

In the car home, with George fast asleep on the back seat, Siobhan and Ian replayed Dr Stewart's advice with their voices low, just in case he was listening. George stirred, disturbed by a snap of acceleration. Siobhan and Ian glanced at each other. Siobhan mimed *'Is he asleep?'* Ian shrugged a *'not sure'*. They both knew George was a skilled eavesdropper with the chutzpah to act his guilt away even when rumbled.

"Did you find it patronising, what he said?" asked Siobhan.

"No, not at all. It was all good advice and pretty obvious really. It's all that sort of stuff that you don't see for yourself, or may take you a bit longer to accept," replied Ian.

"I know what you mean. It's easy to get wrapped up in that whole competitive parent bit. I hate that round here, it's the only thing I dislike about this part of London," Siobhan reflected.

"It's that whole conveyor belt isn't it? There seems to be only one path – get into a good school, a ridiculous number of A-stars at GSCE, a big-name uni and then something swanky in the City."

"With a silent S?" quipped Siobhan.

"Good one – I suppose we have to put a lid on all of that and change what 'good' is. I doubt it's what Chugs wants anyway. It's an environment where he would get eaten for breakfast. Like Stewart said, we need to get George happy and confident to be able to thrive."

"So we do all we can to take the pressure off him. He goes back to school in the autumn but only when he is ready, we reduce his number of subjects and anything to do with exams, homework and expectations, we just relax on. Can you do that?"

"I think we have to," replied Ian with conviction, knowing the question was meant for both of them and not just him.

For the next few days, George's future was often on Siobhan's mind. Over supper Siobhan put a thought out there, one she had been mulling over for a while.

"You know how angsty teenagers can be?"

"What? – do you mean all that stuff about fitting in, being accepted, having five hundred friends on Facebook?" Ian replied.

"Yeah, mostly. I don't see much of it with George, do you?"

"Hmm – not really. He seems pretty self-contained to me," Ian agreed.

"True, but I do remember a few months back asking him about friends and who he hangs out with. I got the impression he has a few good mates but not loads."

"That would fit. He's not a life-and-soul type though, is he? I could never see him being a people-gatherer. He just not that warm a person – until you get to know him of course."

"He is very kind-hearted. It's one of his qualities everyone mentions, so he is warm in that way," Siobhan disagreed.

"Absolutely. I'm not sure what I mean. Not sure warm and kind-hearted are the same thing."

Siobhan paused to think through the emerging theme in her head. She took a different tack. "When I was speaking about angsty, I was thinking that George rarely checks what other people are thinking."

"Can you give me an example?" Ian wanted to understand.

"I'll try. Can you recall George checking or asking about someone else's well-being? Things like *'Are you cross with me?' 'Is it something I've said?' 'Is there something on your mind?'"*

"Are we being hard on him? He is only fourteen, and a young one at that."

"Fair enough, and I grant you he will ask *'How are you? How was your day?'* But that's just politeness and mostly programmed. There's rarely any depth or emotional connection there. Is that right or wrong?" Siobhan pushed for a firm view.

"No, no – you have a point. It does feel like he's going through the motions."

"It just feels to me that George is either supremely comfortable in himself, so he has no need to seek validation of his behaviours, or he's not really thinking about it. I'm not sure what I'm saying, just an observation really."

"It could be a boy-thing or a maturity-thing," fished Ian, realising he was stumbling toward a minefield of having to defend the emotional shallowness of the entire male population. Siobhan let him live for another day, pulling Ian back from his self-sacrifice.

"We need to keep an eye on it. It's something that is not natural for George and maybe he will have to work really hard at it."

By the end of supper, Siobhan needed to break her own introspection and lift her mood. Better have some fun and affection. Rather bravely, she set her sights on her eldest son.

"C'mon Ben, give us a kiss," she wheedled. "Kissy-kissy for mee-eee,"– she was not giving up easily.

"Look, you annoying woman, get back in the kitchen where you belong and leave me alone!" It was not looking good for Siobhan. The combination of a stroke on his arm, the bush baby eyes and creeping towards him along the sofa was enough to tip him over the edge. He leapt up, grabbed his mum by the shoulders and splotched a massive snoggy kiss over the bridge of her nose, then a slurpy full tongue ice-cream lick on each cheek. She squealed in revulsion and pushed him away.

"That is disgusting, you revolting boy."

"What are you screeching about now, you witch? It's what you asked for."

"That's what SHE said," quipped Siobhan gleefully, mimicking the typical teenage lad-mag exchange.

"Great banter – it really is," was Ben's usual response when he failed to get his customary last word with a back-at-yer.

Chapter 13

> Whatsoever house I may enter, my visit shall be for the convenience and advantage of the patient; and I will willingly refrain from doing any injury or wrong from falsehood.
>
> *Hippocratic oath (Original Version[34])*

Michelle the transplant co-ordinator walked Ian through the necessary background on kidney transplantation. It was part of a process to educate and inform so that potential donors were fully equipped to make decisions on their future health. Michelle took her role very seriously, priding herself on her thoroughness and efficiency. She was not there to be your mate, but she would hold your hand through it, leading down paths you might not choose.

Ian had a habit of cutting off the last five percent of each point she made – as if he knew it already or had somewhere more important to go. Dismissive was too strong a word, but his restlessness irritated her a lot, as it devalued her considered and prepared words. She could see this becoming an issue for her.

She gave him a booklet explaining the current state of play, highlighting a few key items for him. "Kidney failure cost the NHS in England more than £600 million[35] in 2004-05 – about one percent of its total budget. There are close to 21,000 people on dialysis. The number rises by about five percent annually. There are 7,951 patients on the transplant waiting list: 6,867 need a new kidney. In total, 3,489 patients across the UK received a range of body parts

---

[34] It is a popular misconception that the phrase "First do no harm" (Latin: Primum non nocere) is a part of the Hippocratic oath. In fact the phrase is believed to have originated with the 19th-century surgeon Thomas Inman.

[35] The Guardian Tuesday 4 March 2014

ranging from a kidney, liver or a heart to both a heart and lung in 2013. They were able to do so because organs were recovered from 1,323 deceased people. Among the 3,489 recipients, 1,955 received a kidney."

On the back of the data, she established the importance of specialist transplant teams and their accumulated experience in a manner intended to reassure. She introduced a supportive element by explaining to Ian the body of evidence to show how a transplant from a live donor is more successful than a transplant from a cadaveric one, even if the latter is a much better match.

"This is more obvious than you might think – by simply being alive, a kidney from a living donor is an instantly healthier prospect." She backed this up with the evidence on living donors, adding that "there were also 1,127 living donor transplants[36] last year in which a living person donated a kidney, usually a relative or friend, but sometimes a stranger."

This was all interesting stuff, and reinforced the decision Ian had made in his own mind. Unfortunately, it was a decision he had made weeks ago, without the full grasp of the information, so more evidence made no difference to him.

Similarly, the family conference the day before had made no difference to him either. Ian was determined to donate to George, and had driven the outcome of the discussion to his ends. He felt it was his duty and the right thing for a father to do to shoulder his fair share, knowing that in their marriage Siobhan had already given birth three times, twice naturally and one by caesarian. Deep down, his desire to protect and care for his wife and son weighed greater than personal discomfort. The last thing he wanted

---

[36] The Guardian Tuesday 4 March 2014

to see was Siobhan in pain in a hospital bed when it was within his control to prevent that. It was an automatic response, for him anyway, so he did not need the debate others sought.

Siobhan knew Ian's thinking on the matter and loved him all the more for it. But she did not agree. Despite Ian's positivity and conviction, she sensed a train wreck to come. She suspected that a kidney operation that Ian had had thirty years ago as an eighteen-year-old was not as easily cast aside to the mists of history as he wished. Factors like scar tissue, repaired vessels, disturbed anatomy may all come into play and she felt Ian was being short-sighted not to fully consider them. Now was not the time for the reality check – he was not ready to listen and would not be swayed by her instinct. It would take a transplant surgeon and a battery of unequivocal tests to convince him.

What Ian and Siobhan did agree on was to keep their sons Ben and Fred at arm's length from any decisions about organ donation. Ben and Fred were instantly discounted. Their parents played up the fact that you have to be eighteen to be a donor, so it was an unequivocal NO. At eighteen and seventeen respectively, they were at key stages of their education, with moves to university imminent. To ask either of them to put their life on hold at such a formative time was too much, irrespective of the implications for the future. Skillfully, the family conference navigated around these options so that they did not come up for debate.

At the next transplant clinic appointment in November, Michelle prepared for her routine session with Ian. She had all the test results in front of her and she dreaded the conversation to come. Despite Ian being one of her most motivated potential donors, she was not sure that she liked him. He seemed too pushy, too motivated, if that was possible. She could not put her finger on it; he just seemed a bit desperate and too keen to move to the next stage. He would be crushed by what she had to tell him, provided he fully listened. They got through the *'hellos, how are yous, fine thanks'* quickly, with Ian itching to get onto the results and next steps.

"Ian, you can potentially be a donor, but the surgeons would prefer it were someone else," explained Michelle, trying to mirror Ian's directness with her own.

"Okay, I get the bit that I can be a donor, but prefer someone else? What does that mean? I would prefer it's me." Ian thought his own words sounded petulant or bombastic or both, but couldn't help himself. "It's my kidney and I want George to have it. I have been very clear from the beginning, Michelle – I may not be the perfect donor but I have to have more than just a preference. How can I explain to Siobhan that she has to be the donor because the doctors prefer her? I can't do that. We keep going with the tests until you show me in black and white, with data, why I can't be a donor. We have to get to the bottom of this." He stopped abruptly, partly to make his point, but mainly to avoid the indignity of a soon-to-be-fifty-year-old stamping his foot.

Michelle ploughed on, trying not to make the furrow deeper. "I hear what you are saying. Let me try and explain better. There are many factors on paper which make you an ideal donor. We know you are a good match for blood type and tissue type. You are motivated, clearly; you are fit and well with no underlying disease, kidney function is good but a little imbalanced and no cardiovascular issues. But – and this is a big BUT – the surgeons have reservations about your earlier operation when you were eighteen. Your right kidney is an odd shape, the vessels have all been sewn back on once before and may be scarred. It presents a bigger challenge for them, so that's at the root of their preference."

Ian nodded, acknowledging her well-made point. "That makes sense and I recognise that, but we still carry on. I need to know categorically if that preference is … I dunno … choosing between two viable options but one takes a bit more effort, or if that *'prefer someone else'* truly means they would not touch me even if George were at death's door."

Michelle winced at his directness again and hated his insensitive analogy. It was his son he was talking about, for goodness' sake. Keeping her own judgments in check, she was aware of his belligerence preventing them moving forward and made one last point before offering a solution.

"Ian, also do remember that the surgeon may have a different obligation from you. If he can avoid a risk to George then he will take that path. Similarly, a risk you may be prepared to take or find acceptable – for example, leaving yourself with a borderline viable kidney function is not a risk a surgeon would entertain. It may be your wish, but he would not grant it if he felt he were doing you harm or jeopardising your future health – does that make sense? Would it help if I arranged for you to meet the surgeon, so he can explain his preference himself?"

"Yes please – that would help. I'm not having a pop at you, Michelle, or doubting what you're telling me. I just need to hear it from the guy who would do the operation to really get to grips with what this preference means."

With that, the appointment ended with the next steps sewn up.

It took a further two months and into the New Year to push the door firmly shut on Ian as a donor. It was a dispiriting time, with the outcome fairly predictable, but still having to commit the energy to drive the process and review each option to reach closure. The surgeon had sat him down and walked through the options and implications. The unavoidable truth was that Ian's right kidney was not good enough. It was misshapen and baggy from the earlier surgery and contributed forty-five percent of Ian's kidney function, which was borderline viable if he was left with that and nothing else – a risk Ian was willing to take. So the surgeon admitted he could technically be a donor. But what swayed the decision, and the crucial evidence Ian sought, were the risks to George as the recipient. X-rays showed Ian's kidneys had multiple arteries going to them, which was a surprise but not uncommon. Sketchily-remembered classroom lessons would remind you that a kidney has three tubes locating on it – an artery, a vein and a ureter. For many people, the blood supply could feature two, three or even more artery branches serving each kidney. For Ian it was no more difficult to extract it, but for the surgeon, this meant a far more complex plumbing exercise to attach the donated kidney to George, with the risk of part of it dying through poor blood supply. The risks all landed in George's lap. The surgeon gently stated that *'only the best kidney will do, so that when we do a transplant we get the best possible chance of success'.* The last thing either of them wanted was to put George through a transplant operation at fifteen and then have to repeat it within a year. In the face of hard facts and clear reasoning, it was jointly agreed to demote Ian to Donor of Last Resort – technically viable but only if George was in a life-threatening situation where the risks and compromises of a baggy, only-90%-good-enough-Ian-kidney were worth considering.

Only the best will do – that could only be one person. Siobhan.

It hurt, it really hurt. It was his pride and self-worth that took a beating. His shoulders slumped with the thought of explaining it to Siobhan. He knew his rejection effectively committed Siobhan to the course of events he wanted to shield her from. She would have to do all the tests he had already done, but go onto major surgery, then the pain and discomfort that would take three months of convalescence to get through.

When he did tell her the situation, Siobhan knew what he was going to say and had prepared for it. Her reaction was matter-of-fact, unemotive and pragmatic to deliberately gloss over the emotional wallow Ian was in. It did not make him Husband of Last Resort or Father of Last Resort, just not much use for donating kidneys. She focused on the next steps, the scheduling of the tests and cracking on. This could have been mistaken for enthusiasm but that could not be further from how Siobhan felt. Honestly and unguardedly, she dreaded the thought of the operation.

Perhaps it was Siobhan's more worried than normal expression that prompted Sheila to act as she did. Sheila was a formidable woman, but only for the first ten seconds of meeting her. She acted out a northern brusque stereotype quite well, but she was a far better Sister than actress. It was true that she was formidable in the standards she set on her ward and to several generations of nurses she had trained. She was tough and demanding, but respected and loved for it, according to many of her trainees, who all remembered her, both for the stern words but also the support and guidance she dispensed freely. They described her as part of the institution with *'nothing she doesn't know about the care of renal patients'*. As Sister, Sheila had authority over anyone who stepped onto her ward and that was everyone, just in case you had any doubt, no matter what org charts said.

So when Sheila called Siobhan into her office, shut the door and sat her down, Siobhan felt she was in for it. After a few pleasantries, Sheila, deep in character, went for brusque to package the sensitive subject she wanted to raise.

"One thing the years in this job has taught me — with renal disorders, you are in it for life. Think about that."

Siobhan did as she had been told, to think, but remained unsure whether she was still in trouble. Sheila pressed on to explain herself to Siobhan's nonplussed expression.

"I mean, think of the long term. The expectations we set now, the good practices we build now, all of that helps in the long term. Most of all, it helps us accommodate the disease and accept it doesn't go away. It just steps into the background for hopefully long periods. How are you coping?"

Ouch, that felt blunt for Siobhan, but she replied honestly. "Pretty well, I think. Now that we are here and over the worst. We tick along, until the next thing ... "

Siobhan's unfinished answer told Sheila all she needed to know. Sheila's next comment went beyond brusque to downright brutal but, as Siobhan came to realise, it was one of the most insightful and useful thoughts spoken to her.

"You will break down at some time. Everybody does. I'm not being hard or cruel, just realistic. No matter how resilient you are or how well you cope, at some point it will all become too much for your slim shoulders. When it happens, you will feel overwhelmed — by the latest wave going over your head, pushing you under. It's not a failure or weakness of yours if it does. So if and when it happens, we can sort it behind a closed door, here in my office, you and me. We will face it together and I will help you. It will seem better on the other side."

At that moment Siobhan saw in Sheila a melting compassion you would not ever have expected.

"Oh Sheila — now look what you've done!" Siobhan crumbled into tears with full squelch of mascara and drips everywhere. Overwhelmed yes, but not by despair and stress, just simply from the shining commitment Sheila had made to her. "I hate it when people are nice to me. I can't stop myself. I'll have the tough Sheila back please; she's much easier to deal with."

What Sheila showed was the experience of a lifetime spent caring for patients and their families. She may not have explained it herself, but her intuition told her the grind of long-term illness was the toughest thing. She knew the storms that rolled through were horrible; the infected lines, the spiked infections, the collapsing blood pressure and wavering creatinine levels. All of these took their toll but only in the short-term. The real battle was the relentless energy-sapping toil of just keeping everything together.

If a trained counsellor had opened the lid on the Birks family, what would he have seen?

A mother trying so hard to keep a stable, happy home environment together, juggling work, three dialysis sessions per week, the emotional roller coaster of a battery of tests and the ever-present fear of the transplant on the horizon.

A father running up a sleep debt from four trips to America in eight weeks. Waking at three in the morning with an anxious brain tripping through scenarios that might never happen. Being spread so thin that he could not remember the last time he had dinner with his wife — just the two of them.

A youngest son just surviving each gruelling day. Permanently exhausted, often feeling truly dreadful, but coping with school. Preparing for exams seemed so important to everyone, but not to him in the scheme of things.

Chapter 14

Jean was skimming through the Daily Express. "This looks really good! Listen to this," she chirped.

Dave was reading his book. Dave wasn't listening. He had the ability to totally tune out his wife's words. He was used to her running commentary on a newspaper that only she was reading. Not to be discouraged by being ignored, she carried on regardless with her unresponsive audience.

"The Inspirational Mother of the Year awards – there's an advert for it here. Look, there are six or seven categories. The closing date for applications is in four weeks – we can still enter! I'll read it to you: 'The Inspirational Mother Awards[37] is an emotional and uplifting event. Treat your mothers and join us for champagne and afternoon tea with musical performances.' Oooh, that sounds good," she went on, bubbling with excitement. "'The Patron for the Inspirational Mother Awards is Gloria Hunniford. These awards acknowledge inspirational mothers and raise money for The Caron Keating Foundation. Caron lost her tenacious battle with cancer in 2004 and subsequently Gloria and her sons Paul and Michael set up a fund in Caron's name – The Caron Keating Foundation – which gives grants to all types of cancer charities.' I like that Gloria Hunniford – you know, the Irish one. She smashed her elbow playing tennis – just like mine. I swear her daughter used to be on Blue Peter. Shall I do it, Dave?" Jean asked hesitantly.

As she had not used Dave's name before, her introduction had completely passed him by, so Dave, at the mention of his name, was behind the start line, searching for the last thing she had said that he could recall. He was guessing at the Awards thing, which had wheedled past his inert defences, but it could be anything. Dave's slowness to

---

[37] Promotional Material issued by The Caron Keating Foundation

respond became the confirmation Jean wanted, so she filled in the gap.

"There's nothing to lose and I can tell Siobhan if anything comes of it. I'm sure nothing will, but we can give it a go."

With no other dissension, Jean squirrelled herself away with a cup of tea, two chocolate Hob-Nobs and her iPad mini, and went to work on the online nomination form. Dave went back to his book, wondering what was keeping Jean so quiet.

INSPIRATIONAL MOTHER OF THE YEAR.

Nominee: SIOBHAN BIRKS.

This past year has been very difficult for our family particularly for our dear daughter-in-law and her 14 year old son George.

George was critically ill with Meningococcal Septicaemia and it was due to Siobhan's recognition of the symptoms that George was rushed to the doctor, where he was put into an induced coma And rushed to hospital.

The next few weeks were touch and go but George survived and during the next 4 weeks in Intensive Care he faced the possibility of toe amputation or skin grafts. After a further 5 weeks George was allowed home but was left with kidney failure which means he has dialysis 3 times a week.

All this has been life-changing for Siobhan, her husband Ian and their two teenaged sons.

Their marvellous mum has been a tower of strength throughout this trial, supported by Ian. She has comforted, reassured and devoted her time to George and tried to ensure family life was maintained as much as possible and always remained positive.

In July George is due to have a kidney transplant ... .donated by his MUM.

In the last 6 weeks Siobhan has raised over £5,000 for the Evelina Children's Hospital in recognition of their wonderful care and support. Ian, George's dad, and 4 friends are running in the Paris Marathon in April to help fundraise.

Siobhan is truly inspirational and much loved and admired by all who know her.

Jean clicked on 'Submit', satisfied she had got the nomination spot on. Now she just needed to wait – and think up what she would tell Siobhan.

Chapter 15

Our lives take turns, we age, we leave and we return, we win and we lose, but many of those spots remain identical and somehow provide comfort.

Michael Barry, Professional Cyclist

Being in hospital, being around hospitals – it's not normal. When I think of my time at school, I can't remember anyone who has been off school as long as me. There has been the odd broken arm, a few acts of monumental muppetry, like falling off roofs and stuff, but nothing that could be called a long-term illness that affects their lives like mine. Fred knows of some kids at his school who are into drugs but he thinks they are idiots and steers clear of them. Those don't count as they did it to themselves.

I am not saying it's unfair, just that shit happens. It just happened to me and there is nothing I or anyone else could have done about it. I don't know the stats (I must Google it) but long-term illness is rare in kids. Like I said, I can't think of anyone like me...

Coincidentally, Siobhan was also thinking about serious illness in kids. It was all around her, part of her everyday existence now. She knew full well that very sick children go to specialist hospitals, but spending most days in one was a dramatic change. It saddened her outlook.

She watched the mum and buggy struggle out of the lift. Like an unruly supermarket trolley, the buggy would not go where the mum wanted and it pissed her off. Just one of many things that pissed her off, judging by her face. Siobhan felt uncharitable thinking that the mum had the most careworn face she had ever seen, the wet cloak of resignation weighed her down, giving her the stoop of a geriatric. Her clothes were grey; her eyes said nothing, no determination, no tears, no plea for help, just emptiness of colour and feeling. She was as detached from other souls as she was from her own – just surviving.

The Careworn Mum's severely disabled daughter in the buggy was a contrasting riot of pink and sparkles – on her pink jacket, on her rosy face and on the jazzy bangles in her hair. She giggled up at her mum, putting up her hand palm uppermost to which her mum stooped down further to brush touchingly with her lips. If a smile can't be read, then warm lips pressed to a palm makes feeling affection better than showing it.

Siobhan's own long stares into space, lazy eyelids and with nothing sparking upstairs, all gave her a hint at the leadenness that mum must be feeling. The absence of any energy, drive or idea was depressing. She speculated on what it must be like to live with no hope, nothing to look forward to – no path to being happy. Such a contrast to the distilled sanitised timelines on Facebook with postings of chocolate-box lives with detached smugness – '*look at me with my exciting exotic life with loads of friends (many of whom I have never actually met or shared an experience with)*'.

The mum in the lift was not the only example. Siobhan had spoken of another potential donor she had met with four kids under ten – how on earth could that ever work? No easy happy ending there.

Or the grinding drudge of a one-parent family on benefits. Having to attend dialysis three times per week meant holding down a full-time job was nigh on impossible. Add in a two hour commute each way to get to the nearest specialist dialysis unit. Add in money worries as relentless as the loan sharks threatening for payment each week. Add in an unhappy teenager who thinks his life is rubbish before it has truly begun. Just how do you hold it all together and not simply crumble?

Siobhan shook her head, more to shake away the images of sadness and despair than to rouse herself. Game face on to visit George.

Along the corridor to George's bed bay, Siobhan could hear Sheila's stern voice.

"I left you in charge, young man! So what's been happening?"

"Not a lot as far as I can see. My staff are running amok!"

"Look at these three standing about laughing. This is a hospital, you know; we don't have any of that."

George looked on, bemused and surprised in equal measure. Becca, Emily and Lois laughed and apologised to George for their tardiness.

I wake to the sound of my name. It is Mrs. Webster's voice. The feeling of dread her English lessons gave me washes through my body. I feel guilty straight away for being asleep.

"GEEorge ..." It is more insistent now, with an elongated hiss in my ear. I am in my dialysis chair, cocooned in a blanket. I rub my eyes so I can focus on Sheila. Sometimes she makes me feel guilty like Mrs. Webster.

I like Sheila a lot. She makes me jump but she doesn't mean it and she treats you like an adult. She's the boss but I don't mind that, at least you know where you are. Mum came out of her office the other day with smudgy mascara, she looked a wreck. Obviously Mum had been crying. She talked a lot but the only thing I took away was that kidney failure is a life-long thing and you have to live with it.

Doh, that's not big news for me, sorry.

I know my kidneys are stuffed. They're not coming back –period. When Mum and Dad go through one of their phases of measuring the amount I wee, I know they are hoping my kidneys have started working again. How can I tell them there is no point in hoping?

The thing I have learned is just to go with it. Today I have to have dialysis, there's no point throwing a hissy over it. I just accommodate it. It doesn't hurt. It doesn't upset me, and it's just a nuisance. Tomorrow might be different but I don't think you can look too far into the future – well I don't, there's no point. I remember Dad encouraging Fred, as a midfielder in football, to get into the attacking penalty box. Fred said, "Nah, there's no point going much further than the centre circle as the ball always comes back there sooner or later."Sounds good to me.

The only thing I can do really is accommodate it. Until I have a transplant there is no cure. After my transplant I'm sure I will recover a good bit, but it won't ever go away. Kidney failure won't ever leave my life. So I accommodate it and it becomes part of me. Hopefully not the first thing you see, but something beneath the surface that I deal with in my way.

Chapter 16

> Writing down the values of the Trust, making them part of our culture and demonstrating them throughout the organisation helps us develop a shared way of acting – not just in what we do but also how we do it. This impacts on how we care for our patients, how we interact with each other and how we make decisions.

Evelina Website: About Us

Spookily, it was as though the Head of the Evelina Children's Hospital had been watching Siobhan on CCTV as she observed the Careworn Mum from the lift and tapped into the same thought. When you are in mired in the depths of despair, how do you give people opportunities to make life better? Not that it was written in a manual anywhere or some cringe worthy corporate poster, but the ethos of the institution was tangible, even from a few hours in the building. It could have said *'we have all the expert doctors and nurses to deal with the bad stuff, but while you are here you can be happy, have things to look forward to and have hope'.*

Values[38] are easy to write down, but only become meaningful when you operate to them instinctively all the time. George, more than anyone, could articulate what values meant to him.

Dad always says that Granddad is big on values and it is the best thing a parent can give their child (apart from kidneys of course). He judges a person in three ways: do they get their round in? He always rattles off jokes like 'short arms, deep pockets' (I am not sure what that means

---

[38] See YouTube video of the Evelina at
http://youtu.be/H2aWMSeJVcM

but smile when I ought to anyway) or talks of tricks like holding the pub door open so last to enter the room and so last at the bar. He is also big on how you treat waiters – I guess that must mean that all men are equal and you should respect others. He makes it sound like the Commandments According To Granddad. Lastly there are the Granddad Rules of Golf. Let me just say I'm not a big fan of golf, but I do like walking in the countryside and looking at the wildlife. The rules are ALWAYS in place even when others aren't looking. I guess the lesson I MUST LEARN is that values only mean something when you have to act by them.

Unless you've been there, most people don't know what dialysis is like.

I know.

Of course there have been some bad bits, but I've done stuff that I have loved. The everyday routine is not that bad.

During term time, I spend three hours each dialysis session with Tamsin from the Hospital School, although I am plugged in so I can't get away. It sounds awful but it does make me focus and we talk through things at my pace. It works for me so I go with it. Other times, I can watch TV, play X-Box, and watch films with everyone else when we have the projector set up on Saturdays. Often we have the radio on and Tinu shows us her latest moves shakin' her booty – you don't even have to ask her! We get the odd visitors – the lady with the hospital dog Nala comes in every now and then. It's meant to be good therapy for sick kids but I'm not sure why. I just like the dog. A clown comes in but he can sod off as he is not funny and gives me the creeps. I get to do cooking, which I love. Some stuff I have done before, like brownies or muffins, but also unusual things like pretzels and sushi – but not together, obviously.

There is also the Medicinema – I saw 'Malificent' with Fred. It can take eighty people, with even some beds wheeled in.

So all in all there is a lot to do so it's never boring.

When I look back, I have done some really cool stuff. Some of it I would never have had the chance otherwise.

I've been a DJ on Radio Lollipop and I got to play all MY favourite songs. I've been to Number 10 and advised the PRIME MINISTER. I saw Spiderman and Superman abseil down the building to clean the windows. I've danced on Strictly Come Dancing and wowed the 2012 Bake Off winner with my muffins. I've scored a goal at Wembley and bowled for Surrey. I have danced with Pixie and sung with Ollie at the Albert Hall. I have even seen tiger cubs in the park. And best of all, I filmed AND presented Springwatch on the BBC.

Impressive stuff.

Ok, well maybe I exaggerated a little but everything is true. I never tell lies. I was on Radio Lollipop – they are a really friendly bunch and let me have a go. One of the girls told me about lomography cameras and helped me make a heart-shaped box for Mum, which made her cry again. I went to Number 10, but David Cameron was called away to Nelson Mandela's funeral in South Africa. I never actually saw Spiderman myself, but Sheila told me they are better known as Paul and Nick from All Clean, the window cleaning contractors for Guy's and St Thomas'. I don't think anyone would be brave enough not to believe Sheila. I was in the audience when Strictly came to film the Christmas Special but I did not see myself on the telly. My muffins were good but John Whaite's, the Bake Off winner's, were better – so light and crumbly. Fred and I got some free tickets to Wembley and for the Oval with Dad. I danced in the aisle with Pixie Lott and sang along in the audience with Ollie

Murs at the Ray of Sunshine Concert at the Royal Albert Hall. The tiger cubs were in London Zoo – free tickets from Lois; she is good fun and cheeky. Dad reckons she fancies him, but he says that about all the nurses. He is such a saddo. I touched the actual camera for Springwatch and sat in the studio (but they weren't filming – shame).

Some truly special memories and ALL OF IT IS TRUE.

They say money can't buy you happiness. Really? I'm not so sure. I'll have the cash and see how I go with being miserable, thank you. I did get an iPad Mini – from Dad's work colleagues – which I think is brilliant, especially as I don't have to share it with Ben and Fred and they have not got one. I also got my Nikon D7100 – it's totally awesome. I suspect this would never have happened if I hadn't been ill. Dad kept saying I should go on a course first and use his camera for a while – to practice and get good, that sort of thing. For some reason he changed his mind and let me have it. I don't know why. Mind you, it was only after using nearly all my own money.

One of the characters in 'The Fault in our Stars' talks about Cancer Perks. He describes them as 'the little things cancer kids get that regular kids don't'. This is a horribly cynical phrase but I get what he means. I have been given things and had the opportunity to do stuff that would never have happened if I had not been ill. I call them Sick Kid Specials (SKSs) as they were special things for me.

I quite like the book but not a lot happened, it wasn't that cheerful and it was a bit intellectual if you ask me. Not sure I will bother seeing the film.

Two of the perks I have in my life are my two brothers – NOT. Honestly, they are a pain in the arse. Both Ben and Fred are older and automatically think they are better than me and boss me about. I guess it's the same with all older brothers. We get along but they are annoying so I tend to do my own thing.

When I was in hospital they both came to visit and tried their best, even if they did twiddle with my machines and copy the alarm signals on their phones.

Fred took me to the cinema one night. Ben brought me sushi for lunch. The playlists Fred made were really good. Mum can't listen to that 'Payphone' song without having a blub. We often watched films they had downloaded, sat on my bed with headphones in. We had some games of table tennis out on the atrium. They were lucky there was no net as I would have whupped them. When my dressings on my legs were really painful, Ben went and got a nurse to give me painkillers.

I really appreciated the lots of little things they did.

So they are still annoying, but less so and even quite nice. But I don't feel like telling them.

Chapter 17

Success should not be measured in how high you can
climb, but by how many people you can take with you.

Kevin Knibbs –Headmaster at Fred's school 2014

Getting back to school had been George's keystone in
his bridge back to normality for all of July and August.

In the month before going back to school, George and
Siobhan popped in to see Catherine at the GP practice. It
was like a celebrity visit – the receptionists spilled out of
their office to join the milling group of nurses and staff in
the waiting room. Although George was walking better
now, he was in his wheelchair, still very pale and frail. He
held a bunch of sweet peas for Catherine, which he had
been thrust into choosing earlier that morning.

It was a very emotional meeting for both Siobhan and
Catherine especially, but not for George. The strong bond
between the two women was unspoken but acknowledged
nevertheless. They had shared a dramatic event that had
thrown them together and shaken then both into
vulnerability in doing so. Predictably, Siobhan had had
sleepless nights and days of worry. But so too had
Catherine; few had realised it beneath her veneer of
professionalism. Siobhan guessed from the regular calls
into PICU at St George's and the palpable relief she could
see in her.

On Siobhan's insistence, George trundled forward and
shyly gave the bunch of sweet peas to Catherine. He had
chosen them as the bright colours and delicate frivolous
flowers would be perfect for her. He liked Catherine.
Siobhan had teased him once about Catherine being a
hottie, but was not brave enough to do it again.

"Thank you Doctor, for everything you have done for me," said George. Although the delivery sounded mechanical, he really meant it. He knew from his Mum and Dad's conversations that she had saved his life.

"No, it's me that should be thanking you, George. It was an honour to treat you. You have been my best patient ever."

Catherine meant what she said from the bottom of her heart. Although George had been the most harrowing and worrisome patient she had ever had, her connection with him had been one of the most affirming moments of her career.

You could see that George was a little thrown by her response. 'She's *thanking* me?' A half-smile spread slowly across his wide face, like a sunrise. He glowed with pride as his understanding of what Catherine meant sank in. She was thanking him for surviving, for his toughness for coming through it, and that pleased him. If she could have added to the awkward smiles, fumbled posy-giving and shy embrace, she would have thanked him for being here today as a shining monument of the human spirit she had helped to preserve. That was what she really meant.

Catherine cooed over the flowers, thanked George warmly with a hug for his kindness and one too for Siobhan. As mother and son exited in a nifty three-point turn, Catherine looked down at the sweet girlie flowers. She did not like her own ungrateful thoughts.

"That's just peachy! – I only ever get bought sweet peas, freesias or pansies. Why is it that people always buy me these?"

Catherine is a very good doctor. I feel a plum giving her these flowers – it's so embarrassing. Mum made me do it. I did get a really nice hug though.

There are two types of hugs. The most common one is barely more than a greeting. With Ben and Fred or Dad it's a quick clasp and release, more of a chest bump with arms waggling about. We have a rule of no clinging as that doesn't look right, if you know what I mean.

The other type of hug is much better – it has warmth and comfort. So as you can imagine, it's with Mum most often. It's so supportive that I swear if I took my legs away, she would still hold me up.

I get hugs from Nan and Gran, but not many hugs from other people. I expect some are wary of my chest pipes.

Ben looked over at his Mum and Dad on the other sofa, engrossed in a tense conversation about George going back to school. It had dominated their evening; bags packed and repacked, uniform set out, logistics discussed, coaching George. He didn't get why it had to be such a drama, said so, and regretted his words immediately.

"Well, son," heralded a *'this is how it is'* lecture from Dad. "It's a big thing for George; he's set his sights on it from the moment he started getting better. I know it's not like a new school, but George wants to show everyone he is back." Although Ian didn't say as much, the underlying hope was that the George with odd and out-of-character behaviours was also a thing of the past. "Do you remember your first day at big school?"

"Yeah yeah, all right Dad?" said Ben dismissively. He did not want to dredge up cute memories from when he was a kid. He was an adult now. Cool and edgy was a helluva lot better than cute and nice. Ian carried on anyway.

"Your tutor Mr Fowler told us all about it. When you were asked to introduce yourself to the class that first morning, you stood up to your full height and said *'I am little Ben today,'* then stood on your chair and said *'But one day I will be big Ben.'* That made us laugh."

"Yeah, right," and with that, Ben's headphones went back on to end the conversation.

Ian so hoped George would have the same ability to judge the moment. In that one simple gesture, Ben had shown the rest of the class his sense of humour, humility and put a marker down of his fierce determination. His classmates had loved him for it.

Siobhan and Ian were both nervous about the next day. It was George's first day back at school in five months and they both secretly prayed *'Please God, let it go well'*. Their forced optimism frothed over into a hysterical cheeriness that was false and desperate. They knew it and so did George.

Despite Dr Stewart's sensible advice to take the pressure off and set timelines and expectations that were right for George, they still could not help but feel that this was Last Chance Saloon. George has to go, he has no other choice. Otherwise he will get left so far behind. Then what? What of his future? What of his chances of a decent job, being able to support himself? It all seemed a domino tumble of consequences, all set off by tomorrow's school run.

"Do you think he will be all right?" asked Siobhan, seeking reassurance.

"Yes I do, he's really looking forward to this. He has set his heart on this and it's a huge milestone for him – we've talked about this with him so many times now." Ian tried to keep the frustration from his voice and mask his own doubts. "It's not a *'one hit and you're out'*, anyway. The school understands the situation and will cut him some slack – well, more so than in the past I hope. We can't think too far ahead. If we have a goal to get to half term and then see how he is doing … if he's not happy or struggling, we take him out."

Neither of them were religious, but both thought the same. *'Please, God – just let George be happy.'*

School tomorrow.

Please God tell me I don't have to go.

It has been on my mind for a while now. I know what it will be like, so that doesn't bother me. My mates will be cool about it and there will be some who'll be a pain and ask me stupid questions. I can deal with that.

It's me I worry about. Just thinking about that English classroom gives me a wobble. I struggled to do the right thing before – it's even harder now, being the novelty act all of a sudden. I don't have the confidence I once had and that's scary. What if I get a brain freeze or my anxiety cloak comes back? Brrr, doesn't bear thinking about.

What if HE comes back – I still dream about Him sometimes. Not every day like I used to, but now and then I feel He is there. I end up looking over my shoulder and being distracted. Sod it, if it happens I'll deal with it – what choice do I have?

I can't let Mum and Dad down again. It would really upset Mum and drive Dad nuts. I'll go along with the day and just get through it. As Clarkson would say – 'How hard can it be?' Shit, whenever he says that they usually balls it up and it ends in disaster. Oh God, I hope not.

You can say with certainty that George's black rucksack is heavy. Despite the stoop it gave him, the bag was also a support. It had everything a brittle confidence would need for any eventuality. Instead of an App for that, George had the real thing – a bird book for answers, a photography magazine for ideas, a measuring bottle for fluid, a notebook for responsibility, a phone for Mum to find him, a pencil case for important notes, a key for a locker no longer his and a dosset box of tablets for the rest of his life.

The house phone rang.

"Shotgun not me," shouted Ben.

"Shotgun not me," shouted Fred.

"Off you go Chugs." George trudged to the phone with a face like a slapped arse.

"Hi George, it's Granddad. I'm glad you picked up the phone, it's you I wanted to talk to."

"Hi Granddad, how are you?"

"Good thanks mate. I hear it's your first day back at school tomorrow. You looking forward to it?"

"Yeah, it'll be good to be going back," replied George unconvincingly.

"It will. Well, I just wanted to wish you luck, not that you'll need it. You've done so well, George, to get to this point. Nan and I so admire how you've taken on every challenge. You've been amazingly tough to cope with your illness – so you have our respect, son."

"Thanks Granddad, that's nice of you to say."

"But most of all, George, we wanted to tell you how brave you are, going back to school tomorrow. You might be a bit nervous about it, or scared even, but the nature of being brave is facing up to it and dealing with it. To still go on when you're scared – now that's what I call brave, and that is you."

"I am a bit nervous, but I will be ok. It's not as if it's a new school, and they all know me there," replied George, boosting his own resolve. They chatted some more, George gaining from the thoughtfulness and support from his grandparents.

It's good of Granddad to call. I wonder what age you have to be, to be that wise. I remember my Dad telling me about Granddad when he was a fireman. He said Granddad went into a burning smoky building to find a baby in an upstairs bedroom. As he entered the bedroom, a butane canister full of lighter fuel exploded like a rocket and hit him on the back of the head, ripping off his fire helmet. Dazed and disorientated on his hands and knees in the smoky darkness, he had the choice to get himself out or stay. He stayed and began a systematic search of the bedroom, crawling his way by touch. By sheer luck, his crawling was exactly what the baby had done to escape the heat and smoke. He found the baby alive under the bed and rescued it. That's what I call brave. I know it's not the same thing, but maybe if I have a little of that tomorrow then it will all go okay.

By the Friday of that first week back, George was exhausted. The dark shadows beneath his eyes made his face ghostly pale. Yet he had done it, he had got through it. He had held everything together and felt proud he had been on time, fully prepared and doing everything asked of him. Although his teachers, parents and doctors all praised his strength, it was George's own quiet assessment that boosted his self-esteem. He knew he could do it.

Mum leaves a leaflet about fundraising on my table. I don't know if she meant to – maybe she was just clearing out her handbag, or had it put in her hand, or maybe she wanted me to read it?

It's mostly stuff I know anyway.

Like, the Evelina was opened in 2005. The plaque on the wall tells you that.

Like, 100,000 children are treated every year. Just walk through on a clinic day and you can say hi to every single one from everywhere in the world.

Like, a quarter of all kidney transplants and dialysis in kids are done here. Kay told me that ages ago.

Like, the Head of Something or Other saying that 'our mission is to provide world-leading treatment and care for each child and every family'.

But what I don't know is how much gets raised and what they spend the money on. I know what we've done as a family. Mum has a Just Giving website where she has channelled loads of activities and I think the total is about £8,000 so far. We did the Paris Marathon – well not me, obviously, but Dad, Sally, Sarah and cousin Tom for the first time. That was a great weekend in Paris. A family friend, Josh, did a Half Marathon and raised loads from the school where he was working. None of these people have ever met me, so I was amazed they were so generous. We've baked enough cakes to feed a small country – Gran did two cake sales, Nan, Aunty Debbie at her work, my whole class at school and we did 400 muffins in one go. What's really surprising is some people I have never met sending money. Oh, and the messages on the Just Giving site were really sweet.

So just being really nosey and all, I flip open my laptop and get the wifi working. It's really slow in here but there is no other option. I want to see what they spend the money on.[39] I go onto the Evelina website and there are pages of good news fundraising stories; 35 runners did the London Marathon raising £85,000, each cake sale raises £100 on average, and in 2013, 112 people took part in a sporting event to raise money for ECH.

What I can't find, though, is the total amount raised in 2013. This is really annoying as it must be somewhere, I just can't find it.

I click on 'donations'.,

> Every donation we receive goes towards improving care for sick children. From life-saving research and the latest medical equipment, to the little things that help make the hospital less scary for our youngest patients.

I click on a big 'Thank You' bubble.

> We want to say a big thank you to all of our supporters as we look back on the amazing year we've had. Because of your generosity, we've been able to:
>
> **Buy equipment in the Neonatal Intensive Care Unit** including incubators, a ventilator and Baby Nests and Zaky Hands which cradle and support extremely premature babies.

What's a Zaky Hand? Click.

> Zaky Hands are weighted hand-shape cushions so the baby feels as if they are being held while they are asleep.

---

[39] If you wish to make a donation to the Evelina, then please go to their website. The ECH sees 300 children come through their doors every day, each needing specialist care. £1000 pays for 4 wheelchairs so kids get home sooner. £5000 means 10 home blood pressure monitors so life gets back to normal faster. £15,000 means a neonatal incubator to give life-saving warmth. "Together we can make a difference to thousands of young lives."

Quickly detect genetic diseases. A new piece of equipment detects inherited disease in newborn babies in just 15 minutes, which means children can get treatment faster that saves lives and prevents disability.

Provide safer spinal surgery for children. The Jackson Table is a special spinal surgery table that keeps patients perfectly positioned during incredibly complex and delicate operations. Nearly 200 complex spinal surgical procedures have taken place at Evelina London each year.

We couldn't have done it without you.

Thank you to our dedicated volunteers who allow us to do so much more as a team. They've cheered on our marathon runners, sent out important invitations, helped out at events and organised fundraising events of their own.

Thank you to all our inspiring runners who have taken part in the Virgin London Marathon, Bupa 10K, Brighton Marathon and the Royal Parks Foundation Half Marathon; our intrepid cyclists who took part in the 100km Nightrider challenge and our fearless fundraisers who abseiled 100 feet down the Golden Jubilee Wing of King's College Hospital this summer!

And thank you to everyone who has shared their stories with us. The dedication, bravery and compassion of Guy's and St Thomas' staff, patients, friends and family and volunteers continue to inspire us and motivate us to do more. We're proud to be in this together. We wish you all the best for 2014.

I read the screen with a smile on my face. I am so proud of what everyone has done. It feels like we have given something back, even if only a little. The last bit makes me feel a bit humble too – there are some nice people in this world, you know.

Every Tuesday first thing, I have double Food Tech and then we drive up to Evelina for dialysis for rest of the day. I really enjoy these lessons. Normally we take in the ingredients we need to cook our latest assignment. This term it's cakes, which always go down well. I usually try and do one box for home and one for Evelina of whatever I have cooked.

We always give first dibs to the security guard on the Evelina car park. He's from Mauritius and has just had a baby boy. I wonder what he likes best out of profiteroles, Chelsea buns, brownies, flapjacks and Victoria sponge. He seemed to like them all so it's hard to tell. He always looks out for us – if there isn't a space, he allows us to wait or drop off out of the way without being hassled.

What makes the difference is we are here so often we become part of the scenery – the people you see every day, you say hi, have a chat, munch on a cake and swap the stories about your life that fit into a short chat. I like that, you meet some kind people.

Chapter 18

Over the years, Siobhan had acquired the role as cultural attaché for her teenage sons and husband. She was most proud of the progress she had made with Ian, reaching as far back as when they were dating. It had taken an inordinately long period of gentle coaching to get him to where he is now. He enjoys ballet as an art form, having an appreciation beyond fit birds doing the splits. He willingly reads books that Siobhan recommends, even if they don't have a tank or fighter plane on the front. And – get this – he even rates a chick flick like *Love Actually* as one of his favourite films – but understandably keeps that to himself.

As part of Siobhan's campaign to get the family back to normality, like doing normal stuff together that everyone could enjoy, sharing the experience, she had booked a West End theatre outing. That was the plan, at least, although the play Siobhan booked with the ticket agent might not have been a natural choice. It appealed to Siobhan as it piqued her interest in unusual behaviours in adolescents, a subject never far from her thoughts.

The Curious Incident of the Dog in the Night had received critical acclaim for its inventiveness and treatment of difficult subject matter. The play is about a fifteen-year-old amateur detective named Christopher Boone who appears to have Asperger's Syndrome, [40] although the condition is never explicitly stated in the play. The curious

---

[40] *Asperger's Syndrome (AS)* is a developmental disorder at the "high-functioning" end of the autism spectrum. Children with AS – more frequently boys than girls – may have obsessions with particular objects or subjects, be stiff in their social interactions, speak in a monotone, or otherwise display eccentric behaviour. The disorder was named for Hans Asperger, an Austrian paediatrician who first observed it in 1944.

incident in the title is the mystery surrounding the death of a neighbour's dog. While searching for the dog's murderer, he encounters resistance from many neighbours, but mostly from his father, Ed Boone. Christopher argues to himself that many rules are made to be broken, so he continues to search for an answer; he compares himself to Sherlock Holmes. When he discovers that his father killed the dog, Christopher fears for his own life and travels from Swindon to London to find and live with his mother, whom his father had told him had died. He encounters many problems during the journey, but is welcomed by his mother. However, the road to his ambitions leads him back to Swindon, where he wants to pass important maths tests. Everything seems to be an obstacle, but Christopher is eventually reunited with his father and this improves his own future.

On the night of the play, Thursday 19th December, the plan was to meet in Chinatown in Soho for a meal, then walk over to the Apollo Theatre on Shaftesbury Avenue. Siobhan and George got there first, coming from a dialysis session at Evelina, with a little shopping detour in Convent Garden. Ian arrived next, having driven in from work. Hungry and hassled, the priority was ordering, which he got on with, head down in the menu. Ben and Fred were last to arrive, due to train delays at Vauxhall. It was more of a refuelling stop than a relaxed and savoured meal. The revolving-table centre made the battle to get more than your fair share of the Crispy Fried Duck more intense than usual. With four males, Siobhan had long given up on the politeness of offering the last morsel to others – a sure sign of weakness if ever there was one. They bustled through the bill, onto the theatre and up to their seats in the Gods, only then drawing breath to take in their surroundings.

It was a small theatre with four steeply-banked tiers of seating, with the Gods wedged beneath the ornate plaster ceiling and its spectacular chandeliers. By curtain-up, it was perhaps two thirds full, but enough to generate the buzz of anticipation as the curtain rose. The staging was striking – all surfaces were covered with large-scale black graph paper with fluorescent elements that would reveal themselves with clever lighting. This could be anything from the outline of a house to the stars at night or a world map. Straightaway it was quirky. The staging and action pulled the audience in, both to keep up and to find explanations for what was unfolding.

So when the audience in the Upper Circle and the Gods started fidgeting, a murmur of muttering filtered around the air and the odd person got to their feet, it seemed part of the eccentricity of the play. It can happen that an actor is placed in the audience, to break down the barrier of the stage itself and bring the action into the auditorium. People went with it, intrigued rather than concerned for what would happen next.

Up above, a low groan from the building, not a person, tilted all eyes skyward.

A loud crack like a beam breaking was heard by everyone, including the actors.

The murmur shattered into a staccato bark of '*MOVE, MOVE, MOVE*' echoing against the ceiling.

Then the panic and screaming started.

I keep being distracted by the people over to my right, about five metres away. They keep moving and it's annoying. Just watch the play, will you! A few people rise to their feet, hemmed in by everyone around them. They look like they are desperate for the loo but keep glancing upwards. I follow their eyes upwards and in the gloom can hear cracking and wrenching.

"MOVE! MOVE! MOVE!"

Still looking upwards I see the ceiling give way, white lumps falling like an iceberg crashing into the sea. A three-metre-wide juggernaut of fast moving air in a vertical cylinder hurtles past us. The rumbling in the floor, the air and the handrail build until a rolling barrage of thunder swamps those down in the floor of the theatre, to be replaced by the outpouring of screams.

The screaming makes me panicky. The coldness in my stomach feels like anaesthetic as it bites. I am really panicking now; it must show on my face. What if our balcony gives way or maybe it's a bomb in someone's bag? I look to Mum next to me and her huge blue eyes are round with terror and maybe mine should be too. It goes well with my panic.

She is up fast and moving, and so am I.

Tied together by our family elastic, we grab, support, drag and pull each other out of the row and into the aisle. I try not to push other people but you can't help it. We sweep down the concrete stairs, limited by the close-packed people in front and pressured from behind.

Don't trip, just don't trip.

We go round and down – it takes forever. I just want to get out. As we near street level, the clear cold air dilutes the grey fog around us and we burst like a human avalanche over the pavement. Only now can I see people around me, no-one from our staircase is hurt, thank God, but they are all traumatised and holding onto each other for safety. Mum is like an octopus, with arms everywhere holding onto me, Ben and Fred all at once. She is frantic, eyes darting everywhere.

"Where's Dad? Fred, were you last? Where is he? Was he with you?"

I look over my shoulder, under Mum's arm and there is no-one else coming out of the Exit door of our staircase, just grey clouds. The pavement outside is crowded now. I see injured people for the first time – one man looks like a coal miner, coated in black soot, his hair, face, jacket, all of him. His eyes are white where the soot has been washed away by his tears. He has an inverse panda face. The side of his head is red with blood which has spread to a sooty gory grey mess on his shirt. He looks staggery but won't stand still until a fireman grabs him upright and takes him away.

I look again and Dad appears in three big steps. He too wraps his arms round us all so we form a Birks island in the chaos that swirls around us. I feel a bit shaky myself but I don't let the others see it. I have been through a lot worse than this. Being a bit wobbly is nothing compared to really hurting when you can't get away from it or speak. You just have to get through it, endure it, but it's not much help telling that poor man that.

Ian was in the middle seat of the row nearest the balcony edge. Unless he used his strength to clamber over women and children, he was going to be the last one out of the Upper Circle. When the panic hit him like everyone else, he certainly considered it. He was relieved to see all his family linked together, ahead of him and barrelling toward the exit. He too felt the almighty whoosh of debris and sooty air go past barely two metres away, but thankfully for him, going down and away. He felt a stab of guilt, knowing relief at his own salvation meant the poor souls in the stalls had nowhere to escape to.

As he neared the top of the staircase and the route to safety, he hesitated as rational thought overcame the barrelling panic. He took four steps back into the Upper Circle so he could see all the empty seats. This was no time for heroics, as the building could collapse for all he knew. His three seconds of delay, and definitely no more than that, was enough to verify that he was truly the last one out. He did not want the Rescue Teams wasting time searching this section if there were no casualties to find. His mind photographed the essence of people left behind – coats, handbags, hats, umbrellas and shoes. Who on earth leaves their shoes behind? Later he would know, and kick himself for leaving his jacket, wallet and car keys under his seat.

Ian scooted down the empty staircase, to find his family huddled together right in front of him. He hugged them briefly, kissed Siobhan's hair and shot off again to collar the Watch Leader as he swept past. Ian told him the Upper Circle was clear and to focus on the floor of the auditorium as that was where the serious casualties would be.

They stood around on the pavement for about twenty minutes, not really sure what to do with themselves. From the buzz of fear and adrenalin, it all sort of fizzled out to dust. They weren't hurt; they could not help anyone; they had nowhere to go – so they went home. Ian and Siobhan got through the muddle of missing keys, shared the spare set and headed for home in two cars.

"Hey Dad, shall I put the radio on – see if we made the news?" suggested Ben, all bright-eyed from the after-effects of the excitement. Ben and Ian were driving back from the Apollo, along the M4 towards the Chiswick roundabout.

"Sure – go for it."

Ben twiddled the tuner, catching snippets across the channels, until he settled on a live news report, from LBC

" ... The London Ambulance Service are telling us 90 casualties, 6 seriously injured. St Thomas' designated as focal receiving point for this crisis ... witnesses earlier said they had seen people leaving the building, covered in dust and plaster ... some bleeding and crying." The presenter's authoritative and clear voice came on, injecting a half-tone of excitement with a live eyewitness report.

"We have a caller on line two, who was there, Sir, can you tell us what happened?"

"Hi, yes, I was in the Circle when the balcony above collapsed. We thought it was water ... We thought it was a part of the show. People started screaming. The theatre suddenly went dark with dust clouds everywhere. I grabbed my kids and ran." The poor guy sounded shaken, and the sirens in the background placed him at the scene. It was radio gold, getting across the human impact and live sounds together.

"That's bollocks! It wasn't the balcony," Ben shouted at the radio, full of indignation.

The newsreader carried on, calm and unruffled, unfazed by the abuse he was getting from Ben.

"Thank you, we will stay with this story live, here on LBC as it unfolds. If you were there, if you saw it, then please call in to the LBS Newsroom on 0345 60 60 973. London needs to know."

"Shall I call in, Dad? What do you reckon?"

"Go for it, just don't say bollocks or fuck on the radio." With the go-ahead from Ian, Ben dialled. In two rings, Ben went straight through live on LBC.

"Good evening to our next caller on Line One. What is your name and can you tell us what happened at the Apollo?" There was a slight hesitation as Ben's eyebrows shot up in surprise and the mouthed the words '*Is this for real?'* in panic to his dad. All he got in reply was a silent hand swish to usher him into speaking, and off he went.

"Well er ... hi, my name is Ben ... ..the entire dome roof fell down on the audience just in front of us. It wasn't the balcony at all, as we were on it. It was the ceiling that came down ... " With that, Ben was away, giving a vivid description, full of energy, doing the newsreader's job for him with his punchy and mature responses. The interview went on for fifteen minutes, live and not a single falter. When Ben did hang up, he let out a huge puffed breath in relief and pent-up tension. They listened in to the rest of the bulletin so Ben's heart could stop pounding. At the top of the hour, the announcer gave a summary to pull together the emerging facts and ended with a crisp sound-bite.

"A 29-year-old audience member, who only gave his name as Ben, said: *'It was about halfway through the first half of the show and there was a lot of creaking. We thought it was part of the scene – it was a seaside scene – but then there was a lot of crashing noise and part of the roof caved in. There was dust everywhere, everybody's covered in dust. We got out fairly quickly; I think everyone was quite panicked.'"*

"Hey, that's me!" hollered Ben, recognising his own voice and high-fiving his Dad at the same time.

"Nice one, Bud –you obviously sound older on radio."

20 December 2013 : News Report[41]

Seventy-six people have been injured, seven seriously, after part of a ceiling in London's Apollo Theatre collapsed during a show. The Met Police said more than 40 walking wounded were treated at the

---

[41] From BBC News website http://www.bbc.co.uk/news/uk-25459567

nearby Gielgud Theatre, while three London buses were used to transport others to hospitals.

The venue in Shaftesbury Avenue was packed for a performance of *The Curious Incident of the Dog in the Night-Time*. Eyewitnesses heard "a crackling" noise before the collapse at about 20:15 GMT. Theatre-goers left covered in debris.

The Apollo's owner described it as a shocking and upsetting incident and said an investigation was under way. A spokesman for the company, Nimax Theatres, said "thoughts are with the audience and staff".

The London Ambulance Service said 25 ambulance crews and an air ambulance rapid response team attended the scene. Incident commander Maria Smith, who was one of the first on scene, said: "When I arrived it was dark and extremely dusty and people were lying on the floor of the theatre. We very quickly set up a casualty clearing area in the foyer of the theatre and the walking wounded were assessed and treated there for injuries such as cuts and grazes, breathing problems and head injuries."

Eight fire engines and more than 50 firefighters attended the incident in London's busy West End theatre district, along with hundreds of police officers. Firefighters said the theatre had been almost full and 720 people were watching the performance. The Apollo's ornate plasterwork ceiling collapsed and brought down part of the lighting rig. London Fire Brigade said its 'search is now complete' and the theatre has been sealed off.

Guy's and St Thomas' NHS Trust said 34 adults and five children were being treated at the accident and emergency department at St Thomas' Hospital. The majority had cuts and bruises, and a small number had fractures. The three most serious cases had injuries to the neck and back, or head. The trust said at this stage there were no life-threatening injuries. In a statement it said: "We have had a fantastic response from staff – both already on-site and those who came in from home – to help."

One of those fantastic responders who came in to help was Carmen. She didn't even make it all the way home.

While the Birkses were on the pavement outside the Apollo, Carmen had her headphones in, listening to the evening news on her phone. It had been a long day for her and the slow bus wasn't helping as she headed for home at the end of her shift. It always was when they were almost at capacity on the Dialysis Unit. It was not helped by one machine playing up, necessitating a full reset, losing a cycle as a consequence.

She was saddened by the devastation which the radio presenter ably conveyed in words and interviews. The eye witness vox pops brought home the confusion and fear for those trapped in the stalls as the roof collapsed upon them. In her own mind, Carmen immediately flipped the switch from sympathy and inquisitiveness to one of response and action. She and her team had trained for this – she had a ward to clear and preparations to be made for a possible influx of patients. She hopped off at next stop, crossed the road and caught the next bus straight back to the Evelina.

Once back on Beach ward, she initiated a set of almost automated behaviours, programmed by repeated drills. Over the next two hours, the day-case section would be cleared and prepared to free up fifteen beds. By postponing several scheduled inbound patients and ushering the discharge of the nearly-well, she freed up a further ten beds. Some other changes gave a capacity of thirty beds to cope with whatever casualties would be bussed to them.

Once she felt comfortable they were ready, Carmen took a deep breath to run through a mental checklist to make sure she had done all she could. Something was nagging at her, and she was annoyed with herself for succumbing to the tiredness which slowed her thoughts.

'*OMG, the Birkses!*' She recalled Siobhan and George telling her about the theatre trip that night. '*Please God, do not let it be the same one.*' Carmen stabbed out a speedy text to Siobhan to check they were all safe.

Through the evening, three double-decker buses with the majority walking wounded and fourteen ambulances with the more serious cases arrived at St Thomas' A&E. Luckily few children were hurt, and those that were received treatment straight away and no overnights were needed.

At work the next day, reports of the Apollo Theatre roof collapse came up on the flat screens in the cafe. Ian drew attention to himself with his '*I was there*' routine. His colleagues bombarded him with questions of disbelief, concern, curiosity, all at once. A few of his close team members knew the significance of the theatre trip, so their questions were more focused.

"Was George scared, after all he's been through?"

"Were you able to get George out ok?"

"How is Siobhan taking it?"

As the top-of-mind questions died down and the conversation started to dry up, a more reflective joker quipped that the Birks family must be due for a lottery win. He got a polite chuckle but then the chat moved on and Ian's brief flit in the spotlight was over. People dispersed back to their To Do lists.

While Ian waited for the lift back to the third floor, that last comment beetled around his head, gathering ill-formed thoughts. These randomly stuck together into a nugget of insight, comparing the probabilities of contracting meningitis and being in the audience of the Apollo that night and winning the lottery. He got a bit bogged down in the mental arithmetic and rather pathetically gave up by time the lift came.

Back at his desk, he persevered to look up the actual numbers.

1761[42] cases of Meningitis B per year out of UK child population of 15 million[43] – that's a probability of 1 in 8,500.

720 theatregoers [44] out of 8.3 million London inhabitants[45] – so, 1 in 11,500.

1 six-figure lottery pick out of 14 million permutations.[46]

This was interesting – catching Men B and the Apollo event had nearly the same probability as each other.

Having both independent events happen to you – catching both Men B and the collapsing ceiling – had a probability of 1 in 98 million.[47]

He blew out a breath, surprised at the conclusion. That meant that winning the lottery at 1 in 14 million was SEVEN TIMES more likely than the events George had endured in the last year.

---

[42] Average annual cases of MenB cases in UK from
http://www.meningitis.org/facts

[43] From Office of National Statistics. UK population 64.1m and <19 years is 15m.
http://www.ons.gov.uk/ons/taxonomy/index.html?nscl=Population

[44] Capacity of Apollo Theatre before the ceiling collapse

[45] From Office of National Statistics. As above

[46] There are 13,983,816 possible combinations of six numbers from 49 numbers so the lottery odds of winning the jackpot are 1 in 13,983,816. From http://www.lottery.co.uk/lottery-odds.asp

[47] Suppose probability of happening of an event A is = p1 & probability of happening an event B is = p2. If both event A and B are mutually exclusive, then probability of happening both the event A and B together is = p1 x p2 (i.e. you are multiplying both the probabilities)

Whatever the odds, he just thought themselves very, very lucky that George was still on the planet. He vowed never to ask for luck, happy just to settle for a normal life back again.

Chapter 19

When I count my blessings I count you twice!

Irish blessing

Ever since Ian was cast aside as the Donor of Last Resort, he became attuned to articles and stats on who donates and why. He spent many late evenings researching. He scanned across many websites, bookmarking articles and papers as he went. Some articles he snipped to save as separate files to which to add his own notes. He read FAQs to get his basic questions answered and build up his knowledge. He read personal stories from donors, recipients and meningitis sufferers, with a mix of sadness and inspiration. From patients, some of it was desperate. Others shared their experiences, highlighting their learning or asking for advice. Often they were self-deprecating of their own qualities and making light of their suffering. Medics tended to be much more strident, buoyed by the evidence of their data or righteousness of their argument. They demanded, not asked and rarely sought help or advice, preferring to make recommendations for others. It was two different species of human beings.

It was the collection of scraps of knowledge that would come to inform his views about 'opt out legislation' where it is assumed you are a donor, unless you proactively opt out.

He became a sponge, developing an awareness of the changing picture relating to donation. The headlines shouted a positive picture of record numbers of critically-ill patients who had their lives saved or extended in the last year. New NHS figures[48] revealed that the largest ever

---

[48] All data apply to the UK between 1 April 2013 and 31 March 2014 taken from http://www.organdonation.nhs.uk/statistics/

number of people were donating their organs after death. He read a transcript of a NHS Blood and Transplant (NHSBT) Report stating the number of people donating has risen year-on-year over the last decade from 709 in 2003 to 1114 last year. He was encouraged by the rising number of people who had signed the organ donor register – from 8 million in 2001 to 20 million – about 30% of the population. So all in all, the figures he saw reflected changing public attitudes towards organ donation and NHS measures to improve rates, including creating clinical leads and specialist nurses in hospitals and setting up dedicated organ retrieval teams.

Another journalist had an opposing view, bursting Ian's bubble. He saw a situation that looked dreadful when you consider that the UK has one of the lowest donor rates in the western world and the number of organs available for transplant in the UK has remained static over the past five years. About 1,000 people a year die waiting to receive one. Despite the NHS schemes, this was not going to improve any time soon. Traditionally, organs have come from road accident victims and brain haemorrhage patients. Improved road safety and medical intervention mean fewer are dying.

The frustrating thing is that around 65% of British people say they are prepared to donate an organ after their death – but only a quarter are registered donors. The latest trend bore this out. In 2013, 58.6% of families who were asked about the possibility of donating their relative's organs agreed, up from 56.5% in 2012. The NHS wants to reach 80% consent from families by 2020. Clearly there is a gap between intention and action. Figures from NHSBT reveal that families are more likely to agree to organ donation going ahead if they were aware of their loved ones' decisions to be a donor[49]. Far more work is needed in the area of 'soft consent' to ask people to spell out their donation decision

The only conclusion in Ian's mind was the need for more live donors and family donors. The solution had to come from within the family, and in George's case that meant Siobhan. So, Siobhan it was, and she entered the same cycle of tests that he had undertaken. Ian was not wholly comfortable with the path forward, but logically there was no other option.

Dad asked me to research donors the other day. Not sure why, he never said. He spends hours at his desk up in the loft doing exactly that, so I don't know why he needs my help. There is usually a message in there for me to work out. It could be one of three things – to keep the old grey matter ticking over, a prompt for me to do something useful with more fundraising, or a nudge for me to have an opinion of my own. He is sooo predictable and I can read him like a book.

---

[49] Kidney Life, Autumn 2014 Issue. The magazine of the National Kidney Federation

Chapter 20

> Too often we underestimate the power of a touch, a smile, a kind word, a listening ear, an honest compliment, or the smallest act of caring, all of which have the potential to turn life around.

> *Leo Buscaglia*

I look up from my dialysis chair and I don't believe what I see.

What the hell? Those four hairy-arsed bikers shouldn't be in here. What are they doing? Jesus – I reckon they've stolen those Easter Eggs from the kids' ward. I don't believe it, what is the world coming to? Oh no, they're coming my way – I'll pretend to be asleep so they pass on by. Thank God I've got my iPad under the covers so they can't nick that too.

"Hi fella, I saw you were awake so we've come to say hello. We're giving Easter Eggs to all the kids and thought you might like one – take your pick!" said Pipes enthusiastically.

Pipes and two of his mates shuffled over to George's bedside, standing like the Shrek family, all dressed alike in denim, black leather, studs, tassels and tattoos. Their intimidating presence made the ward go still, waiting for a fight to start. George opened one eye and looked them up and down suspiciously. His earlier judgment of *'thieving pikeys'* still sat more naturally than one of tough Samaritans whose generosity you dared not refuse.

Siobhan gave George the hairy eyeball, which, on this occasion, meant *'just pick an egg, don't tell them you can't have chocolate, and smile politely'*. George was a little slow on the uptake, wondering what he had done wrong, but never one to refuse chocolate, went for the biggest, flashiest egg that Pipes was eclipsed by.

"I'll have the Easter Bunny one please."

"No problem, fella. Would you like to see a picture of my Harley? It's parked outside."

Pipes offered George his iPhone with a series of photos of his motorbike.

"Nice bike! I've seen this bike before," said George. "Well, not this one actually, obviously, but I have photographed it in black and white. The engine has *Live to Ride* on it."

"Wow, that's cool – guessing photography's your thing then? I love it too and have a Canon 650. What's yours?" said Pipes, trying to slip into what he thought was teenager-speak.

Little did he realise the monster he had awoken in George, who launched into a diatribe of the virtues of a Nikon D7100 versus the Canon. He sounded like a barrister sentencing the Canon to life imprisonment reserved for patently inferior cameras. Pipes rose to the challenge, taking on the cause of Canon-owners everywhere, to push George with his good-natured banter and gentle mischievous digs. Winning the battle meant less to Pipes; instead he relished the animation and enthusiasm coming from George. The nerd-fest of techno-jousting went back and forth with a quick-fire of *'Ah yes, but can yours do this?'*. They ground to a stalemate, each convinced they were right but only George voicing it. Pipes conceded defeat but with a smirk behind his eyes, knowing he had got George fired up and engaged. George missed that completely and felt sorry for drilling the misguided biker into the ground. So George tried to give Pipes a bridge to retreat over.

"That was a really good chat, thanks Pipes. Will you come back with more photos, so we can compare lens quality?"

"What, and have another dose of shame? 'Course I will, fella –bring it on. It was great to see you and to speak to someone who knows their onions."

"Yeah, right," said George, wondering if his reference to onions had anything to do with Shrek. "Thanks again guys," he called, and waved to the bikers as they ambled onto the next bay of beds, beyond his eye line.

Allyn, one of the renal consultants, looked over at Siobhan. He put a finger to his lips to shush her. He could see she was itching to take the chocolate egg away from George, as she had been told countless times that dialysis patients were not allowed chocolate due to its high potassium levels.

"The Hells Angels come in every year. They are a great bunch and the kids love it. Here on the Renal Unit, no-one has the heart to tell them that our kids can't have chocolate for all the reasons you know about high potassium content. We are very sneaky cowards. We tell the kids to take the eggs so their families can have them. If there are any eggs without a home then the nurses have them – that's why nurses have big bums and thin legs."

"That's awful, they'll kill you when I tell them," threatened Siobhan.

"Knock yourself out. I've told them loads of times – thin legs from being on their feet all day and big bums from too much chocolate. I'm only saying what's good for them. I'm amazed the Hells Angels come in, but they do every year[50] and it's an invasion. There are over forty of them in the hospital today, judging from the bikes I saw out front when I came on shift this morning. It can't do much for their rufty-tufty biker image, but you saw what it meant for George and the enjoyment they all got from it; just to make a kid smile and brighten up his day. We don't tend to publicise it as most people wouldn't believe us. I guess prejudices are too strong sometimes. Anyway, sermon over. Are you going to eat all those Bunny Ears?"

---

[50] Easter Egg Run Lakeside Chapter of Harley Owners Group April 19, 2014

Chapter 21

Bad news is sudden and dramatic

Good news is gradual and unnoticed.

Matt Ridley, transcript from BBC R4

Spring is always a surprise – it just appears like a guest you weren't expecting. Accustomed to drab and lifeless winter, then suddenly daffodils appear, leaves sprout, birds sing and there is freshness in the air that is crisp with watery sunshine. Spirits lift in anticipation of a summer to come. In the same way, the Make-a-Wish Springwatch day came round so quickly, they were barely ready.

A few hasty phone calls recruited the troops, finalising on Mum, George obviously, Gran Mags and Nan Jean. Celia from Make-a-Wish had made all the arrangements and would accompany them on the day. The day before, they had a rendezvous in Essex at Dave and Jean's so they could have an early start up the M11 to Minsmere on the Norfolk coast.

Celia met them upon arrival mid-morning to go over the final arrangements for the day. They would tour the Minsmere Nature Reserve and the film set, meeting the presenters before lunch. They would watch the rehearsals for most of the afternoon and were allowed to watch the live broadcast in the evening if they wanted to. It all sounded great and they were all excited.

George loved every second. He became the tour guide as all locations were recognisable to him from the TV and he knew most about them. Add in his impressive knowledge of natural things and he edged towards the slightly annoying, but none could begrudge his enthusiasm. The camera man, Ed, was a charming young man according to Jean, and the wink was not lost on Siobhan. Ed and

George got into a technical Q&A, which allowed the ladies to have a seat and a sneaky rest. George had a go on the camera, filming a short sequence with Ed hovering over his shoulder, guiding his actions.

"You look good in front of the camera, Ed," said George as he squinted through the viewfinder.

"Er, thanks …" said Ed, the oddness of a fourteen-year-old complimenting a man on his looks sitting uncomfortably with him.

Halfway through the afternoon rehearsal, energy levels had started to flag. George was done in and all out of excitement. Both Mags and Jean had had enough of walking but neither would admit it. Mags was unsteady on broken ground, with a real fear of falling. Jean was fine on broken ground but her hip was sore from too much walking. So in comparison to anything too bumpy or too far, a sofa was a winner. Siobhan was just shattered, being driver, organiser, bag-carrier, enthusiasm stoker, and behaviour coach. She sensibly floated the idea to watch the live broadcast from the comfort of the hotel and got unanimous approval.

They were all impressed with the plush rooms and celebrity treatment. They had a pleasant meal, and then barely made it to the end of the program before crashing into bed. Siobhan and George got one room, with Gran and Nan in the other. As Siobhan put out the light, she kissed George.

"How was today then?"

"Really good, but I've got to sleep now, night."

Siobhan would have to be grateful for such high praise indeed.

Whilst George was at Springwatch, Ian got updates by text throughout his working day. As Ian travelled home, he flicked on the radio and let his mind wander. He was aware of the news but then the DJ launched enthusiastically into his next item.

"Matt Ridley,[51] columnist for *The Times* and author of *The Rational Optimist*, has something for us."

The author then started speaking in a measured and scholarly voice, getting Ian's attention with his first words, which hit a chord.

> "There is a lot wrong with the world at the moment. Is this what 1914 felt like, or the end of the Roman Empire? After 200 years of rising living standards, are we about to experience collapse?
>
> It's always possible. Nothing guarantees the future will be better than the past. And mad men and bad men can do mad bad things. But perhaps we should remind ourselves that there is a lot going right in the world too?
>
> Living standards are rising rapidly all over the world, but especially in Africa, Asia and much of Latin America. The percentage of people in absolute poverty has fallen by two thirds in the last fifty years. Child mortality is down by the same amount. Malaria's retreating and so is AIDS. Technologies that seemed like magic keep falling into our hands. Undreamt-of knowledge is a click away.
>
> I could show you statistics that unambiguously demonstrate that, on the whole, we are cleverer, cleaner, kinder, healthier, happier and safer than we've ever been. Contrary to what most people think the world is getting more equal all the time, as people in poor countries get rich faster than people in rich

---

[51] Transcript from Broadcast on Radio 2 Mon 13th October. Actual work was published in May 2010

countries. Global warming is currently happening more slowly than we feared it would. So maybe we should pause to count our blessings?

It's a funny thing, but every generation thinks it stands at a turning point in history and that life will stop improving and our children face misery. As a general rule, bad news is sudden and dramatic while good news is gradual and goes unnoticed. Why is it, said Lord McCauley, that with only improvement behind us we are to expect only deterioration before us. Not every silver lining has a cloud in it."

"Thank you," the DJ came breezing back in to take the praise. "What about that, did you like that?"

The *'good news is gradual and unnoticed'* phrase formed the kernel of Ian's thoughts. Life felt tougher than pre-illness; the grind of dialysis, the absence of holidays, the permanent impatience and the debilitating effects for George. But improvements were there and sneaking up on them. He made a mental note to ask George how he felt when he got home.

What is dialysis like?

Dad asked me the same question a few nights ago over supper.

Dialysis means four to six hours in hospital every other day. You have to plan your week around it, you have to change your diet, and you have to be very strict about the amount of fluid you take on board – 400ml tops for everything. Dialysis becomes the focus of your life and, however much I deny it, I am defined by my illness.

It is not so bad; mostly it's just boring being stuck in one place for half a day. The two pipes or Hickman lines[52] in my chest do not hurt and the nurses are very gentle when they change the dressing every two weeks. It really freaks Dad out when I swing the pipes around like tassles – he goes nuts and runs away! It still gives me the creeps when they open the taps and the transparent tube changes from clear to bright red as my blood charges out of me into the machine.

The odd thing about kidney failure is the effect it has on the bodily functions you normally take for granted. As one of the kidneys' main jobs is to turn waste products into urine, when they stop working, you don't pee so much. I still pee a bit – maybe 200ml per day when I am asked to measure it. But it is not 'good' piss, as the urea, creatinine and other stuff gradually accumulates in my bloodstream as my kidneys do not do their job to filter it out. So all the liquid that comes in has to be taken off by dialysis, and my blood filtered.

The biggest torture is thirst. You just try 400ml of liquid per day – that's a bit more than a can of Coke – from the moment you wake up until you go to bed, irrespective of how hot it is or what activity you do. It includes everything – so yogurt, sauces, fruit and ice-cream. I am easily the best on the Unit at managing my fluid. I have my 400ml and that's it. I know as I measure everything and write it all

---

[52] A Hickman line is a central venous catheter most often used for the administration of medications, as well as for dialysis. Under general anaesthetic the catheter is pushed through a tunnel in the chest wall and advanced into the superior vena cava, preferably near the junction of it and the right atrium of the heart. Throughout the procedure, ultrasound and X-rays are used to ascertain the positioning of the catheter. From http://en.wikipedia.org/wiki/Hickman_line

down. We have so many measuring bottles all over the place; in drawers, cupboards, handbags, glove boxes. I am always thirsty and craving liquid. Sheila says that if she were ever trapped in a desert, she would want to be with a dialysis patient as they would always find water. Mum and Dad are convinced I cheat and take sneaky drinks – I don't, but they don't believe me.

I must avoid all foods with high potassium content or risk damaging my heart or worse. So bananas, avocados, melons, tomatoes and orange juice are all off the menu. Chocolate – forget it. As a treat I can have a little in the first thirty minutes of dialysis, as the harmful bits are filtered out straight away. It's quite an unhealthy diet as I need to whack in the calories, so bizarrely, fatty junk food is ok.

You wouldn't think that being plugged into a machine for so long would be so tiring. It seems to just drain your energy so I'm a Master-At-Sleeping whenever I get the chance. Seriously though, it can just leave you completely washed out for the rest of the day. You don't eat much on dialysis so you don't grow much – there is some science to this but I'm not sure what applies to me. I think growth hormones are affected – so many kids on dialysis are much smaller than they should be. One of the nurses told me that higher creatinine levels suppress your appetite so it's hard to take on the calories you need to grow. Either way, I ain't gonna be playing basketball any time soon.

I do manage to keep up with my schoolwork though, which keeps Mum and Dad happy. The Hospital School are brilliant and work with me one-to-one. They also back off if I'm feeling rough. My own school is a bit patchy. They think being supportive is taking stuff away. I have to chase the teachers to tell me what is coming up and chase them for what I've missed. It pisses me off that my teachers don't follow the routine and think ahead, as they could make it so much easier for me.

When George had gone to bed, and Ben and Fred were in their bedrooms working, Ian and Siobhan finally had some quiet time to themselves. Siobhan sipped her wine, which was a repeat prescription to help her relax, according to Dr Ian, who secretly hoped she would get into the magical three-glass realm of Wondrous Possibilities.

"Do you think George cheats with his liquid?" asked Siobhan.

"Hmmm – if you'd asked me a few months back I would have said no way. He was meticulous with measuring and noting everything."

"That was a long hmmm?" she pressed him before she gave her own view.

"Now I'm not so sure. I keep catching him looking really guilty. He's pushing the boundaries and he knows it. You watch him cleaning his teeth – there is far too much slurping going on. His latest habit is rinsing his mouth out with an eggy *'I'm NOT DRINKING it'*. I caught him with bubbles on his chin in the bath the other day. I bet he was scooping bath water into his mouth."

"Well, get this, you know when a bowl gets flipped over by the jets in the dishwasher ..." Siobhan wrinkled her nose in disgust.

"Don't – and grey greasy rinsing water gets trapped?"

"Yep – saw him drinking that this morning. I don't mean to be catching him doing things wrong when he has so much to deal with, but we can't ignore it."

"I know, I know. Trouble is, there's no hiding it when he gets weighed every other day and he comes in heavy. He gets a long dialysis session to take the max fluid off him they can."

Siobhan changed the subject to George's school work, or more accurately his attitude to his school work. "So what about George's Spanish oral tomorrow then? It counts, you know, to his overall GSCE," she wondered.

'*Sod it,*' thought Ian, recognising that her thoughts were still at Two Glasses –Opinionated and Feisty. "I honestly don't know. There's no lack of work there. You know what he's like; he will spend hours doing work but I always feel it is junk hours. He is either not concentrating or it doesn't stick."

"Maybe," she paused, thinking. "He just seems so unprepared to me. He's not in the least bit fazed by it, like he couldn't give a toss."

"I think you're being a little harsh, darling," nudged Ian, aware that Two Glasses Feisty was still a dangerous opponent.

"But how can he stand up there in front of the examiner? What is he going to say? Just stand there dumb, or even worse just drop in English words like you do with French? There's no fear, no responsibility, no setting his own standard. His attitude is '*so what*'. There's not even any embarrassment." Her voice rose toward a squawk as her frustration stoked. Ian tried appeasement.

"I can remember being ridiculed by a teacher. I hadn't prepared a proper answer so instead I gave a very honest spontaneous response. In front of the class I said I was really sad that Boxer in *Animal Farm* was taken off to the glue factory and that Communism was unfair and exploitative. My English teacher went off on one about prejudice, weak thinking blah blah. He ridiculed me so much in front of the whole class that I never contributed again so he had nothing to criticise. Doing the minimum meant I lost all love for the subject. So my point is that I gave so little and got back so little – which is where George is going."

"Grrrrr – he drives me nuts, that boy sometimes. You coach his bloomin' socks off and you still feel you aren't getting anywhere. Well, let's just see how he does and see if he learns a lesson from it." Siobhan gave a shoulder shrug a Frenchman would have been proud of.

Over supper the next day, Siobhan could not help herself.

"So George, how did the Spanish Oral go?"

"Yeah, good."

"And?"

"Good – it went really well. The Examiner was really nice and chatty. He gave me a few prompts but we talked of all the things I knew about and could say. "

"So it was a back-and-forth conversation?"

"Yep, all the way."

"No silences or big pauses?"

"Nope."

"Well, that sounds really good, well done you, Chugsie." Siobhan's wide-open eyes flitted between George and Ian, flashing two different meanings. For Ian it was *'Jesus, can you believe that, who would have thought?'* For George, he took it as genuine praise.

Siobhan excused George from the clearing up, recruiting Ian to load the dishwasher. As soon as George had left the dinner table, she hissed at Ian, "So we must have completely misread his behaviour. When he does nonchalant, maybe it's not '*I don't give a shit',* maybe he is confident and knows his stuff."

"He's like a bloody poker player, and just as hard to read. He feigns he doesn't know things so no-one expects much of him. I bet he'd even lose a hand or two. It's his way of taking the pressure off and hiding his true ability if he can't consistently produce it."

They clattered through the remaining plates, feeling they had been hustled.

Chapter 22

Never engage in battle of wits with an unarmed person.

Anonymous

The signals were loud and clear, but the comfortable routine lately meant they went unheard. It all kind of crept up on George, unseen by Ian and Siobhan, so when the wheels fell off, they all hit the road hard.

It began with a tough week at school. George had been stressed by his English teacher demanding he repeat his planning for his controlled assessment. She had never given George a second chance after the *Top Gear* debacle. She did not waste time giving George the clear simple instructions he needed. So he had no idea what 'good' looked like but gamely kept trying, sinking in bewilderment with each near miss. He had not been feeling great either, his back ached and it burned every now and then when he peed. He told his mum, but his usual stoicism made light of the symptoms. By the end of the week he was shattered, at his lowest ebb since restarting school.

Saturday came and proved to be a grueling dialysis. His blood pressure dropped below eighty and he nearly passed out. It left him spacey and washed out for the rest of the day. Ian and Siobhan just put it down to tiredness.

Sunday was a family get-together for Ian and Jean, whose birthdays were one day apart in May. A warm early summer day seemed to be perfect for a sightseeing trip to the viewing deck at the top of the Shard. Afterwards they went for a meal at a bistro on the riverbank by Hays Galleria, with Tower Bridge backlit by the sunset. George was distracted and quiet all through the meal, making no effort towards conversation. Even subjects he liked, such as talking about cameras, met with a dollop of indifference. Both Ian and Siobhan commented on it in the car home.

The tipping point was an explosion on Monday, mid-morning. George's guts launched his breakfast over the desk. To avoid the collateral splatter, the class shot from the classroom, leaving poor dazed George in an island of vomit and rejection. The school secretary was all of a twitch, mobilising the Head of Year and the School Nurse, and repeat-dialling Siobhan and Ian until she got a response.

They got there speedily, to find a dejected and disorientated George in the school library with a dithering teacher, who was keen to find the fastest way to discharge his responsibility. George was in meltdown, disheveled from the hasty clean-up, missing his socks and carrying his blazer stuffed into a bin bag. He was shaky and unable to explain what had happened with any coherence. Siobhan wrapped him up in a blanket as she bundled him into the back seat of the car and got in alongside him. George laid his head on her shoulder. He did not have to hold it together any longer, so he closed his eyes and visibly melted in her arms, his resistance gone.

It took seven minutes to get to A&E and then ten hours of torture and anguish before they got back home.

He has a clipboard, he must be important. He has a checklist. I can see him ticking me on it. I'd better give him the right answers. Sit up and focus – I stare at his face but the words he says just merge into each other like 'liaison' in French. I'll just tell him what he wants to hear. Why are they asking me all these questions and looking at me as though I'm mad?

You've just asked me the same questions the last four doctors did, and I bet you will compare checklists to catch me out. You say you are trying to help me but why keep asking the same things over and over when you know I don't know the answers – it's just cruel.

Leave me alone.

Who is Mr. Green, why are you giving me his address? Am I to see him or what?

Why are you asking me who Mr. Green is? Don't you know? I have never met him and I do not know his name so don't ask me, numb-nuts.

How the hell do I know where he lives? You should put him in your contacts on your phone so that you remember and stop keep asking me.

I've had enough of this, get your hands off me, NO you can't examine me, I don't want you to. My back is really sore, low down around my kidneys, like a tube is blocked or something. My tum is really tender but you seem to be ignoring that or think I am putting it on. I am not answering any more questions. I look across at Mum and Dad and ask them with my eyes to get me out of here. I want to do what they want but I don't know what that is, please let me go home, please. I just want to be me.

Siobhan and Ian looked at the computer screen over the doctor's shoulder. He talked to the screen and pointed at some tiny white dots.

"Well, here on the X-ray, we can see small kidney stones. Some are the size of peppercorns, others the size of Nigella seeds." The doctor could see the blank looks, so he explained further. "Like poppy seeds – you have to know your condiments to work here." His feeble joke fell flat. He reverted back to safer ground. "It's likely he has been passing these for some time. The small ones would be irritating, perhaps some soreness when he urinates, but the larger ones, they would be really painful – is that right, George?" George nodded, looking back at the doctor with distrust. "It's horribly unfair, isn't it. You have dialysis three times a week because your kidneys don't work, but you still get kidney stones."

"This guy just can't stop digging, can he?" thought George.

Looking back, what derailed the diagnosis was the mix of symptoms; some serious, related to chronic kidney failure but others linked to mundane kidney stones. Similarly, the symptoms of behavioural meltdown were set against the background of the recalcitrant and belligerent teenager in front of them. What concerned them most was George's mental state and how he could potentially act. He could not be discharged until they were sure he would not harm himself or others whilst so disorientated.

The fifth doctor got the brunt of it. Being kept waiting for a change of shift for this on-call psychiatrist to arrive just ratcheted up the tension. The psychiatrist tried the same basic test to see if George was disorientated. His version was similar, but slightly different to the previous four doctors, which confused George into thinking the questions were more contrived that they actually were. The doctor explained carefully.

"George, I'm going to give you a man's name and address. Please can you remember them for me?[53] I will ask

---

[53] Standard mini-mental state test is useful for assessing the level of mental impairment a disorientated person may have. From

you about the man and where he lives later. The man is Mr. Joe Green and he lives at 20 South Street in Wimbledon. Clear?"George nodded. "Good."

Of course, when it came to asking George to recall Joe and where he lived, twenty minutes later at the end of the examination, George did not stand a chance and quickly became confused and upset. The repeated questions to George he couldn't answer seemed like persecution. Seeing his son suffer in bewilderment was as intense and as cruel as physical blows. Ian felt a tremendous surge of anger, wanting to protect George against the bully that was hurting him so. He stood up decisively, glowering at the psychiatrist with no idea what he was going to do. His bunched fists and bluster forced him into a non-violent act of removing George.

"That's it. You are getting nowhere. It's the same questions five times now and you are guessing like the rest of them. Can't you see the effect you're having on George? We are taking him home now – so get the discharge notice done. I'll sign it – he is my responsibility and he is in my care."

I am determined not to cry in front of people who love me. I clench my jaw and stare fiercely ahead. When I have got a grip, I stare hard at that person so I look still and untroubled. I think this works most of the time. I haven't cried, not once in all the time I have been ill.

I never cry, ever. There are some people who cry when they've had enough or can't take any more. Others cry because they have to carry on. I just want to move on and be me again so I don't need to cry.

---

http://www.nhs.uk/Conditions/dementia-guide/Pages/dementia-diagnosis-tests.aspx

Maybe there was just once when I got upset, it was in the A&E department at Kingston. I had been there nearly ten hours and loads of doctors kept asking stupid questions I didn't know the answers to. I got myself in a state, just confused and disorientated and I hated it. I just wanted to be me again, just to be how I normally am.

Tuesday, the next day, was George's routine dialysis session. The toll of the previous day was clear to see. George had retreated into his shell, unwilling to speak to anyone. Little Katie was right to call Laura, the psychologist who saw George's shattered confidence immediately and asked her colleague for his professional input.

"Hi George, I'm Paul. I am a doctor but not like those other doctors. I don't prod and poke you, or give you injections, or nag you for drinking too much. I am the talking doctor... and yes, I do talk a lot and guess what the good thing is? By talking to each other, we can listen to what's troubling you and we can find ways to make it better. Is that a deal? Can we have a talk now?"

Ghost George stared back at Paul. Siobhan felt her spirits dip, wondering which George would turn up today...

Calling George a ghost felt cruel, but he was a dilution of his usual self. His colour and essence had been washed out, leaving him devoid of any vibrancy. He responded to Paul's questions when he had to, but the effort of thinking and speaking showed in his breathy words.

By the end of the day, Paul had visited George three times, building and refining his diagnosis, each time gaining George's confidence and supporting his parents with his quiet assurance. He was clear that George had suffered a one-off psychotic event. The stresses and exhaustion had accumulated through each dialysis cycle of the previous week and had left George raw and vulnerable. At his lowest ebb, the chronic low-level pain of kidney stones had ground him down further. He could take no more. Unbeknownst to him, his brain initiated an in-built safety mechanism, tripping into a neutral gear of partial shutdown. All the good, interesting, lively, engaging parts of George's consciousness were protected and closed for now.

Paul prescribed an anti-psychotic drug, mainly to calm George down and reduce his anxiousness. There was the downside of drowsiness and loss of drive to consider, but on balance, George needed to be stable for the time being to regain his perspective. Siobhan was hugely grateful for the care and decisive action shown by Paul. Something was being done and she felt at least they had a grasp on the amorphous cloud of George's behaviour.

Over the next few days, George climbed back from his ledge. He responded well to the new drugs and seemed calm, serene even. He slotted back into his dialysis routine and seemed to lock away the unsettling events. He remembered a Mr. South from Hambledon but was not sure why.

A week later Paul turned up on the Renal Unit and plonked himself down next to George's bed. "Hi George, do you mind if I just stop here for a tea break? I've been rushed off my feet all morning and was just passing through." The Renal Unit was a dead end corridor.

"Sure but I can't have one with you," said George, nodding in explanation at his machine. He unplugged his headphones and sat up. He liked Paul and trusted him.

Unusually, Paul did not ask the battery of questions you would expect. So none of the *'how do you feel? What has changed? What happens when you feel anxious?'* His experience of George was that he did not know himself, and so there was little chance of him explaining it eloquently. He wondered, not for the first time, if child psychiatrists and vets had much in common?

Paul started gently, ambling through the events of the last year. He talked of the trauma and challenge that George had never faced before with such raw intensity. He built George's confidence, getting him to realise his toughness and attitude had got him through. Paul's respect mattered to George and he grew for it. With this foundation, Paul changed direction to get to the true purpose of his contrived counselling session.

"With all my years in medical school, even then sometimes we can't explain why the body does what it does."

"Okay." George looked surprised. It was the first time any doctor had told him he did not know the answer. That explained a lot and was strangely reassuring.

"Perhaps your body's way of responding to the trauma is by shutting things down, stopping you doing things, almost as a way to stop it happening again. It may be a safety valve to release the pressure you're under. When I say trauma, it doesn't have to be the flashing blue lights and sirens type of trauma. It can also be the small things that add together to weigh you down and sap your will."

In Paul's mind was the knowledge that PTSD and short-term behavioural problems amongst children commonly last for up to one year post-illness. He knew of one study that showed 62% of children followed up at 3 and 12 months after PICU admission reported symptoms of post-traumatic stress, commonly nightmares and hyper-arousal, while 10% fulfilled the diagnostic criteria for PTSD.[54] He

---

[54] Judge D. et al., *Psychiatric adjustment following meningococcal disease treated on a PICU*. Intensive Care Med, 2002. 28(5): p.648-50

chose his words carefully for a fifteen-year-old to understand.

"So think of it this way, George. Your body is a very clever thing. I think it's resetting itself with a pattern of behaviour that it feels comfortable with."

The barista took Siobhan's order and asked her, "Do you get staff discount?"

"No, no, I don't work here, I just come here a lot," smiled Siobhan, acknowledging to herself, *'I suppose I am part of the furniture round here'*. She stood in the coffee shop queue, waiting for her skinny latte and George's Froffee. He had been good with his fluids and was allowed 300ml whilst on dialysis – a real treat and reward. Siobhan turned at the voice next to her.

"Hello Siobhan, good to see you – how are things and how is George?"

"Oh hi Dr Inger, it's great to see you and thanks for asking. We've been a bit up and down the last two weeks," replied Siobhan, who felt Dr Inger would wrap her up in a hug, but would never close the two-step gap of diffidence to make it happen. Siobhan would have so appreciated the hug right then.

"I sort of heard, so I'm glad to have caught you. I was speaking to one of the Renal Physicians on the Unit and he hinted George was having a tough time. It is such a shame, considering everything he has been through."

"Well, Paul the psychiatrist was brilliant. He spent practically a whole day with George really getting to grips with what had derailed him so badly."

"That's great, and I'm so pleased George has responded. I do admire those psychiatrist types, don't you?"

"They are like detectives piecing together clues," Siobhan agreed.

"It's funny, isn't it – you spend enough time around us doctors and you start to recognise the different species."

"I know," responded Siobhan, enthusiastically but wary of the boundaries, letting Dr Inger go first if there was any denigrating of the profession to be done.

"Now just take anaethetists – they keep their patients quiet so they don't have to talk to them. That's the last thing they want to do."

"Surgeons – they always seems a bit posh to me," offered Siobhan.

"Too true –either old and pompous or young and uppity."

"*Ouch,*" thought Siobhan, worried that Dr Inger had gone too far and was on a roll.

"And physicians – now they have a tough job; chronic illnesses, clinic after clinic to follow up. I know I couldn't do what they do. I like to see what I'm treating, slap on some jollop, all mended, job done. So less messy." Siobhan laughed at her jolly-hockey-sticks humour, and felt confident enough to put a full stop on a tough few days – until the next time.

She said goodbye to Dr Inger. The coffee shop was half full so Siobhan took both cups and magazine to the window for some space, if only on the other side of the glass. The flipped pages did not hold her attention. Bored, she gazed up at Big Ben in the distance, following the track of pigeons flapping past.

Out on the walkway, three metres away but deadened by the glass wall, she noticed a huddle of people forming around something on the floor. Their movement had the same excitable, agitated furtiveness as school kids in the playground. Within the pattern of feet, there was one pointing upwards – a woman's bare foot. Siobhan moved to the edge of her seat to get a better view, something was not right. The huddle was getting bigger.

A man waved urgently, beckoning unseen shouters to join them. Two burly paramedics wrestled into the huddle, pushing back the onlookers. A third arrived pushing a gurney on her own. Blankets were held up as makeshift screens.

As quickly as they had gone up, the blankets were swept aside so Siobhan could see a large African lady reclined on one elbow, holding a bundle of blankets. The ones used as screens? She turned to the lady on the next table; they looked at each other quizzically

"Did you just hear a baby cry out?" They both nodded to each other, not believing their ears. "Oh my god! That poor lady's just given birth right there."

The baby was born quicker than Siobhan's daydream. The huddle moved off as one, circling the trolley. Siobhan puffed out her cheeks in amazement. She could not believe what she had seen through the window, like a TV screen with the volume turned low. There were no sirens, no drama at all for such a momentous event. That wasn't as bad as it could have been. A pair of tatty sandals with butterfly buckles were left behind. Not a bad day at all; you lose your shoes but bring a new life into the world. Siobhan went back to her coffee, a little shamefaced at her voyeurism. It was tepid, but she had a warm glow all the same.

Back on the Dialysis Unit, Siobhan set aside George's Froffee to wait for him to wake up. As Katie popped her head round the corner to check they were settled, she asked, "You guys okay? Nice coffee, Siobhan?"

"Not really, I let it cool down too much. You see, this lady gave birth right outside the window."

"What? Noooooo, I don't believe it ..."

The TV burbled away, only George paying attention. A former Household Cavalry Captain, Mauricio Gris, was being interviewed.[55]

"Loud bangs are bound to make you jump if you aren't expecting them and are just back from a war zone. It's natural. But there are some sounds which will still get you when you've been back a while, depending on your experiences while on operations. The whistling of fireworks going up and the thud of either a distant firework or heavy door shutting occasionally makes me start, or feel a bit sick. That's a hang-up from my second tour of Afghanistan. For me, the thud of a heavy fire escape door is always worst, because that sounds like a mortar being fired from a distance, meaning it is more likely to be the enemy firing it, rather than our blokes because then it would sound more like a bang. I haven't been mortared much at all in the scale of things, but I found the experience very unpleasant."

"I heard that firecrackers are another sound that can make a veteran flinch," the interviewer empathised.

"It happened once to me," the Captain agreed, "One fireworks night while I was out with a group of friends. Like meerkats, all our heads popped up and scanned about,

---

[55] Interview with Mauricio Gris on BBC Newsbeat, 5th November 2014. From http://www.bbc.co.uk/newsbeat/29921640

then we caught each other's eyes, shook our heads, and laughed and went back to our pints. The rest didn't take notice. It immediately separated those who served from those who didn't."

"Is that what I have, Dad?" George asked matter-of factly.

"What do you mean, George?" replied Ian casually, trying to buy thinking time for where on earth this could possibly go.

"P-T-S-D – Post Traumatic Stress Disorder," said George, spelling it out without any hesitation for his pupil, as though it was still about the soldier rather than himself.

"The soldier on the telly just said that only those who served really understood it. That's the same for me. None of my friends know what it is like. No way at all."

"Okay ... so George... ... tell me, where did you first hear of PTSD?"

"We did it in English last year. It was Owen Wilson, the poet from the First World War. We studied his poems and he had to come back from the war as he was suffering from PTSD and wrote about it."

"Ahh – I see now, George. Isn't Owen Wilson the blonde guy from *Behind Enemy Lines* and *The Wedding Crashers*?" The latter was one of George's favourite films and he could quote the best lines in a flash.

"No, it's the same name but they're two different people." Still no hesitation from George, but the glance away was the tell-tale that he was bluffing.

"Right, ok," replied Ian, going with George's confident reply.

Making sure Siobhan could not see, Ian googled Wilfred Owen. Normally George used the phrase 'POS' to mean Parent Over Shoulder when he was on his computer and a nosey parent was around. Ian thought it applied here too – Piss-taker-Over-Shoulder.

He knew all about Wilfred Owen, it all came flooding back as he searched page-by-page online.

He clicked on a link to PTSD.[56]

> It is an anxiety disorder caused by witnessing or being involved in a frightening or distressing event. People naturally feel afraid when in danger, but the legacy of some traumatic events is a change in perception of fear. They may feel stressed or frightened in day-to-day life.

Click: What triggers it?

> Any traumatic event has the potential to lead to PTSD, including military conflicts, serious road accidents, disasters, and harm to self.

Click: How is it diagnosed?

> We rely on the judgment of a doctor speaking to their patient about their symptoms. There must have been an initial traumatic event involving a near death experience or violence. Then there are four criteria which must be present:
>
> - Re-experiencing the event – commonly known as flashbacks
>
> - Avoidance behaviour – people will not talk about the event and avoid anything that reminds them of it
>
> - Sleep impact – they will have poor sleep quality and be irritable

---

[56] Taken verbatim from BBC News article, 11th May 2014

- Mood change – commonly a perception that something bad is always about to happen.

Click: How is it treated?

It has to impair day-to-day function. Cognitive behavioural therapy can help change the way people think about the traumatic event in order to control fear and anxiety. This involves going through the event in detail with a therapist. Drugs such as anti-psychotics and antidepressants are used if psychotherapy does not work. After a long time period, symptoms are very unlikely to clear up without treatment.

Ian let out a whistle. This was uncanny. It fitted George and his recent breakdown at school to a tee. He took a breath to weigh it all up. Maybe this was just like reading a horoscope? A skilled writer could easily craft scenarios broad enough to bend to your circumstances if you wanted to. Was he doing the same bend-to-fit approach for George?

Ian and Siobhan were both reading in bed, just before lights out.

"Have you had any discussion with George about PTSD?" Ian asked Siobhan.

"No, not at all. He must have been hovering, listening to our conversations again. He does it all the time and he has the ears of a bat, that kid. There's nothing wrong with his hearing, that's for sure – and he misses nothing."

"I'm not sure, you know – he raised it with me earlier. He said they had studied it in English and he knew all about Owen Wilson and the First World War poets."

"Do you mean Wilfred Owen? You great plum," cackled Siobhan, sensing a rich seam of piss-taking.

"Yeah, I thought the name sounded odd but it was near enough that I believed him. Let's move on, shall we?" said Ian, regretting his slip of the tongue and trying to maintain a shred of dignity.

"Are you saying you think George has PTSD?" asked Siobhan, serious now.

"I think I am. The symptoms fit and so does the treatment he received. Rather than me play armchair psychologist, why don't we ask Barbara?"

"Yeah, she can tell us if there is any substance to this."

Chapter 23

"Stone me — listen to this, Shiv. This is an almighty U-turn, " said Ian in amazement. He read the paragraph to Siobhan.

> "The UK JCVI recommends use of Bexsero, saying the vaccine is effective in preventing meningitis B and should be rolled out subject to it being made available by the manufacturer "at a cost-effective price". It has recommended Bexsero be added to the existing immunisation schedule, starting at two months of age.[57] Around 700,000 infants will be eligible for vaccination each year."

"How is it a U-turn?" inquired Siobhan, nonplussed.

Ian went onto explain how the government-appointed body, the JCVI, had originally restricted the use of Bexsero and refused to make it available for everyone as it was so expensive. This latest public statement blew that out of the water and their negotiating position with it. Not only were the JCVI confirming the efficacy of the vaccine, they were recommending it should be widely available — and to make that easier, it should fit in with the existing immunisation schedule.

This was a huge success for parent groups, scientists, lobbyist and charities that had all pressurised the Government. One of the most pleased had to be the Meningitis Research Foundation to see the decades of research and campaigning for a vaccine against MenB finally paying off. A whole raft of members and supporters helped bring this about, having taken part in research, signed petitions, fundraised, shared their personal

---

[57] From
http://www.ukmi.nhs.uk/applications/ndo/record_view_open.asp?new DrugID=5391

experiences, helped the cause with their professional expertise and supported lobbying work in Westminster.

Although the expectation was for this vaccine to have a major impact, there remain other kinds of meningitis and septicaemia that still cannot be prevented by vaccination. Ian's enthusiasm wavered at this. Raising awareness of the symptoms and reminding people to be vigilant still had to remain a priority.

"The trouble is, Shiv, this isn't the finish line for MenB. Getting that price agreed will take forever. Then the vaccine must be rolled out – so parents and doctors will need support and information."

Good news was landing in Essex too.

"Hello, is that Jean Birks?"

"It is. Who's calling?"

"Hi, I'm Celia from the Fundraising Events Limited and we are working for the Caron Keating Foundation. You may remember a few weeks back that you nominated your daughter-in-law Siobhan Birks for the Inspirational Mother of the Year award 2014. Well, I am pleased to tell you that Siobhan has been shortlisted."

Jean squealed down the phone, surprised and elated by the news. "That's fantastic! It's so exciting! So what does short-listing mean and what happens next?"

"Well, Siobhan's nomination will be assessed by the judging panel against ten others in her category and the most worthy will be presented the award at the Mayfair Hotel later this year[58] – you can come, can't you?"

---

[58] The Awards Ceremony was on 29th March but was moved to August

They sorted out the arrangements between them. This meant all the important stuff like what to wear, how to find the hotel and which celebrities would be there. Lastly, Jean skipped through Siobhan's home number so she could be contacted directly. When she finally put the phone down, she said to Dave, "Oh my God, Shivvy has made the shortlist and I haven't even told her. I do hope she doesn't mind."

Less than twenty minutes later, the phone rang again. It was Siobhan,

"Jeee-eeean, a nice lady called Celia just phoned me. Anything you want to tell me?"

"Well, it was like this," Jean started, without a shred of embarrassment. She was so excited about the forthcoming Big Day Out, just the two of them.

"We get a ride in a limo, big hotel in London, Gloria will be there, we might be on the telly, imagine if you won ..."

Photos II

13: ECH in wheelchair

This is just after I came out of PICU and transferred to ECH. I have my seat belt on – safety first and all that. I found it almost impossible to stand, as my legs were so weak and my feet so sore, as they had no skin on them.

14: My first walk

I can't believe how thin my legs are! They look like skinny little Twiglets – no wonder they couldn't hold me up for long. The first time I walked into the Evelina foyer, from the car, I got a cheer and clap from the security guards. That was really cool and I felt proud I could do it.

15: Me and Dad on Westminster Bridge

Mum took this of Dad and me on Westminster Bridge. This is our first escape from Evelina whilst an in-patient. We trundled along the South Bank – people look at you differently in a wheelchair. Anyway, we saw a cool bunch of street dancers showing off to Gangnam Style.

16: Me at Physio

This is one of my early physio sessions. I found them really tough as my legs were so numb from not moving and I couldn't feel my feet too well. Odd to say it, but I liked the physio sessions – they were tiring and painful at times but at least I felt I had achieved something and made progress.

17: Spiderman man at ECH

I told you it was true. I haven't seen it myself so I Googled this and found Superman and Spiderman abseiling down the side of the Evelina. I am glad the nurses weren't making it up.

18: Atrium at ECH

The Evelina is a really cool building – really bright and airy. On a windy day, you can hear the indoor trees rustle – quite a juxtaposition (extra marks for good word in an English essay!). We spent a fair bit of time in the atrium, playing table tennis, doing schoolwork, visiting the Radio Lollipop team and sitting in the patio area on a sunny day.

19: Hells Angel logo

I didn't take any photos of the Hells Angels as I didn't have my camera in the hospital. I could have shown the guy a proper camera. Afterwards all I could find was their club logo. They seemed so out of place when I first saw them, but chatting to them, they were such nice people that they seemed right at home at Evelina. I remember getting a huge chocolate bunny thing but I don't remember eating it – must ask Dad?

20: Harley engine

I took this photo of part of a motorbike in Montpellier. I loved the shiny chrome which caught my eye. The logo is a great sentiment to have in life. I think it looks better in black and white, as though the words have stood the test of time.

21: At Yo! Sushi for first time

I don't look too cheerful, but believe me, it was great to be out of the hospital, even for a few hours. It's not too bad in the wheelchair, but people do tend to look for a half-second too long, which makes me uncomfortable. I still have that tube up my nose. Sushi is my favourite and I can make loads of different sorts now.

22: Strictly Come Dancing at ECH

I tried to get into the picture so I could see myself on telly, but they missed me. The footage was used in the Christmas Special.

23: Pixie Lott

24: Ray of Sunshine Concert Poster

I have to be straight, I'm not an Olly Murs fan. But seeing him live, seeing him chat with all the sick kids, he really is a top bloke.

25: Apollo exterior

This looks still, but so much was happening. I saw and heard the ceiling crack and then fall in. We ran to the stairs and down as a human waterfall. Then we saw all the sirens, police cars, and firemen who went straight in with no hesitation. Scary stuff, and we were very lucky.

26: Apollo injured theatergoers

Once we got out of the Apollo, we waited on the pavement for half an hour. We were all a bit dazed and just milled about getting in the way – there was nothing for us to do, so after a while we went home.

27: Apollo buses

The news reports said three buses of injured people went to St Thomas'. Carmen called us that night to check we were all ok. She remembered us saying we were going and was worried for us.

28: Sarah and Dad at Paris Marathon

This was a great weekend in Paris in spring. What would their speech bubbles say? Sarah's would say 'I can see the finish line, not far now' in a cheery way. Dad's would say 'Can I stop now? Where is the first aid tent?' We were Team Evelina, all with our Smartie tops on, including Gran.

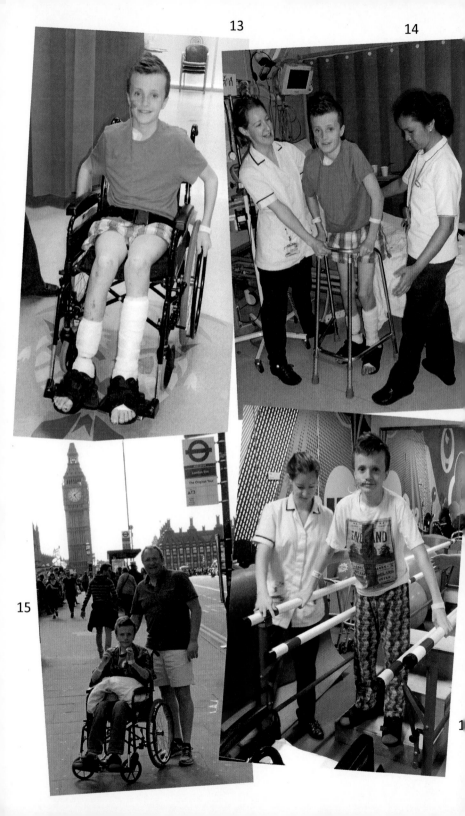

17

18

19

21

20

22

23

THE FRAGRANCE SHOP RAYS OF SUNSHINE CONCERT

OLLY MURS
PIXIE LOTT ELIZA DOOLITTLE
ELYAR FOX FLAWLESS

24

25

26

27

28

PART 3: RESURRECTION

Chapter 24

When the fight begins within himself, a man's worth
something.

Robert Browning 1812-1889

*Since I was ten, kayaking has been my favourite sport. I
think I am pretty good at it too – my carve turns look really
cool and my paddling technique is smooth and powerful. So
all those certificates I worked so hard for have been worth
it. I love being out on the water and so close to birds and
wildlife. It's a good laugh too – they are a great bunch at
Albany, especially John and Falcon, the instructors. They
make it fun as well as teaching you skills and how to be
safe. I was really touched when they gave me a blue
Instructor's t-shirt with the real club logos on it and signed
by everyone. I can't wear it though, as I'm not a qualified
instructor, and the ink will run.*

*After my transplant, I have already decided what kayak I
want. I will sell my Wave Runner on eBay and then there's
my birthday money from Gran, Nan and Granddad. It's a
Jackson Rockstar in lime green. Dad says the red looks
better. He says cars, bikes, skis all go faster if they are red –
scientific certainty, he says. Load of crap, I say. Hmm, the
green does look sooo cool...*

*I can't wait for that first day back. Imagine me in my
playboat, my sleek green reflection, the sun shining on the
water, dodging the sail boats and bashing through the
wakes of the river cruisers. I do want to get qualified as an
instructor one day.*

*I am pretty good at my numbers. Not so much Maths –
well, actually I'm not bad. I mean my medical numbers,
where I should be; what is good or bad. I read my charts, I*

listen to the nurses and I question them all the time so I know what is what.

I notice that every kidney doctor always gets me to look up and off to the left so he can see my neck stretched. They then murmur about being full or empty. I asked Caroline the consultant, and she told me she is actually looking at the jugular vein close beneath the skin to assess the jugular venous pressure – a way of telling if I am wet or dry meaning full or empty. If you can see the big vein then I am full and need dialysis to take fluid off. Clever stuff.

I know my weight to the nearest 100g as I am weighed all the time. I always do a poo before being weighed. It all makes a difference (well, a big one can). Shoes usually weigh about 400-600kg, my belt is 200g and a big hoodie can be 700g. It all comes off so I'm as accurate as possible.

Blood pressure is a good one. If I have two readings greater than 130 then I get investigated, as it's too high. I know exactly when it is too low. It's a bit like a thermometer scale when you write it down:

90 – I'm fine and the nurses will let me go home after dialysis.

80 – I don't feel right, light-headed so I stay sitting until I feel better.

70 – by now I'm horribly spacey and I'm on the edge of chucking.

60 – I'm close to blacking out, feel awful and breakfast is likely on my shoes.

50 – I've been here a few times, but only knew when I woke up afterwards.

Creatinine is a really important marker. The level will rise and rise in my bloodstream, getting up to 700+ if allowed to accumulate. After a dialysis session, it will be around 150. Then there are the chemicals like potassium, urea, and phosphates. Potassium needs to be less than five. If I come in at the top end of the range then I have been eating too much spinach, chocolate etc. I never even have banana or mango. I daren't, as they are not good for my heart and blood pressure. Phosphates need to be in the range of 0.5 to 1.75. If I am at the top end of the range then I've been eating too much cheese and dairy. I sometimes come a cropper with pizza and mozzarella, as you can never tell how much is on there.

Chapter 25

I am grateful that you were born, that your love is mine, and our two lives are woven and welded together!

Mark Twain

The kidney is not a glamorous organ. It has none of the attributed feelings of the heart, the boggling complexities of the brain or the tangible power of the lungs. They are there to filter the blood, to regulate levels of fluid and salt and to remove waste products like urea and dead cells, through passing urine. All very important stuff, because if the blood is not properly cleaned, tiredness sets in, the hands and feet begin to swell and vomiting is common. Without medical intervention, kidney failure is ultimately fatal.

Kidney dysfunction can be a gradual decline over years or decades, to the point where symptoms become noticed and diagnosed. For others, like George, it can be as a result of trauma, damage or poisoning. The cliché for Intensive Care teams is that the kidneys are the first organ to fail and the last to recover function. Unfortunately for George, clichés become so as they reflect the statistics.

For some time now, Ian and Siobhan had known that Siobhan would become the donor for George, once he had fully recovered his strength from the original septicaemia. She was a good tissue match, had compatible blood groups with George and she had passed the initial screens for rude general health. Counter-intuitively, the long-term survival rates for kidney donors are better than for the general population, but this makes more sense when candidates with underlying health issues of high BMI, hypertension, concomitant disease are rejected so only the healthy cohort are considered.

Ian had tried to put himself in pole position, adamant that after giving birth three times, Siobhan had already done more than her fair share as such. He had now accepted that he was Donor of Last Resort. For Siobhan, there was the lengthy process of medical tests to get through – more blood tests, scans, ultrasounds, glomerular filtration rate tests and many more besides. There were also the psychological and ethical aspects, in which the potential donor is quizzed on their motivation (a no-brainer for any parent), expectations, and understanding. An independent ethics review, following rules set out by the Human Tissue Authority, ensured that the stipulations of the Human Tissue Act 2004[59] were followed, in that no coercion or monetary gain took place.

From February onwards, Siobhan entered the series of tests to see if she could act as a donor for George. When friends and family heard what she was doing, most were amazed at her strength, surprised that it was not Ian, and all of them commented in different words on the special gift she was bestowing on George. If Ian was telling the story, he always spoke with pride that his wife was going to be the donor, his admiration and deep respect for her shining through. Siobhan barely ever mentioned it herself, and squirmed slightly when he did.

Siobhan sat in the Transplant Clinic waiting room with perhaps twenty other people. They were waiting to have cannulas fitted for the battery of tests awaiting them throughout the day. Although they were all connected by the giving and receiving of a kidney, none of them spoke. Already, each of them would have taken a journey of facts

---

[59] Human Tissue Act 2004 provides the legal framework for organ and tissue donation across the UK

you would rather not know, discussed it with loved ones, taken some of the biggest decisions of their lives, and maybe were feeling fearful right now. Siobhan was.

The lady next to her must have sensed it, or just mistook Siobhan's *'don't worry it might never happen'* face.

"Are you donating too?"

Siobhan welcomed the conversation opener and turned to face Gail, appraising her in a glance. Gail was a bit younger than Siobhan, with a sparky face, assured and comfortable in herself.

"Yes, I am, for my fourteen-year-old son George. And you?"

"If all the tests go well, everything crossed, for my husband, Tim."

They got chatting, finding out that they lived a few miles apart in south-west London (a posh bit of Twickenham), that Gail was a photographer (George would be nosey), Gail would be going first (Tim's transplant was four weeks ahead of George's) and that they both loved quilting.

"I saw that gorgeous quilt in the book you were reading, Siobhan – are you making one?"

"Do you mean this one? It is lovely, isn't it. The colours go so well together. Yes, I am. I've got two quilts on the go, another three promised and my stash of scraps exceeds my life expectancy."

Their bonding was interrupted by a call for Siobhan to have her arm done. As they were on the same program of tests, the pattern was set for the rest of the day. Hello, Wait, Chat, Call, No Goodbye. By late afternoon, they greeted each other theatrically like long-lost old friends, with faux surprise and *'mwah mwah'* air kisses. Fortunately, Siobhan had the foresight to swap details so they could keep in touch. Their quick emails, snatched coffees and shared experiences became a great help to them both in the weeks ahead.

Most people do not really get the compatibility thing. Usually there is the assumption that you have to be the kind of match that you get from a blood relative. The truth is that immuno-suppression drugs and transplant medicine in general are so sophisticated now, that you no longer need to be. Compatibility is based on blood type and six antigens. Histocompatibility antigens are molecules on the surface of all cells in the body. The specific types of histocompatibility antigens present on a person's cells determine their identity, and distinguish each person. They are a 'fingerprint', as each person has a unique set of histocompatibility antigens. If the antigens on tissue or organs from a donor do not match that of the recipient, a rejection response can occur. The recipient's immune system will detect the difference between the two sets of antigen and start a rejection response to kill the donated tissue. Except in the case of identical twins, no two people are identical in terms of their histocompatibility antigen types. However, the closer two tissues come to matching, the more likely the recipient will accept the donated tissue or organ.[60] For Siobhan and George, neither had antibodies against each other that would mean George's body would reject her kidney.

As well as testing her compatibility, the doctors needed to be sure that Siobhan's kidneys functioned well enough to withstand one being removed. They also wanted to check that she had no lurking health problems of her own.

---

[60] From http://www.faqs.org/health/topics/93/Tissue-typing

Over a four-week period, Siobhan underwent a battery of further tests. It started with a chest x-ray and general physiology, then moving on to Glomerular Filtration Rate testing, where a fluid with a radioactive trace was injected into her arm. She then had a blood test every hour for three hours to see how much of it had been filtered out by her kidneys. The bit they don't tell you is that you start the test with a bladder full to bursting – but you are not allowed to pee. It becomes a red-faced desperate test of holding it in until you can't take any more and bolt like Usain for the loo. After this came a scan to check that both her kidneys worked equally well. Her heart was monitored with an ECG, and they also performed an angiogram of the blood vessels in her kidneys with a CT scanner.

So at the end of it all Siobhan was inured to being poked, prodded and pricked by medical staff while in various states of undress. She was no longer squeamish or embarrassed. She was a dead shot at peeing into plastic cups, and developed superhuman bladder control for a lady of middle years. Even wafting about in a hospital gown that flapped cheekily at the back was handled with the aplomb of a ballerina.

Ian supported her as best he could through the process, sitting with her in the waiting rooms of various hospital departments. Her name was called out instead of his. He winced with her as a cannula was stuck in her vein, but her grimace was not acted like his. Seeing her being the hospital patient suddenly made the concept of her actually going through with the surgery horribly real. It became even more real after a call from the live donor team. The tests were positive; there were no more barriers to jump, no more plastic cups to fill and no more indignities. They had the final go-head and the date was set for July 8th.

Ian and Siobhan read through the entire blurb about the operations themselves. For Siobhan as donor, the keyhole approach meant that incisions would be smaller and scarring kept to a minimum. It seemed quite run-of-the-mill that a donor may be out of hospital within three to five days and back to work within three months. That seemed a long time compared to a Caesarean, which Siobhan had bounced back from quickly. Both knew Siobhan was a tough cookie and secretly thought she would be fine within a month. It was a good job that neither of them mentioned it out loud.

There would be no lasting physiological damage – the remaining kidney would shoulder the full burden of filtering her blood. Despite all the reassuring facts, it still seemed inhuman to Ian to contemplate putting the person he loved most in the world through this.

On the surface, Siobhan appeared very chilled and balanced about the whole thing. She absorbed the facts and knew what would happen. She did not go into the detail, or question Michelle the transplant co-ordinator too deeply. Was this being blasé or choosing not to know? Ian was not sure, but was not brave enough to tease out the distinction. Siobhan shared the same determination as Ian to be a donor but dealt with it differently. Ian was more gung-ho, less concerned about the physical aspects of the operation, seeing himself as invincible with an overly-optimistic take on the outcome. Siobhan was just as adamant; she was unshakeable in wanting George back. She saw his life ahead of him and hated the thought of mourning George's future. In truth, she was willing to do whatever it took but perhaps more comprehending of what that meant. As a mother of three, she knew what the pain would be like. Maternal amnesia is a myth invented by midwives to try and make it bearable; you don't ever forget how painful childbirth is. Her anxiousness and fear of post-op nausea was real now, and would only build. Her bravery meant that she kept these feelings to herself, partly as a self-preservation mechanism but also because she did not have anyone to discuss it with, not even Ian.

For George, he had Laura, the Evelina psychologist, who spent several sessions one-on-one with him talking through the operation itself. They even visited the empty theatre and the recovery room so there would be no surprises. They talked of how the anaesthetic would be administered, who would be there when he went to sleep and when he woke up. George drew an oval on his tum for roughly where the new kidney would go, and a smiley face for where the scar would be. Laura asked the things he feared most and what they would do about it, writing it all down in George's Transplant Book. George knew the operation would take about five hours and that he might be able to pee straight away. The nurses told him they would get him on his feet within a couple of days, that dialysis would stop and he would have to drink three litres per day – this was more fluid than he was allowed in a whole WEEK on dialysis. He was promised he could eat whatever he liked, but must never eat grapefruit ever again. So in the weeks running up to the operation, George was the most knowledgeable, seriously chilled and nonchalant about the whole thing, so much so that Ian and Siobhan doubted he had really taken it all in until they saw his Transplant Book with it all mapped out.

"Hey Shiv, this is an interesting stat – a 55% jump in kidney donations by strangers in the last year."[61] Ian threw the figure over the top of his paper without checking whether he was interrupting her, which all people do. He continued, quoting from the article. "In 2007, the year such donations became legal, only six procedures were recorded. In the 12 months to April, 118 people gave an organ to a stranger while still alive. I love this case, listen to

---

[61] From Times 20th Aug 2014. Article by Chris Smyth

this one – what a girl!" He read on, smiling. "An 85-year old woman has just become the oldest living kidney donor, saying, '*why do I need two kidneys to sit at home knitting and watching television?*'"

Ian went quiet for a moment, his enthusiasm tempered as he read out the last line of the article. "There are 5847[62] people waiting for a kidney." Siobhan looked up – she had been paying attention after all.

"Well, that just makes the case even stronger for opt-out donor legislation. They say it would clear the waiting list in less than two years. I'm sorry, but I rate the real suffering of those 6000 far greater that the handful of philosophical objectors."

Ian nodded his agreement but did not comment for the moment. He knew one of his wife's greatest strengths was her clarity of thought and conviction, once decided. She would listen to the counter-arguments, but there was no splitting of hairs or backsliding. It was not the time to bring up the complexity of the issue[63] in scenarios where no clear donation wishes were known, or where the deceased family are not consulted, or possibly do not even need to be if it became a 'hard' law. Maybe that was part of the problem – too much consultation and not enough leadership? It was typical of Siobhan take a stance.

"I agree with you. But would you have had that opinion a year ago?" Ian didn't wait for an answer. "I'm sure I wouldn't have done. I'm not making a counter-argument, just that in the past I hadn't even thought about it. Other than carry a Donor Card since my student days, I have never

---

[62] Kidney Life Autumn 2014: The magazine of the National Kidney Federation. Figure as of 2nd July 2014

[63] To see recommendations of the Organ Donation TaskForce, go to http ://www.organdonation.nhs.uk / newsroom/statements_and_stances/ statements/opt_in_or _out.asp

given organ donation a second thought. I had no experience of waiting lists, and knew of no-one in UK needing a transplant."

Now, though, it was different. He felt pretty confident that he could describe what life is like for thousands of people on the waiting list for an organ transplant.

Siobhan challenged him, intrigued to hear what he was saying. "So, are you saying you're going to wave a placard and lobby for a change to our system of organ donation to one of 'presumed consent', or hand out leaflets to encourage people to join the UK organ donor register?" [64]

"Slow down, love, brain at work here and it takes a while. Oh, I dunno, cut me some slack, will you? I'm just saying at least I have a view now. And you're right, what am I going to do about it?" He paused, without an answer. "You've done your bit and I can't match that. They are welcome to the rest of me, but I will have to pop my clogs first."

"Don't say things like that." She touched the door frame and whistled.

Siobhan's challenge snagged him. Its hold was that same inadequate feeling when you see a derelict tramp in a doorway. In the time it takes you to wrestle with your indecision, you have walked on by, avoiding eye contact. *'Christ, he looks in a state, he must been frozen on that concrete, if I give him a fiver he'll only spend it on Special Brew, maybe if I get him a sandwich or something if he's still there at lunchtime? There are places he can stay, surely? Someone must look out for him?'* On the rare occasions when he did drop some washers in the hat, it was more to quieten his own guilt, so he didn't have to think about it.

---

[64] To join the NHS Organ Donor Register visit www.transplantweek.co.uk or call 0300 123 2323

Unfortunately, the *'surely someone must be doing something'* bubbled to the surface, so when Siobhan wasn't looking, he flipped open the iPad and searched for organ donation.

We need organ donor 'opt-out' system urgently[65]

Seven years ago, the Government ordered a review of the UK's organ donation system. Figures showed that the rate of demand for organs was far outstripping supply, leading to hundreds of needless deaths every year. The Organ Donation Taskforce found that countries using a presumed consent, or 'opt out', system had far higher donation rates. The United Kingdom was not in the top 10. Tragically, nothing came of the review. Since then, 7,000 people – including children – have died. With recent advances in science have come increased potential, and demand, for transplantation. The gap is today greater than ever.

Despite laudable registration campaigns, the opt-in system can no longer be expected to fulfil its purpose. Organs are donated from just 1% of the numbers of deceased each year, while healthy organs from half a million people are cremated or buried. As a result, being on the transplant waiting list has become a game of Russian roulette. For example, if you're waiting for a liver, there is a 20% chance that it won't reach you in time. For heart patients, the figure is even higher. Children suffering kidney failure are having, in some instances, to wait for five perilous years.

In Wales, they are finally moving forwards. After a period of careful public consultation and debate, an awareness-raising programme is underway ahead of the implementation of a new 'opt out' system next year. Those who object to organ donation can rest assured – as can their relatives – that their wishes will be respected under the new system.

For now, there are 7,000 people in the UK – many young children among them – waiting for a lifesaving transplant. While we wait for the rest of the country to

---

[65] From The Guardian, Monday 7th July 2014.

catch up with the Welsh, we can at least ensure we are properly registered on the NHS's donor database.[66]

Ed Goncalves, Director, KidneyKids UK

He put the iPad down, digesting what he had just read, and tried to relate it to his own experience. By pooling their memories, Ian and Siobhan could recall eight transplants, all from mothers, fathers and uncles, in the year George had been on dialysis. There were at least ten children and babies on the waiting list, lives on hold. One little chap went for his transplant and they never saw him again. It did not go well after the surgery. Another had the crushing disappointment of having three family members fall by the wayside as they stumbled in the selection to be donors. In all of those children, they could only recall one transplant as a result of the waiting list – from a deceased donor.

Siobhan stated the reality. "And that's with children supposedly going to the top of the list as priority cases."

"Surely there is a minimum size or something for putting an adult kidney into a kiddie?" asked Ian.

"I think the weight is ten kilos, so little Millie was three when she had her transplant from her Mum and she's doing great."

"I know," confirmed Ian, " I saw her in clinic the other day and she is such a poppet. Her mum says she's grown five centimetres in four months."

"That's one of the biggest impacts – not being able to put on weight," said Siobhan, passing on knowledge picked up from the dialysis nurses. "The high levels of creatinine and urea in the blood suppress appetite so getting to the

---

[66] For details, go to www.organdonation.nhs.uk.

minimum weight becomes a huge challenge and growth is impaired. Look at her now she's able to eat normally."

And then there was George. If all went well in the next few days, his life would be transformed, potentially realising George's burning goal to get back to normal. The feeling of guilt returned – *'my ticket has come up, but hard luck mate, yours hasn't, maybe next time, eh?'* and Ian tried to imagine walking back into the Dialysis Unit, to the swell of good wishes, and trying to be non-committal. To not show joy or happiness or relief or hope – to then say goodbye because, guess what, we're not coming back again. He cringed at the thought, tempting fate. He, too, touched the wood of the coffee table and whistled.

In early June, the scheduled date of the transplant was moved from 8th to 25th July. The reason was not clear, either the lists were full that day or a surgeon was unavailable. It could also be that a deceased donor kidney had become available, so George got bounced to another day for someone whose need was greater.

It was not a problem. George had waited long enough and three weeks would not make a difference. Siobhan had more time to think but hid it well.

Chapter 26

So wake me up when it's all over
When I am wiser and I'm older
All this time I was finding myself
And I didn't know I was lost.

Lyrics from Wake Me Up by Avicii

The decision to go out for the evening before the operations was an inspired one. The *'let's go somewhere really expensive'* was not so popular with Ian but it did make it different, special. Newly opened, the Oblix restaurant and lounge on the thirty-second floor of the Shard appealed to the young and trendy of London or those with corporate expenses accounts, out to impress.

The cityscape at dusk reminded Siobhan of the view from the Rainbow Room in the Rockefeller Centre in New York, pre-9/11. Hopefully, the same mental Polaroid would be stored away and referred back to as an evocative memory of a happy time just before George's transplant. Siobhan shuddered, welcoming the thought but wary of tempting fate in the next twelve hours.

The meal itself was joyful, with everyone making an effort, but mindful to keep well away from the sentimental. They all sensed that this was a night to remember. There were no speeches, just a simple toast to Siobhan and George to wish them well. The meal ended and they descended from the rarefied world in the clouds to the pavement and reality. There was no postponing it.

I can see Big Ben from the Shard.

Big Ben is the world's most famous tourist attraction. Think of London, and I bet Big Ben, a red double-decker bus and a black cab will be in your mind's eye. What I bet you don't know is that Big Ben is the bell only – the Tower itself was renamed after Queen Elizabeth in 2010 as part of her Diamond Jubilee, but no-one remembers that. When you walk over Westminster Bridge in the summer, you have to fight your way through the crowds of tourists. All of them wanting to take a little piece of it home with them, but I do not mind.

You see, it's my Big Ben, just mine. When you use something a lot, it becomes your possession, doesn't it? I know that doesn't stand up, not for real, but I like to think so. It's special to me. I would listen out for its chimes marking the grey early hours, when the ward was still and I was alone. I can picture its yellow tower, standing 100m tall, a white clock face on each side, topped with a fairy tale spire. I loved the gold highlights casting a magical sparkle in the sun light.

That was when I first saw it, first truly noticed it, almost with eagle vision. In the spring sunshine, the gold glinted in majesty. It was my first trip out of the hospital on a warm day but I shivered anyway, my heart beating faster at the stimulation of cool breeze, newfound sights and the joy of living. Small things, but precious to me then.

As summer passed, whenever I was wheeled though the main corridor of St Thomas', I would steal a glimpse of Big Ben through the trees across the river. Its face became as familiar to me as Jen's, my best friend's. In the winter, I saw a different personality, its face without make-up, outlined by bare trees. At night, the balcony below the clock face was lit up bright green against the night sky. It became my lighthouse, my beacon shining in the distance. I remember Dad telling me of his fear sailing across the Bay of Biscay. With a wave of his arm, he told me of a lighthouse he could see sweeping the horizon, pointing the path to safety. He said he will remember it always. I see Big Ben across the water, glowing, and it makes me feel safe too.

Tonight, I look down on Big Ben from the Shard. It must be the same view as angels have. It looks smaller but still stands strong, its spirit dominating the skyline. Mum stands next to me as we look to the far horizon. I know now, I'm not sure why, but we will be okay tomorrow, my mum and me.

Earlier that day in the flurry of packing bags in the hall by the shoe rack, with never-to-be-found-again stuff like chargers, lip balm, slippers and flowery Thank You cards, not much thought was given to the logistics of saying goodbye. After the restaurant (good idea), the plan was to drop Ian and George at the Evelina (bad idea) which was on the way home for Siobhan, Ben and Fred (also a bad idea). It was not as if saying goodbye had to be staged, but there is a right way to do these things – as a natural full stop, unhurried and including everyone.

But when it came to it, on the pavement outside the Evelina, it was rushed as the engine was running. They wanted to prolong the magic of a pleasant evening. George and Ian did not want to go, and Siobhan hated to leave them. It all became a bit functional and they were left with the feeling of missed opportunity, of words unsaid for a set of circumstances that would never happen again.

It would be the best part of a week later before Ian found the flowery Thank You cards in one of his boots on the shoe rack and Ben squashed his toes on the Lip Balm at the end of his Nike Free.

George had not said it to anyone, but he thinks all lip balm is slimy and the Thank You cards were girly. Sneaky so-and-so.

With uncharacteristic forethought, Ian had left a card for Siobhan on her bedside table so she would find it when she went to bed the night before the transplant. She opened it as soon as she got home. The picture of a demure angel with *'You deserve angel wings'* was sweet, and a bit schmaltzy, if she was completely honest. She cried. Not big sobs or anything, just a quiet solitary cry that she kept to herself.

My darling Siobhan

The outside of the envelope says 'Open on your Own' but as you often skip to the last page to read the cliff-hanger, I bet I have not even made it to the car before you are reading this!!!

I tell you each day that I love you — it is as true today as when you chucked red wine on me and said yes to marrying me. But oft-used words can become a 'catching a bus kiss' — the everyday perfunctory action that loses its meaning. Well, not to me and not today — here and now.

There are so many things that you have done that make me love you more and more — our life together, full of fun, passion and the best of times, three fabulous sons you brought into the world and made fine young men, your strength and support when I really needed it, but above all your special warmth, compassion, mischievousness and sparkle that is so you and so intoxicating.

I look on in awe, admiration and pride at what you are doing for George. A very precious gift from a very special person. I can't think of a more selfless act than to give George up to twenty years of normal life at such a formative time for him. Even getting to this point would not have happened without your instinct and conviction – I am certain that you saved George's life that day in April and are doing so again. You truly deserve angel wings.

So, I expect you are feeling shaky and nervous about tomorrow. Easy for me to say, but just scroll through the times when your qualities have served you well – your strength and toughness, your unquenchable values to make the right decision and your tenacity to overcome the physical and emotional challenges that will come in the next six weeks. Maybe it is some comfort and rock-steady foundation to know how much you are loved and cherished by us all.

I'll see you when you wake up in Recovery. I will hold your hand. I will be there for you.

All my love

Ian

Ian had a card for George too. It was a breezy colourful card with *'Be Bright, Be Happy, Be You'* across the top. The intent had been to give it to him on the morning of the transplant. In the nervousness of getting everything prepared, and with characteristic lack of forethought, Ian forgot. When he remembered two days later, the moment had been lost.

To Chugs

Big day today, fella –we have all been wanting this day to happen for so long but now it is here, you may be feeling a bit nervous and excited perhaps?

This day will be the next chapter of your life, George. As you know, this transplant will give you back your life and allow you to do all the things you love — kayaking, chocolate, long cold drinks!!!

When times are tough, that is when we really find out about ourselves. You should be very proud of what you are made of:

- Tough as Nails — to cope with what you have been through and never complain or whinge.

- Positive Attitude — to get on and make the best of things. I have never heard you wallow in self-pity or ask why me? Sometimes shit happens that has no explanation, but you have just got on with it.

- Enthusiasm — I love it that you get all nerdy over cameras, wildlife and stuff. You can be an expert in your field with so much to offer if we can harness this.

- Top bloke — people like you, George, for who you are. They sense what a kind-hearted person you are who wants to help others and do the right thing. This is such a great quality to have.

So think of this, Chugs, especially if you are feeling grotty or sore or desperate to pee an ocean, you can dig deep, show the grit we know you have and take comfort that it will be short-lived and you will get through it.

I will be there when you wake up in Recovery and Mum will Skype you as soon as you get back on the ward.

We love you, George, and have huge pride and admiration for you – the bravest and toughest bloke we know.

All our love

Mum and Dad

PART 4: REPAIR

Chapter 27

> If we are ill and in hospital, fearing for our life, awaiting terrifying surgery, we have to trust the doctors treating us – at least, life is very difficult if we don't. It is not surprising that we invest doctors with superhuman qualities as a way of overcoming our fears. If the operation succeeds the surgeon is a hero, but if he fails he is a villain.
>
> *Henry Marsh[67], consultant neurosurgeon*

"How does this sound, Shiv?" Ian handed her the iPad for her to review a draft email.

"Looks good to me."

"I was thinking of sending something like this every few days, purely to cut down on the number of calls and messages. People will want to know how you and George are doing but we won't have the time to reply, at least at the beginning."

Hi Everyone,

We all know Shiv is a far better communicator than I, so this is an attempt to keep you all updated over the next few days.

I hope you do not mind the 'group' email. Email is not reliable in the hospital and I may not be able to pick up calls at certain times.

You have all been very thoughtful with messages of good wishes and have asked for updates.

It is all getting real now, with Siobhan, George and me packing bags to go in on Thursday. Friday is 'operation day' and Saturday is often a day with a fair amount of discomfort for both. If you were thinking of visiting, could I ask you to email/text me before you do ... would hate it to be a wasted trip.

---

[67] From Do no Harm, Stories of life, death and brain surgery by Henry Marsh

Love to all,

Ian and Siobhan

I wake up again at 04:00 am. I'm not sure why; I'm not nervous or anything. There is no point; I want the operation. All attempts at going to sleep fail, so I sit up in bed. Emily pokes her head through the curtains.

"You ok, George?"

How does she know I am awake? She must have been watching me.

"I'm going to get a cup of tea and some toast, fancy some?"

We sit and chat in whispers for a while. I don't remember about what. She is a nice lady, that Emily, she has kind eyes. I must have closed mine at some point.

They all agreed that Friday 25th July was an odd day for different reasons. Fred started early, driving Siobhan to Guy's Hospital for seven a.m. The first tears of the day as they said goodbye to each other. Siobhan needed a tissue and Fred said the London air was smoky. In the Evelina, George was so chilled, he fell asleep all morning whilst waiting to go down to theatre. Ben recalled a massive thunder and lightning storm around midday that terrified the thirty kids in his charge at Tennis Camp. Fred remembers having chicken for lunch, but he was making it up, as he always has chicken and could not think of anything else to say. Siobhan woke up in recovery that afternoon and asked the anaesthetist *'have you done it yet?',* as time for her had stood still. Conversely, Gran and Nan claimed the day was twice as long as any other, interminably clock-watching and stewing for something to happen. As mums do, they just worried for everyone, with a sprinter's response on the R of 'ring' whenever the phone went. Above everything else, Ian remembered the warm grip of hands –first with the surgeon in an overwhelming flood of relief and gratitude, then with Siobhan as she put all her love into one squeeze to say she was fine and finally with George, with a knuckle-crusher, as he showed his strength and resolve to get through the next stage of his fight back. Odd, what people remember.

The surgical team operating on Siobhan undertook a laparoscopic nephrectomy. This is a form of minimally-invasive surgery, using instruments on long, narrow rods to view, cut, and remove her healthy perfect kidney. The surgeon, Mac, viewed the kidney and surrounding tissue with a flexible videoscope. He manoeuvred the videoscope and surgical instruments through four small incisions in the abdomen. For poor Siobhan, these looked like bullet holes, but quickly faded from angry purple wounds to tiny scars. The carbon dioxide that was pumped into her abdominal cavity to inflate it for an improved visualisation of the kidney left her with serious bloating and appalling unladylike wind over the next two weeks. Once her kidney was freed, it was secured in a bag and pulled through a fifth incision, approximately three inches wide, in the front of her abdominal wall below the navel. Again, the scar healed well into a thin pink pencil line. Although this surgical technique takes slightly longer, it promotes a faster recovery time, shorter hospital stays, and less postoperative pain for kidney donors.

Once removed, the kidney from a live donor like Siobhan was placed on ice and flushed with a cold preservative solution. The kidney can be preserved in this solution for 24–48 hours. The sooner the transplant takes place after harvesting the kidney, the better the chances are for proper functioning.

The team at Guy's undertook five full kidney transplants that day, co-ordinating donors and recipients, including harvesting Siobhan's kidney to go to the Evelina. It was only on the transplant ward, with its rows and rows of recovering patients, that the realisation hit home of the factory-type enterprise.

The liberated kidney was whisked by motorbike courier through busy south London over to the Evelina, where George's team were already prepped with George anaesthetised on the operating table. He was covered in theatre sheets, with only a square of iodine-swabbed tummy visible under the bright lights. People were surprised that the new kidney goes in at the front, rather than the back, close to the existing kidneys.

During the transplant operation itself, George had antibiotics administered to prevent possible infection. A catheter (a tube into the bladder) was inserted before surgery began; fortunately for George, it was done as soon as he was under, to spare him the indignity. Mac, the surgeon, made his first incision in George's flank, opening the space just below the skin and muscle to implant the kidney above the pelvic bone and below the existing, non-functioning kidney. He then attached the blood supply by suturing the new kidney artery and vein to the George's iliac artery and vein, which would now have to serve his new kidney as well his legs. The ureter of the new kidney was attached directly to George's bladder. A small plastic pipe, called a double J-stent, was inserted into the ureter to help prevent it from becoming blocked after the operation. George's existing, useless kidneys were left in place. It was deemed too much of a trauma to remove them for no gain. The transplant operation itself took about four hours.

At different times, both donor and recipient, mother and son, were tidied up and wheeled off to Recovery in their separate hospitals to begin the disorientating journey back to reality. The recovery teams were geared up to closely monitor both patients for risk associated with any surgical procedure. Possible complications included infection and post-op bleeding. A lymphocele, a pool of lymphatic fluid around the kidney that is generated by lymphatic vessels damaged in surgery, occurs in up to 20% of transplant patients and can obstruct urine flow and/or blood flow to the kidney if not diagnosed and drained promptly. Less common is a urine leak outside of the bladder, which occurs in approximately 3% of kidney transplants when the ureter suffers damage during the procedure. This problem is usually correctable with follow-up surgery.

A transplanted kidney may be rejected by the patient. Rejection occurs when the patient's immune system recognises the new kidney as a foreign body and attacks it. This may occur soon after transplantation, or several months or years after the procedure has taken place. Rejection episodes are not uncommon in the first weeks after transplantation surgery, and are treated with high-dose injections of immunosuppressant drugs.

Whilst the surgical teams were busy with George and Siobhan, the opposite was true for Ian. He had already done all the worrying he could. Fussing was all done too, no bits of paper were left untwiddled, no times unchecked and no updates available. Nothing happened. The day dragged, so long that it lasted forever. Like George's slow-set metronome, the minutes morphed into hours and the hours decided to become days. Ian tried to occupy himself with a newspaper (*fourteen minutes, pictures only, can't concentrate*), a coffee (*seven minutes and scalded tongue*), a walk up to the ward and back (*eleven minutes, utterly, utterly pointless*), reading a book (*one plus two plus two plus three minutes, same sodding paragraph read four times and still couldn't tell you what it said*). Everything he could think of to do had taken just shy of forty minutes and it exhausted him.

Chapter 28

Heart (Noun)

1.1 A hollow muscular organ that pumps the blood through the circulatory system by rhythmic contraction and dilation.

1.2 The heart regarded as the centre of a person's thoughts and emotions, especially love or compassion.

1.3 One's mood or feeling.

1.4 Courage or enthusiasm.

1.5 The vital part or essence.

Synonyms

compassion, sympathy, humanity, feeling(s), fellow feeling, concern for others, brotherly love, tender feelings, tenderness, empathy, understanding; kindness, kindliness, goodwill, benevolence, humanitarianism.

When George woke up from the anaesthetic, he had several tubes coming out of him. These included the urinary catheter mentioned earlier, and a central venous pressure (CVP) line. This is a tube which went into a large vein in the side of the George's neck, and one of its jobs is to measure the pressure of blood inside the heart. It is also a three-pronged cannula to allow the nurses to administer fluid and drugs as necessary.[68] In different places in George's arm he had an additional three cannulas for inbound lines for intravenous drips. These would only stay in for a few days, but were there as a backup if needed. In his abdomen, he had two surgical drains to drain off any fluid that gathers around the kidney after the operation. Although he looked like a pincushion now, these tubes were removed one by one over the next five days. The urinary catheter was left in

---

[68] Evelina: A Guide to Kidney Transplantation in Children. Grainne M. Walsh

place until George's natural urine flows were fully established. The wound drain took more than two weeks before it could be removed, as it did its job too well and persistently kept filling the drain bottle.

It's so noisy in here. Who are all these people in blue suits and navy suits and purple suits? My eyes feel gummy. Jeez, I remember this feeling and I do not like it. I feel quite cold and achey stuck in this position. I hear Dad's voice. I'm glad he is here. He leans in to kiss me and I see his nose come into view. I don't want to be kissed in front of all these people, so I reach up, surprised that my arm works with all the tubes in it, and grab his hooter.

Parp!

"Hello Mister!"

"Bazinger!"

He looks really surprised and his eyes are watering. Maybe I grabbed his nose too hard?

Siobhan's pupils were huge and dark, with one twice the size of the other. Normally a dilated pupil on one side can be a marker of something sinister, but once checked for a response to a pen light, the anaesthetist relaxed. The anaesthetic was still in her system, taking the edge off time and reality. It was a pleasant detached feeling as she lay propped up in her bed before being wheeled onto the ward.

Sometime later, Ian bounded round the dividing curtain. The pent-up frustration of two and a half hours waiting to see her came out with a rush of '*How are you? How you feeling? What hurts? What took so long?*' Siobhan saw a hundred things in the way he looked at her. The surface smile was hopeful in its concern for her pain and the relief for her recovery. She saw his eyes look deep into hers, seeking the connection of love and togetherness she knew so well. His eyes widened, inadvertently signaling his unspoken question, hoping she was where they had left off a few hours ago. With time, he calmed down to match her level of consciousness, ending up quiet and reassured, with her hand clasped in his, as she drifted partly awake, partly asleep. All had gone well.

In a soft and soothing voice, trying to stay on the edge of her consciousness, Ian chose his moment well.

"Do you remember that advert of that Land Rover I showed you? It was brilliant, wasn't it? So I can have my Land Rover then? You know it's a good idea. You'll love it. I bet you want one too. Just say yes."

"Sod off – I'm not that spacey."

Something elemental wells up inside me. I am determined to do this. For me, for me, I am getting well, I am back, I can do this. I grit my teeth and plant my feet on the floor. I push with trembling thigh muscles to get myself vertical. I feel a tugging around my belly button but push through it.

YES, done it – I 'm upright with head bowed and shoulders hunched! I raise my head, square my shoulders as best I can – look at me! I am doing it, I am standing, I am back.

WOAH YES – I am back.

Hi Everyone,

A very busy day but a successful one.

Shivvy went first this morning. The surgeon said it was a big fat healthy kidney. Once out of Recovery at 15:00, Siobhan is doing fine – a bit dozy (careful!) and sore but relieved and happy.

Then George's turn – a longer and more complex operation, but all went well. Back on the ward at 19:00. The kidney produced urine almost immediately, and rate of production is excellent. Blood flows are good so all early signals are positive. He is doing great – pulled my nose when I went to kiss him, and desperate to drink now that his intake is not restricted.

Over the next few days, lots of tests, tubes and pipes gradually get removed, and lots of chill time to speed recovery.

Early days but big smiles and relief all round.

Cheers,

Ian

Chapter 29

Life's most persistent and urgent question is, 'what are you doing for others?'

Martin Luther-King

Any parent with a child going down for major surgery would want the A-team. Ian and Siobhan certainly had the best, that Friday 25th July.

The ever-present Laura and Kay kept in the background. Laura's job as a psychologist was to prepare young minds to accept the unsettling events of their illness and recovery. She had crafted her relationship with George over the last year, so together they built George's Transplant Book to capture the events, his concerns and how to deal with them and his hopes for the future. It meant that nothing was a surprise for George, and allowed him to take everything in his stride to such an extent that he was more chilled than his parents.

In the week leading up to the transplant, Kay sat George down and walked him through what would happen. He knew she was replaying what she had seen and what to look for.

The surgical teams at Guy's did five transplants that day and at Evelina six major operations, including George's transplant. On one level, this gives huge confidence that teams are highly experienced, techniques are fully honed and treatment protocols proven. But who in this big machine looks out for your child so he is not simply the next on the conveyor belt?

This where Becca, Emily, Mac and Caroline stepped up in the order that they appeared as George woke up.

Becca is a very talented nurse – full of ability and focus. What set her apart was her complete ownership of George as HER patient. She spent an uninterrupted thirteen-hour day focused solely on George. She owned every element of preparation pre-op and rigorous care and monitoring post-op. You felt that nothing had been missed and George was given every opportunity to get well.

Emily is deceptive. She looks tiny and timid, but is a giant. The night before the op, she spent forty minutes in the dead of night just chatting with an edgy fourteen-year-old whilst his dad snored with gusto. The next night, George's first post-op, she was on her feet at the end of George's bed throughout the night – continually. Her dedication was thorough – monitoring hourly, calculating fluid flows in and out, giving multiple meds, titrating pain relief and intravenous nutrition.

Mac the surgeon must represent the new breed. Thirty years ago Ian remembered his surgeon as a cliché – the pinstripe suit and bow tie, Received Pronunciation English and a master of the Empire air. Mr Pompous only popped in once, to tell his patient how pleased he was with himself on the brilliant surgery he had done. Mac, on the other hand, was understated but authoritative, again showing real care for his patient to be an ever-present in follow-up, and the next Saturday morning in jeans and a t-shirt in typical relaxed Aussie fashion. Mac even seemed a little embarrassed at Ian's profound and gushy gratitude. It was though a brief encounter was enough for them to be best mates for life. In truth, Mac never wanted to see Ian again, not from some violent anaphylactic reaction to his thanks, but more that with a successful transplant operation, he hoped he would never need to. For a surgeon, success is when the transplant works, the patient returns to normal life and forgets their fear and discomfort and ultimately their surgeon.

Caroline joked that if all transplant patients were as easy as George then her life would be rosy. George had been pretty impressive, generating urine that first evening, standing on his own after breakfast the next morning and hitting all the levels he needed to with no drama at all. He was polite and engaging with the nurses. Even with the unpleasant stuff like blood tests every six hours, and having his cannula cleaned or replaced, he took it all in his stride.

Siobhan was flicking through a magazine, scanning the pictures mostly. She felt awful, far worse than she had expected. Her shoulders were propped up by the raised bed-head as the thought of any kind of tension in her abdominal muscles made her sweat with nausea. She tried to limit pressing the on-demand pain relief pump, but had given up, opting instead to keep her lower half anonymous. The article was irritating too, but there was no pump for that.

> These amazing and courageous people donate one of their kidneys to help a loved one survive. The recipients might have been on dialysis for years, with a very poor quality of life, and no real hope of receiving a kidney in any other way.
>
> Almost from the moment the new kidney is plumbed in, they begin to feel better, but for the donor, they have gone into hospital feeling great and come out feeling terrible. They go through major surgery to bring the chance, the hope of life to the recipient. Of course, there is no guarantee that the transplant will be successful, but the majority are a triumph. Whatever the outcome, this can never diminish the astonishing altruism of the donor in giving them the chance to live a life worth having.

She did not feel courageous. Her only amazement was the change to dreadful nauseating soreness compared to perfectly well just yesterday. The irony of a hospital stay being worse for her health would have been lost on the cheery journalist. Then again she could not write *'don't do it, you will feel crap'* could she? Siobhan gave another pump and tried to sleep.

"Did you notice Mrs Patel in the bed next to me?" asked Siobhan.

Ian's blank look told her the answer. "Sorry, no – should I have?"

"Not really. She's so tiny you could easily miss her." Siobhan let him off the hook and gave him the short version of her conversation with Mrs Patel.

"I got chatting to her, as you do. She is a remarkable woman with impeccable manners. She's back on dialysis after her second transplant. The first transplant from her mum lasted seventeen years, but the second from a deceased donor only lasted a few weeks and she was in to have it removed."

"Poor lady – I guess that means she'll be back on dialysis."

"That's right. It brings home Sheila's words that kidney disease is a life-long thing. Can you imagine? It will be so hard going back on dialysis after so long leading a normal life." Siobhan continued, "I loved talking to her. Such a sweet lady. She told me that *'Mum's kidney is the best kidney'*, and to make sure George knows that. She had another great line – *'look after your kidney and it will look after you'* – we must get that in George's head. It helped to hear she has led a full and happy life, got married, raised kids, gone on holiday – all the normal stuff you would expect. So although life isn't great right now, her message was an inspiring one of a life well-lived despite the challenges. I did ask her about timings, you know, if she thought a family holiday abroad at Christmas would be doable – she frowned and said better next summer. That really surprised me. She also said that even when they do go on holiday, they always book a hotel near to the hospital. Like next door!"

"God, they obviously think about the risks all the time. Maybe that is something we need to get used to," replied Ian. He was rattled as the Patel family approach was very different to his own – and they knew what they were doing – he didn't.

Ian was not spoiling for a row, but he felt he had to develop his own view of risk and see where Siobhan was, too. If they had different views then an almighty dust-up was on the cards. He knew it was more productive to address issues with Siobhan when she was shaping her opinion rather than banging his head against the brick wall of her conviction. He had tried that before and it was painful, leaving him dazed and bruised – literally.

"So Shiv, where do you stand on risk?" Not allowing her to answer, he got his view in first. "The reason I ask is that I can't help but think Mrs Patel seemed overly cautious to me. Which may sound arrogant as she has the experience of kidney disease and I don't," began Ian, sharing his dilemma and inviting a kick in the goolies.

"I know, she surprised me too. I don't know where the boundaries are either. Are you suggesting some sort of criteria or good/bad list? I know you like a good list." Siobhan was a Master of Lists, usually leaving one for Ian at the weekend and for the boys when her unfair share of housework bugged her. When a list was being compiled, Ian had tried hiding the pen (childish) but it did limit the length (effective).

"Maybe. I do want to talk it through with you, though. I'm nervous I haven't thought about it much – and I feel I'm being reckless."

Siobhan took the initiative, introducing the high level principle which was usually where her moral compass and decision-making was founded. She began, "Let's start with George first and what he wants. He's determined to get back to normal. For him, that's getting back to school – he's adamant that he's going to kayak again, he loves cycling and he wants to travel, see different places. But he hasn't given any thought to his limits – he is more susceptible now to infection, any impact to his abdomen makes me shudder, he can never have a suntan ever again."

"All good points," Ian acknowledged. "Wherever we start, we run straight into limits – what he can't do rather than what he can. Don't you see, it's the wrong way round? Do we decide the limits for him or let George decide?"

Siobhan set out her stall, no grey area as usual. "I feel really strongly about this. You have read *Grainne's Transplant Guide,*[69] same as me, so the first six months are the most difficult and uncertain. What was the rejection rate? About 25%, I remember? I know I can be a worrier, but the whole purpose of the transplant was for George to lead a normal life. He says it himself, '*I just want to be me again.*' Life is to be lived, we can't wrap him in cotton wool. "

Siobhan paused, having said her piece, a little surprised by her own views. She was not normally a risk-taker, but that was not what she was advocating. At least she didn't

---

[69] Evelina: A Guide to Kidney Transplantation in Children. Grainne M. Walsh. The 25% figure refers to rejection episodes which may not become full rejection. Evelina's most recent cohort shows after five years 96 out of 100 transplants are still functioning.

think so. It came across as confrontational, demanding either fight or flight. Ian responded.

"I couldn't agree more, and you put it well. How's this, then – me being the dove to your hawk? What about Mrs Patel? As you told it to me, her adventurous view on life is brilliant. But even she has limits – like don't consider a holiday for six months, only books hotels close to hospital in case of an infection. Back to my question, where do we place those limits?" Ian repeated.

"I don't know any more than you do, what about some examples?" pushed Siobhan.

"Let's take kayaking. He has done his drills and is sensible so no risk there. But there is Weil's disease, sewage in the water – that sort of thing. If he cuts his foot, then he is exposed. Do we say no kayaking?" said Ian, still seeking the boundary.

"No, not at all, but what we do say is, you can't go if you have any broken skin, we limit the deliberate dunkings, so no messing around, pushing each other in, makes sense? We get the doctor's advice and make that part of the decision too. Do you think that can work?" Siobhan was confident her solution was workable.

"That makes sense to me. It's a sensible compromise, we reduce what risks we can, but accept there are still some. Christ, you can get hit by a bus, just stepping outside your front door. George gets to do what he loves. The spin-off is the adult discussion with George so he can determine what residual risks are acceptable to him. It's a bit like me with cycling – in thirty years I have broken my thumb, wrist and got a scar on my head which ruined my modelling career. You can say with certainty that I will fall off again, but I try and minimise the risk – I don't cycle with muppets, I stay off A-roads where the traffic is a hundred miles an hour, and I look drivers in the eye at junctions."

"You also dress like a traffic island, all lit up like a Christmas tree."

"Thank you, I know I look cool. But the same principle applies for George. I think we agree, right?"

"We do." Siobhan went quiet, thinking more. She opened the window for some air, allowing an uncomfortable presence to sweep in and drive a chink in their fragile agreement." But what happens when his temperature spikes at thirty eight degrees[70], or his creatinine starts to creep up, or he collapses?"

"We deal with it, we get it investigated, and we get him back in the Evelina. Nothing could be worse that the last twelve months."

Siobhan sighed with acceptance rather than resignation. "You never really escape do you? From the Evelina I mean. You never really get discharged and away."

"I wouldn't want to. We can go back there whenever we need to," Ian replied, concentrating on the road and his own thoughts.

---

[70] At the time this was a prophetic comment. George contracted a suspected Cyclosporidium infection two days after kayaking. He had nearly two weeks in hospital and lost 7kg in 10 days.

Chapter 30

If I know anything about love, it is because of you.

Herman Hesse

The one thing Siobhan remembered more than any other from her session with Michelle, the transplant co-ordinator, was the phrase *'a one-time unconditional gift'*. It was though four simple words were a rule book or code to live by, founded on the experiences of the many people that had gone before her.

She remembered Michelle breaking down the phrase for her to make sure Siobhan understood. The *'one-time'* element was so important for the donor to be able to move on with their stalled future. So phrases like *'remember this for the rest of your life'* or mawkishly celebrating the transplant day itself were ill-advised. For *'unconditional'*, Michelle meant that the recipient must not feel beholden, *'what I have done for you'*, *'the sacrifice I have made'*. Even donors joking about *'looking after my kidney for me'* was unfair. The last part, the *'gift'*, was less relevant for a mother and son. The special bond between mother and child was already a given, based on unspoken lifelong unconditional love. So really, donating a kidney was a piece of tissue in a much bigger tapestry of life.

Up until George fell ill, Ian and Siobhan would have described life as perfect. Not in a boastful way, and admittedly, maybe only in the last five years had it edged that way. Before then life had been a bit frayed around the edges, but nothing different to what everyone else deals with. Three kids under five had been hard work, but memory filters off the gritty bits to retain the joyous milestones and laughter that goes with them. Sometimes they got in a rut of household drudgery and too much travel, with long hours to climb the greasy pole. Mid-thirties had carried the nagging pressure of money worries, somehow managing to combine well-paid jobs with no money. They had routinely spent more than they earned on the mortgage, three sets of school fees, holidays and the hungry mouths of credit card bills.

By their forties, the elder boys were becoming adults, so more good fun than needy. Provided they were within a short commute of a full fridge, they were happy lads. A shrewd financial advisor had given them some discipline and surety that they should have listened to a long time ago. All the boxes for happiness were ticked – love, health, choice, comfort, warmth, fun, fulfilment and, secretly, satisfaction.

There was no *'too good to be true'* moment. Truth be told, it did not all change when George contracted meningitis, it just became different. Once they were through the shock and trauma of the first month, family life crept slowly into *'surviving, not living'*. That whole work/life balance shifted, but no-one told Ian's employers. If anything, he worked even harder to prove beyond question his engagement and loyalty. Accommodating George's illness meant a reprioritisation, inevitably pushing George's medical needs higher. They both regretted spending less time with their older sons, but then again, they were at an age where they sought independence and experiences beyond safe old Mum and Dad. Family holidays were put on hold, so they had fewer opportunities to add to the rich bank of shared memories.

Life now was deeper, more complex than just black and white, perfect or imperfect. It had colour and tone, reflecting an appreciation of each day unfolding. With gratitude that they were all there to live it, but to adapt, taking the best they could. Siobhan relished her cultural ambassador role, booking many events, attending most but not all. Holidays also got pencilled in with a few rubbings out. Work was demoted to a means to an end. School for George was remoulded as a source of fun, no longer an exam factory. What did not change was the expectation, by George most of all, to lead a normal life and do everything that he used to.

With no staff shuttle bus working at the weekend between Guy's and Evelina, Ian exited the Jubilee Line at Waterloo and walked towards the London Eye. On a sunny day in July, the area was packed with tourists who lacked the task focus he had. He dodged through the throng of people, and keen to avoid those in bizarre poses – the 'Holding Up the Eye', the 'Eye in my Hand', the 'Eye as my Halo'. He did wonder how many times he had inadvertently photo-bombed some eager traveller. He wondered more what Mr Yutaka from Osaka would think when he noticed a large tired-looking bloke with a preoccupied expression striding through the background of his photo.

As Ian was packing Siobhan's bag to leave, he picked up the card he had given her and waved it in her eyeline.

"Oh Ian, that card was just lovely, your words meant so much to me."

He was pleased his words had the effect he hoped for.

"Well, I meant every word, and you needed to hear it that night."

"It made me cry, but then it doesn't take much." Her eyes were welling up. "How did you find it? You must have searched for ages."

"Yep,'course ... walked across hot coals and all that. To be honest, it was the second shop I looked in, and I saw it straight away. You know how your eye notices only what's on your mind – so it was either going to be a picture of an angel or a Land Rover on the front. I just saw that angel picture first."

"Great – there's me thinking you're a man of depth and feeling, but you set me straight."

The next morning George also mentioned his card.

"Thanks for the card Dad, it's really nice," said George.

'*Is that it?*' thought Ian. A big father and son bonding moment was too much to expect with a teenager, but even so, he felt short-changed by the lack of emotion from George. It was entirely his own fault. If he had given George the card when he meant to and not two days late, maybe it would have meant more. He added the 'if' and 'maybe' to the burden he still carried.

PART 5: REUNION

Chapter 31

A bit of fragrance always clings to the hand that gives
you roses.

Chinese proverb

As Siobhan and Ian waited for the lift to take them up to
Beach ward to visit George for the first time after the
operations, Siobhan looked at her reflection in the lift doors
and shuddered at what she saw. Her posture was dreadful,
as standing up straight was too painful. The comfy faded
trackies screamed *'elasticised waistband for escaping
tummy'* and her hair – well! She saw the same Careworn
Mum in herself and the image flattened her optimism.

"Wheeeee – hit the brakes or we'll crash the lift." A
mum and her severely disabled daughter came bombing
along the walkway as fast as a battery powered wheelchair
can bomb. The daughter threw her head back at the
acceleration and the pink sparkly bangles in her hair caught
the light. Siobhan recognised the bangles immediately, then
the little girl, but no way could it be the same Careworn
Mum. This one was laughing her head off and sprinting
after her escaping daughter. Their joy and mischief
delighted Siobhan and she smiled back at them both,
stepping gingerly to the back of the lift to let them in,
provided they braked in time. As the lift went up Siobhan
furtively studied the mum, marvelling at the
transformation. Maybe it was no transformation at all? Had
she judged them snobbishly on an off-day? Was this what
she was like most of the time? It could have been one of
those breaking-point days that Sheila had mentioned and
had haunted Siobhan's thoughts ever since. She put the
haunt away for another time and squared her shoulders as
much as she could without it hurting too much – this was

going to be a good day, one she had dreamed about for so long.

Mum is getting discharged today! I am so chuffed she is getting out. I know it sounds selfish and horrible, but I wish it were me. I'm starting to get so bored in here and want to go home.

She is here; I hear her voice coming down the corridor. I crab to the edge of the bed to show her I can stand – nearly as tall as her. I am on my stockinged feet as she rounds the corner and sees me. Her eyes crinkle and fill with tears – I knew she would.

Mum is totally speechless. That's a first.

She grabs my shoulders and we cling to each other. She smells of warm skin and fresh figs from her body lotion. Her embrace is warmth and love. I am overjoyed to see her but I don't cry in front of people I love any more. Mum dips her face forward to kiss me, just on my temple, making my eye scrunch up, squeezing a tear out and my vision go misty in one eye. I hope she doesn't think I'm crying or anything. She snuffles into my neck on my good side, away from the lines in my neck and mumbles and squelches into my ear. I don't know what she's saying, but I know roughly what she means. As we cuddle, neither of us risks touching each other below the shoulders – it's still too sore. We must look like we are making a celebratory arch for others to run through.

I imagined this to be a private reunion, just me and Mum, maybe Dad looking on. Well, everyone has gatecrashed the party. We are the centre of the dance floor. Doctors spill from the office, the nurses' station is suddenly full, all the other beds look on, and even the lady with Nala, the hospital dog, is there. They are smiling at me. I feel a bit of a twonk and not too sure what to do with myself.

Ian retrieved the wheelchair from the atrium and lowered an exhausted Siobhan into it as soon as they were out of sight of the ward. No longer needing to maintain her cheerfulness, Siobhan looked drawn and in pain, grateful to be trundled out to the car. He helped her into the car and left her sitting there whilst he scooted back into the building to return the wheelchair to Beach Ward.

A tap on the passenger window, although shyly done, still made Siobhan start from her stolen moment of shut-eyed stillness. The security guard was framed in the window, smiling broadly and holding a small but carefully chosen posy,

"I've been waiting for you. I have these for you. I have them in my hut for two days in water for when you come back to see George."

Siobhan mirrored his smile, touched by his thoughtful tenderness – a person she barely knew, yet buoyed by his gesture.

"That's so kind, thank you, thank you, they are so lovely," and with that she welled up again.

Ian drove home as gently as he could to avoid gut-rattling potholes. Each one made Siobhan wince. The day had been far longer than planned, as Siobhan had been compelled beyond her limits to see her son on her way home from hospital. It was her own choice, knowing it was at a time when her resilience was shot, but what else could she do? It had been worth it, though, as she replayed George's reaction behind her closed eyes.

"Just get a fucking move on, you useless twat," a cyclist bawled at Ian for repeatedly slowing at speed bumps.

"That's not very nice, now is it," commented Ian to no-one in particular, with none of his normal chin-out belligerence. Driving in London at rush hour brings out the worst in most people, but today Ian surprised himself at his mellow benevolence. He secretly agreed with the cyclist, he *was* driving like a twat, holding up traffic. But hey, they had not had a day like his, nor seen what he had seen, nor retained the glow that finally things were well in his small part of the world. His bubble was known only to him, so he did not expect any accommodation or understanding.

Mr. Angry in Lycra pedaled off in a huff. His arse wobbled as crashed over the speed bumps too fast.

Hi Everyone,

Well, we are now the other side of the transplant and all going to plan ... relief all round!

George is doing brilliantly and took the award for Earliest To Stand Post-Transplant ... proud Mum and Dad! He is no longer under the consultant's nose and now has his own ensuite room plus sofa ... feels like a king and I've warned him not to get used to it as that's not how it is at home!

George has another 7-10 days in hospital and then becomes an outpatient with tests every day in the clinic for the next month.

I came home yesterday after a very tearful reunion with George at his hospital and had my first night back in my own bed, which was wonderful! Am being looked after by my own Supermum, Superhub and Superboys!

So we have moved onto the next stage.

Much love

Shiv

X

Chapter 32

Caroline, the renal consultant, was so pleased with George's progress that her prediction of two weeks in hospital proved to be very close. George was discharged twenty days after his operation. The last few days were waiting for a wound drain to dry up. It was no hindrance to George, as he put the bottle in his jeans pocket and still was able to get around the hospital.

Ian, too, was discovering domestic talents he had hidden for a lifetime. He finally worked out how to use the washing machine, where to find the Hoover and which end of the iron went first (the pointy end). He had the back-up of a freezer stocked with meals prepared by friends, for which he took shameless credit. Mags and Jean took the French view that the only way to preserve or restore health was through gastrointestinal well-being, so they prescribed hearty meals, loads of cakes, sausage rolls, full English breakfast – Ben and Fred were in bulging waistband heaven. Ian could not compete, but was particularly proud of his soup, although the recipe was donated by a colleague at work.

Vodka Tonic and Lime with Chicken Noodle Soup

Ingredients:

1 quart Ice

6oz Premium Vodka

24oz Tonic water

3 lime wedges

1 can Campbell's Chicken Noodle Soup per every two family members

Step 1

Fill glass 2/3 full ice

Pour 2oz Premium Vodka

Top off remainder with Tonic

Garnish with Lime Wedge

Begin drinking immediately

Step 2

Empty canned soup in pot

Add 2/3 can water per each can

Simmer while repeating Step 1

Step 3

Serve Soup to family while repeating Step 1

Enjoy !

Within three days of her operation, Siobhan was discharged and came home to a sofa and enforced rest. She was surprised at how immobile she was. So much was sore that she had no desire to move.

Nevertheless, Siobhan woke up feisty, and she stayed that way over breakfast, intent on solving World Peace over her bowl of bircher oats and fruit.

"It's nuts that we have to travel into the hospital every day for George's blood tests. Surely in this day and age, someone could invent a gizmo that does the analysis at home, links to your smart phone and then beams the results to the hospital. It works for my mum and her diabetes, she does the test herself, with a drop of blood and gets the insulin level immediately."

Ian replied over his iPad, sharp as a tack, which itself was unusual this early. "I know what you mean. It should be easy but so many diagnostic tests today are all about logistics – I mean, transporting the samples of blood to the lab and with a bit of science thrown in. So it takes forever. Instead, do the sampling yourself, automate and miniaturise the tests and then it all becomes about transferring data."

She had expected a *'Hmm yes darling'* not-really-listening response, but did a double-take, impressed with his insight. Not that she thought him a doughnut, but this was way out of his usual league. He warmed to his theme, basking in his own brilliance, but gave the game away by reading from the iPad too much.

"Funny you should mention it, I was reading about this new venture called Theranos,[71] headed up by a ridiculously young girl who they say is the next Steve Jobs – even dresses like him, all in black. She is on a mission to make blood tests simple, timely, unalarming, and cheap. They use tiny blood samples, these secret automated labs for 200 analyses and use the existing pharmacy network. It won't be long before heavyweight investors pile in and we get it in Europe."

Now fully rumbled, Siobhan snatched the iPad. "Give me that, you Sheldon Cooper, you – so, not your own brain then! Is that her? Elizabeth Holmes? She is far too pretty and far too brainy if you ask me. She could do with a nice colourful floral scarf. Just to brighten things up a bit from all that black. Then she won't look so grumpy."

She gave him the iPad back, eyeballing him with chin-up stare. It was either her pleased-with-herself challenge or her don't-mess-with-me look. He wasn't sure which.

---

[71] From http://uk.businessinsider.com/why-elisabeth-holmes-started-theranos-2014-11?r=US

Later that morning when George and Ian got to the hospital for the daily round of tests, there was a mix-up with the blood tests. None had been ordered the night before, the labels weren't ready and so no blood could be taken. Ian tried to push the logic that it was exactly the same tests that George has every day, so they should just take the bloods and stick the labels on, but got nowhere.

When they finally did get to clinic, the session with Dr Amrit was uneventful, with George playing Poster Boy Patient to the max. All his blood chemistry was spot on – within the ranges expected. No pain or unexpected sensations anywhere. All topped off with a smile and chirpiness that was a joy to see in George.

Dr Amrit apologised for the delay caused by the breakdown in communication over ordering the tests. It was not her fault, but her courtesy meant she took the responsibility. She added, "It does seem a palaver to come all this way, to then wait around all morning just for blood tests, which tell us everything is okay. I suppose it's better we keep a very close eye in case anything goes wrong. One day someone will invent a much more convenient way that you can do at home and then call me."

Ian was just about to say *'funny you should mention that ...'* , but hesitated long enough for the moment to pass. He had to ration out his brilliance and not use it too much in one day.

Hi Everyone,

Here's update 4 and the last for a while.

We have now got George home from hospital and it is great to have him back. He continues to be the model patient, hitting all his numbers for urine output, fluid intake, blood chemistry and general awesomeness. He has been trained to take responsibility for all his medication – so currently 17 tablets per day and 8 different medicines all packed in a calendarised box for the week ahead. We still go up to the Evelina every day for blood tests and close monitoring, which will lessen over the next few months as he gets into a stable routine.

Siobhan is doing well, but the bell she was given to summon me when she needs something is going to get lost very soon. Ben, Fred and I have shared the cooking this week. We have been able to rely on some yummy stuff prepared by friends, so provided I hide away the donated bowls, I can claim the credit.

We have been really touched by everyone's kind wishes, cards, flowers, offers of help.

We are very lucky to have such good friends.

Have a great summer everyone.

All the best,

Ian and Siobhan

They sped through the country lanes near Alvescott, already late for Sunday lunch at Gran's. George, in the centre, lolled against Fred who pushed him back upright and got an elbow for his trouble. Ian saw it in his rear view mirror and told them to cool it.

"Handbags, ladies."

"It's him!" protested Fred, "Look, if you don't stop being so flaming grumpy, I'm gonna punch you in the kidney."

"Fred, that's just awful, you can't say that!" Both Siobhan and Ian winced at the thought.

"Just a threat ... and a joke. Lighten up you two. We need more kidney jokes. We don't have anywhere near enough."

They settled back down, with the journey nearly over and a glorious lunch to look forward too. Ben carried on dozing, or so you would think, but the tell of a Bond-villain leer at the corner of his mouth was significant.

On a long straight stretch, the speed went over seventy, which was more than enough to leave stomachs on the ceiling as they took off from a hump-back bridge.

"For Christ's sake, do you have to? You nearly shook my last remaining kidney out," wailed Siobhan.

"What about poor old George, he's got three in there rattling around like maracas," piped up Fred.

"Nice one Fred," acknowledged Ben, for the quip and the inspiration it gave him. He asked George innocently, "So George, I've been thinking, what do they put in maracas to make them rattle?"

"I dunno, dried beans I suppose?" replied George, mystified at the odd question.

"What sort do you think?"

"Kidney beans maybe. Are you trying to be funny?" challenged George, disconcerted as to where this was going.

"No, nothing. You're learning Spanish, right? Say your favourite word for me again."

"Un – shaka – puntas. It means pencil sharpener."

"Excellent, bet that's handy if you ever get kidnapped by a Mexican drug cartel."

Ben carried on with his random questions. "So, what's the biggest hat you can think of? You need to keep out of the sun, right?"

"A Stetson?"

"No, bigger, with a huge brim."

"A sombrero?"

"Gotcha! Say hello to our Spanish-speaking, sombrero-wearing Mexican Kidney Bean."

With that they all burst into song, bouncing around the back seat like a bunch of happy Mexican beans.

"I wear a big Sombrero,

I always wear one,

here in the sunshine ..."

Chapter 33

There are two ways of spreading light:

to be the candle or the mirror that reflects it.

Edith Wharton 1862-1937

Siobhan and Jean had spent many lengthy calls planning for the big day.

George would be monitored by Ian. The nurses demanded regular updates so they could track progress. The level of co-ordination was impressive and proved to be flawless on the day.

But it was not the day of the Transplant. It was the Day of the Award Ceremony.

"It's soooooo exciting." Jean was like a skippy teenager, off to her first dance. She had been the ringleader at the very outset and her energy was unstoppable. Dave may have said *'flaming annoying, she speaks of nothing else'*, but true to type, with still waters that run deep, he kept schtum. He knew when to smile and agree at the right time.

The day began in earnest with a champagne reception at the Mayfair Hotel. They took a flute of champagne each from another *'nice young man'*, according to Jean. They scanned the room, checking outfits ranging from just-come-from-the-pub to full Ascot Ladies' Day outfits with fascinators all a-bobble. They had got it just right, having made an effort but not desperate or showy, which relaxed them both. After twenty minutes of just standing about, they got a bit bored, truth be told. They found a bench seat in the foyer to await their summons.

"C'mon, let's go exploring," said Siobhan, dragging a reluctant Jean with her. Siobhan stole a peek through to the Dining Room, whispering back to Jean keeping lookout behind her. "Oooh, very posh. OMG, a great big stage and lights and everything. Table decorations are spectacular – set for loads of tables for 10 people so maybe 100 to 150 people."

"Why are we whispering?" asked Jean.

"Dunno, work with me on this – it's not every day I get to be so nosey and not get told off."

The Master of Ceremonies, Tim Vincent, boomed across the waiting audience. They both jumped, startled, thinking they had been rumbled, then giggled, realising it was the announcement for dinner. Once the dining room was full and hushed for a second time, Tim gave a short introduction outlining the origin of the awards, thanking Gloria for her patronage and raising a round of applause for all of the inspirational women in the audience.

"I warn you – you will need your tissues this afternoon. I have read the nominations and your personal accounts give an insight to your challenges. There are some heart-warming stories that make you realise what women go through to keep children happy, keep families together and fight overwhelming illnesses. We are here to honour and recognise some of those inspiring women."

He then read out each category and a summary of each nominee. Siobhan was entered for one of six categories.

Each category was awarded in the lull between courses, following a well-oiled schedule. The winner was described with the view of their worthiness summarised by a member of the judging panel. In excited anticipation, the audience looked around for who it could be, before the MC called out the name with a fanfare and explosion of ticker tape. The winner, awkward in the glare of attention, made her way through the tables, delayed by hugs and kisses, to step up onto the stage.

The feeling in the room, buoyed by nervousness and a glass of champagne or two, was light and joyful. The audience arrived full of expectation and came to smile. As each winner was crowned, they revelled in the warmth and support that was rarely felt so powerfully. It restored faith in humanity – its capacity to love, to bring happiness and care for others in need. Each person swam with the current, adding their heartbeat to the noise of the clapping and cheering.

Gloria Hunniford, the Irish TV presenter, rose to her feet and instantly got a storm of applause and cheering. She waved the noise down.

"I'm too old to leap onto the podium. You do not want an elderly leprechaun falling over the stairs. I'll say some words from here."

With humility and the pain of her loss bare for all to see, she introduced the Caron Keating Foundation, set up by her in memory of her daughter, tragically lost to cancer. It was every parent's nightmare to outlive their children, so she drew empathy from every mother in the room for her loss. She skilfully moved the focus away from herself to praise the nominees and her admiration for their achievements.

Jean had liked Gloria before meeting her, warming to her down to earth TV persona. But in person, she could do no wrong in Jean's eyes. Jean whispered to Siobhan in the darkness, "She's just absolutely lovely and chats to everyone. She is such a mum first and celebrity second. It really choked me up when she was speaking from the heart about her daughter. You don't get many people in the public eye willing to show their loss. Can you believe she even asked for the honour of having her photo taken with the winners?"

"Is she your new best friend?" asked Siobhan with a smile, deserving the poked tongue she got in response.

When the overall winners' turn came, the room hushed in anticipation. Siobhan and Jean held hands under the table with everything crossed. As Gloria opened the gold envelope in true Hollywood style, they both wished ...

As the announcement rang out, the audience cheered and clapped and whooped in appreciation. They stood to recognise the winner as she made her way to the stage. Under the dazzling light, she looked uncomfortable and self-conscious, reluctant to be the centre of attention. She visibly squirmed as accolades and compliments were heaped upon her. She had fostered over forty children in her lifetime, giving each the love and safety they had missed out on. During this time, she had fought her own battles with cancer, and you were left with the impression that the war was not over. For perhaps the only time in her life in the spotlight, her glowing smile filled the room, letting all see her humility and selflessness. The standing ovation went on for some time, and finally Siobhan and Jean sat down, eyes damp, hands sore and emotionally shaky.

It had been the perfect end to a special day.

Ian and George had arranged to meet Siobhan and Jean in a Starbucks around the corner. By time they got there, the girls were sipping coffee and a little subdued. George dived in.

"Hiya Nan, Hiya Mum – did you win?" George's enthusiastic question was, to Siobhan, the wrong one but she tried to keep it from her reply, aware that it needed a level of maturity to realise that just being there was a privilege. She hoped George picked up the hint in her reply.

"No, Chugs, I didn't, but then I didn't expect to. There were many people there who deserved to win more than me. We had a great time, though."

"I would have loved you to win, Shiv," Jean said to Siobhan, then adding her views for everyone, "But the winner truly deserved it. She was such an ordinary person but she had done so much for so many for so long – and do you know what? I reckon that's the first time anyone has even noticed."

"Didn't Winston Churchill say something like that?" piped up Ian, being a smartarse and suitably ignored by George. "Did *you* have a good time, Shiv?" He emphasised the 'you', as he wanted Siobhan's take on the day.

"Yes we did, it was lovely. The meal and the awards ceremony was really well done – just like the Oscars but more crying and real tears, not just actress ones."

And Gloria Hunniford, she is just so nice," Jean added, still bubbling with excitement. "The charity auction was daft though – what's the point of selling something for £1000 when most of the audience wouldn't have £100 spare?"

"So will you be on the telly or in the papers?" Ian wanted to know, proud of his wife.

"I doubt it. I got the feeling only the overall winner gets to be the poster girl. It's a bit of a shame, as all the people there have wonderful stories to tell but would never tell it themselves. I know it's a cliché, but taking part was far more important than winning. We had a great day, some free champagne, a giggle and bit of a blub at the end, didn't we Jean?"

Jean nodded and smiled in agreement. As they were leaving, Siobhan felt Ian's hand squeezing her shoulder and her heart swelled with love as he leaned forward to whisper in her ear,

"You get the award for me."

Photos III

29: Me at Hampton Court

Dad and I were on a trip out one afternoon to take photos for my portfolio. Usually I take all the pictures but I let Dad take this one of me. He has focused the perspective lines as a tunnel on my head. Good work!

30: Gloria Hunniford at Awards

Gloria Hunniford, the TV celebrity hosting the Inspirational Mother of the Year awards in 2013. The image behind is of her daughter, Caron Keating, whose death in 2004, from cancer, inspired the Awards of the same name.

31: Mum and me night before transplant

Dad took this one, too, on my camera. It was a memorable but pricey family meal out the night before the transplant operations for Mum and me. Neither of us looks at all nervous.

32: Mum and Nan at Awards

Two very excited ladies. Mum and Nan, who have both brushed up very well, waiting for the awards ceremony to begin. Mum had been shortlisted in the Inspirational Mother category, following Nan's secret nomination.

33: Tower Bridge from the Shard

I took this one from the Shard. As you can see the views are spectacular but difficult to capture the scale of the panorama. One day I will go back at dawn or dusk when the light will have more colour and the shadows longer.

Chapter 34

I'm so bad I make medicine sick.

Muhammad Ali

If you were to shake me, I swear I would rattle like a medicine bottle. People are amazed at the number and quantity of drugs that organ transplant patients must take every day.

Remembering more than three things isn't what I am good at, so I have signs all around the house to remind me to take my tablets on time. I also have a dosette box which is a tablet grid with four compartments per day for the seven days of the week – so I can tell what I have taken and never miss a handful. It's my responsibility to pack it every week. So far so good, as I must take Tacrolimus on time every day for the rest of my life. TAC and mycophenolate mofetil are both immunosuppressants. These are the most important drugs I take, as they stop my immune system from rejecting Mum's kidney.

As my immune system is less efficient than most people's, I'm more likely to get infections. Some transplant patients in places like Thailand and India wear face masks like surgeons do. That seems a bit much to me. I do, though, have to take co-trimoxazole which is an antibiotic. It is always in my system so if a bug does attack then the defence is waiting for it.

I also took a corticosteroid called prednisolone, which also helps with the immunsuppression. Just after the transplant I was on a very high dose for four days only and then it stopped. I was told that it could give me mood swings so knowing I get anxious sometimes, I don't want it, thank you. There's an added benefit that I will avoid chipmunk cheeks, which is a common downside of weight gain from corticosteroids.

Some time ago when I was on dialysis, I took a blood pressure drug, amlodipine. Now though, I don't need any heart drugs. I do have half a tablet of aspirin a day to thin my blood so it can get through the repaired blood vessels going in and out of my kidney.

After the transplant I took a diuretic, frusemide, to help with fluid retention. I was pumped up by 3-4 litres during the operation and this helped remove some of it whilst my new kidney was getting up to speed.

On dialysis, I used to have 'epo' , which helped my body to produce red blood cells. This is the stuff Lance Armstrong used to help him cheat at seven Tours de France. Now my kidney is working, my haemoglobin levels are rising naturally – so this is good news.

I still get quite tired, but not as bad as when I was on dialysis. Back then I reckon I could get a gold medal for sleeping – I could sleep for 12 hours a night and still feel shattered the next day. I can still fall asleep in the car at the drop of a hat and I do enjoy an afternoon nap – but then who doesn't, given the chance.

I've had it drummed into me how careful I need to be. The tablets are my responsibility and I am the only one who touches my dosset box. Mum and Dad check it, but it's my mouth that the tablets go in, so I am the most careful.

The consequences of getting it wrong are all mine too. If my TAC level is too high then toxic damage can occur to my new kidney. A knock-on effect is that my creatinine level is pushed up, leading to tiredness, no appetite and vomiting. If my TAC is too low, then it leaves my kidney vulnerable to *attack by my own immune system. You see it's a fine balance.*[72]

Another odd thing is kidney pain. Kay told me that I may get aches and pains around my new kidney, and to tell someone if I do. She gave me the science bit, that no nerves came with the transplanted kidney so it can't feel pain as such, but kidney pain is still possible. She reckons it's due to swelling and inflammation around the new kidney. She told me that's another big warning signal to look out for, along with high blood pressure and weight gain. All three may mean a suspected rejection episode.[73] *That means my new kidney is in trouble.*

What does the future hold? Dunno really, not thought about it much. I must have heard the phrase 'if you look after your kidney, it will look after you' about a million times. I do not think of it as Mum's kidney, it is mine now. I hope that doesn't sound ungrateful. People ask me if I said thank you to Mum – as though simply two words would do the job. So I don't think I have said so in the way people would expect. At the time, our eyes met between the two of us with no-one else around, and there was a knowingness we recognised. Ask Mum, I bet she says the same. But it is mine now and my responsibility to look after it.

I feel that responsibility and I get reminded of it every day by Mum or Dad or both together or one repeating what the other told me two minutes ago. Every day, I have to take my meds on time, always carry a drink bottle so I drink 2.5 litres, eat fruit and salad, only one hot chocolate (no cream or marshmallows), do some exercise

---

[72] *Evelina: A Guide to Kidney Transplantation in Children.* Grainne M. Walsh
[73] Evelina: A Guide to Kidney Transplantation in Children. Grainne M. Walsh

292

(walk/bike/swim), not worry the scars on my legs, not lift anything heavy and make sure I don't whack my tum. Are you bored by this list? I am. I hope Mum and Dad will lighten up and trust me. There is no point kicking and screaming about it – they are a formidable tag team and I'm not after a fight. I just want my parents to be happy, so I don't say what I feel sometimes, and do what they say as best as I can.

The doctors tell me that my new kidney will last 15-20 years if I look after it. I HAVE GOT THE MESSAGE – ALL RIGHT! That would make me thirty years old. That is ancient and so far into the future, I can't imagine it. I have no idea what I'll be doing then. Hopefully I will be driving a Bugati Veyron and be a world famous photographer.

At one point, I felt robbed of my ambitions but now I have them back. Don't get me wrong, my ambitions weren't clear even to me, but I felt vaguely that all options were open to me. All my bits would work – I would have energy and an appetite to go for them. On dialysis I felt less than whole, somehow fitting in with what everyone said was best for me and tied to that bloody machine – literally. Now all the restrictions are gone. I feel I just need to be worthy of all the effort others have put in for me.

I have not reached an opinion yet but I need to recalibrate (extra mark word again!) my ambitions...

Siobhan, in a reflective moment, thought back to the idea of mindfulness that Ian had raised, rather unsuccessfully. Could it be useful for George after all? If mindfulness is a way of creating enough space in the mind to allow you to be less irritable, more patient and clearer in how you communicate, you inevitably become more aware of others. You listen to what they are saying and understand them better. Could she say that George had matured and learnt this skill?

Chapter 35

The reality remains that there are still a lot of hurdles to cross before babies start to receive the MenB vaccine at two, four and twelve months of age, as the Joint Committee on Vaccination and Immunisation (JCVI) recommended at its meeting in February 2014. The Department of Health is negotiating with the manufacturer, and arrangements will have to be made with GPs for its implementation. Parents and health professionals will need support and information as the vaccine is rolled out.

Currently in the UK and Ireland, stocks of the vaccine (brand name Bexsero) have been made available privately, which means that people who can pay can get it. The vaccine is also available free of charge to people in the UK with medical conditions that increase their risk of the disease.

Results from the vaccine trials are very encouraging, showing that the vaccine triggers a strong immune response in infants, toddlers and adolescents.[74] Studies of circulating MenB strains, looking at how well they match the vaccine, have predicted that it will cover approximately 88% of MenB circulating in the UK.[75]

The actual proportion of cases prevented will depend on other things too, including how widely the vaccine is offered and taken up, whether it prevents the bacteria from

---

[74] 1.Gossger, N., et al., Immunogenicity and tolerability of recombinant serogroup B meningococcal vaccine administered with or without routine infant vaccinations according to different immunisation schedules: a randomized controlled trial. JAMA, 2012. 307(6): p. 573-82.

[75] Frosi G, et al., Bactericidal antibody against a representative epidemiological meningococcal serogroup B panel confirms that MATS underestimates 4CMenB vaccine strain coverage. Vaccine, 2013. Epub ahead of print.

being carried and passed on as well as protecting from disease, how long protection lasts, and whether it works sufficiently well in all age groups.

Real-world experience of using Bexsero is growing. Nearly 17,000 students in the US were vaccinated in response to an outbreak of MenB disease at Princeton University in late 2013 and the University of California, Santa Barbara in early 2014. In the UK, the Public Health Agency monitors all cases of meningitis, looking for trends and potential outbreaks. In George's case, the PHA arranged for all family members to have prophylactic antibiotic tablets. They also wrote to George's school to raise awareness among staff, pupils and parents and stimulate greater vigilance towards symptoms.

So you would think getting vaccinated for MenB would be perfectly doable. Well, no – not at all.

The price has not been agreed and it is taking months to negotiate. The wrangling between Novartis, the Swiss drug manufacturer and the Department of Health makes depressing headline news.[76] The deadlock needs to be broken – it's now almost nine months since the JCVI made their recommendation for the introduction of the vaccine for babies, and three and a half months since negotiations started.[77] The focus must be on the human impact of this delay, not the accusations and counter-accusations that are flying around. The chief executive of the Meningitis Now charity,[78] Sue Davie, who is quoted in the *Independent* article, makes a good point when she says: *"How long can it*

---

[76] The Independent. 20th November 2014. James Cusikk-Health Correspondent. *Wrangling over Men B vaccine may cost hundreds of lives*
[77] As of November 2014
[78] From http://www.meningitisnow.org/about-us/news/end-the-wrangling/

take two parties to negotiate on one product, especially when that product will save lives and prevent disability?"

In the meantime, the NHS list price is £75 per dose (you need 2-3 doses depending on age) but you can pay out of your own wallet, provided you hassle your GP to get it for you.

The immunisation program for babies at two months will come into play in time. But for George's adolescent age group, there is no current recommendation for adolescents to be vaccinated. The JCVI concluded that there was not enough evidence about the extent to which the MenB vaccine would stop teenagers from carrying and transmitting the bug, nor how long vaccination would directly protect this age group.

The most sobering, most saddening point is that there have been 1,000 cases of Meningitis B since the vaccine was licensed. We are fast approaching the second anniversary of that licensing. Every day brings new cases.

Time lost is lives lost.

Chapter 36

With your gift, my life reborn.

Anon

George and Ian were sitting at a booth in Yo! Sushi on the South Bank, just a short walk along from St Thomas'. They sat inside to avoid the bright sun of a glorious summer day. George's bright blue hoodie made his eyes look startlingly vivid, or was it the light reflected from the river captured in them? The sense of déjà vu was real– the same restaurant, the jazzy bowls on the conveyor, the bright sun, walking slowly through the bustling crowd all felt familiar.

"Hey George, what were we doing a year ago? Your memory is brilliant!"

George's eyebrows met as he accessed his renowned memory but nothing came. With a lull in their conversation, Ian drifted with his own thoughts. It all seemed so vivid; the fear and panic he knew were easily accessed just below the surface. He felt his emotional pool was always full to the brim, and just recalling the words *'the sickest person in the hospital'* invited an overspill. But the reunion of mother and son was his most precious memory making him swell with pride.

He thought of a different reunion, for George now with his former self. Would they be one and the same or strangers?

He lost the thought but he knew the reality is that George is back – the real George, the big-hearted selfless one, the quirky sense of humour, the back-at-yer with his brothers, the slo-mo George, the nutty professor and the nerdy expert George. They are all there to make us laugh, drive us nuts, amaze us with facts only George can recall, but most of all, humble us with his strength, resilience and care for others. He has a calm presence now, less anxious, as though he has knowledge held only by him. He knows that whatever challenges life brings him, he can take it on, knowing that it will be small beer compared to what he has already faced. It is the opposite to the pinnacle of a professional sportsman, in that nothing can replace the exhilaration of scoring in front of your home crowd and that life ever more will be washed out, never to scale the peaks again. Instead for George, he has plumbed the darkest depths, seen the far horizon and come out the other side to a beautiful spring day.

"Do you realise, almost a year ago, we came here, with you in a wheelchair and we sat outside? You still had feeding tubes up your nose and your legs were heavily bandaged. You couldn't walk as you had lost all the skin on your feet. Remember it now?"

"Sure do," said George noncommittally and looking down at his feet, either in boredom or not wanting to dredge up a painful memory.

It seems so long ago to me, like sepia photos from a different age. I was a different person then. I was so anxious and worried all the time. Some of it was my own doing, worrying about stuff, but I did think would I ever be better, would I lead a normal life, would I ever get out of this wheelchair? I remember people looking at me like I was a freak or something. Everyone else was having a great time and there was me in a wheelchair. Food tastes so much better now, none of the metallic taste pre-transplant. I notice it most with food like sushi, which has such a clean taste.

I feel so much more confident now, less dependent. I still get the odd phase where I struggle to concentrate, but they are much shorter and I can get myself out of them. I am tough, me. I know I am, after what I've been through and survived. So whatever life throws at me, I can sort it. It can't be any worse than the last fourteen months. Best of all, I am me again, just George and I'm comfortable with that.

I have no idea where this will take me but I know I am ready to move on. The lyrics[79] of my Number Three favourite song say it best.

> Feeling my way through the darkness
> Guided by a beating heart
> I can't tell where the journey will end
> But I know where it starts.

To break George out of his introspection, Ian asked without really thinking, "So, fella, what was the worst bit and the best bit of the last year?"

"Worst bit, has to be intensive care."

Ian would not let it lie. "So, what bit exactly?"

"Shitting myself every ten minutes – well, you asked."

Ian was unimpressed with the distasteful image over a mealtime. Of all the things that have happened to George, this was one thing he remembers? He was not expecting poetry, but on reflection he accepted the absence of dignity, lack of control and sheer unpleasantness would be aspects that would stay with a teenage lad. He moved the conversation on with the second part of his question. "And the best bit?"

---

[79] Lyrics from Wake Me Up by Avicii. Permission sought from Warner Chappell Music Inc.

George stared out across the river, past the strolling crowds, past the busy river boats, toward Big Ben, his beacon. His face lifted and he smiled broadly.

"Just being with you guys." He did not say any more. Father and son just looked in each other's eyes and they knew.

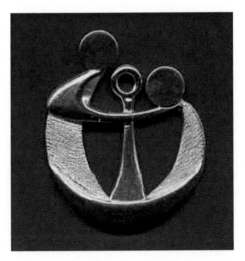

80

---

80 The crossed anchor is a symbol of hope. The Egyptian Ankh symbol represents zest for life.

Epilogue

Georgina

Georgina spent the summer of George's transplant somewhere in Southern Italy, touring for three months in a derelict VW camper van called Teresa[81] as it is small, blue and white like Mother Teresa. It is probably the cleanest and most meticulously tidy camper van in existence. After five unbroken years working at the intensity of concentration needed at her level, and with the emotional roller coaster of a Paediatric Intensive Care Unit, Georgina needed a well-earned break.

Picture the scene, Georgina at a beach side bar sipping a cocktail as the sun dips to the horizon. The pick-up-sticks jumble of straws in a tray at the end of the bar has caught her eye. Checking to make sure no-one is watching her, Georgina steps forward to straighten all the straws...

Catherine

Catherine moved on from her traineeship in Kingston to a practice in the West Country. She has seen two children since with symptoms suggesting meningitis. She has been wrong both times, as their flu-like colds cleared up within a few days. She does not mind being wrong and hopes to be wrong many times more, as it allows her to sleep at night.

She got married to a very lucky chap, according to George. Although George is no longer in contact, Catherine will remember that fateful afternoon for the rest of her life. She can be very proud of what she did.

---

[81] This quip comes from the comedian Milton Jones and has been misappropriated.

Ian

Ian spent the remainder of his 6-month sabbatical without a To Do list, which was a new experience. In his more spare time than usual, he has become a gardener – well, he plants things but then after that, he is not too sure. He is still trying to master the French language but persists in brutalising it instead. He returned to work in January 2015.

Siobhan

After the transplant, Siobhan returned to teaching at St Paul's, but – for now – gives hand stands and cartwheels a miss. She keeps Ian and George on a healthy diet, herself only drinking wine diluted with water, which ruins Ian's schemes. She is onto George's every sniffle, slight temperature or loss of appetite like a shot – her finely-tuned instincts proving to be right every time.

Five months after the transplant, Siobhan received a letter from Ian Trenholm, Chief Executive of the NHS. Quoting his words, *'offering someone (George) the opportunity to enjoy better health and an improved quality of life with a successful transplant is a very special gift'*. He enclosed a silver pin badge, designed by Liz Welch. It incorporates the crossed anchor as a symbol of hope and the ancient Egyptian Ankh symbol to represent zest for life. The designer aimed to distill the essence of the gift of a kidney down to two things – hope and life.

Siobhan's health barely registered a second thought, as she is back to her pre-donor days. A routine blood test at the GP's was anything but, when Siobhan was asked to come in to see her doctor. With a 57% kidney function, the GP expected to see high blood pressure and protein in the urine, both markers of chronic kidney failure, but oddly, neither was present. A nervy two hours passed before Siobhan called Michelle, the transplant co-coordinator, to be reassured that 57% was brilliant for a kidney donor and nothing to worry about. It is all about perspective.

George

George's transplant took place on 25th July 2014 and his future looks very promising. He has continued to be a model patient. He has had two spells as an in-patient, mainly to keep fluids and nutrition under control whilst fighting off infections which took longer than usual to shake off.

He has volunteered for three Clinical Trials: a long-term study with the acronym CHIPS, intended to investigate the impacts of meningitis and its behavioural links; and a second study focused on exploring blood pressure changes during dialysis, hoping to shed light on profiling that the most experienced nurses like Kay use. The output was more refined treatment protocols to guide the rate of fluid removal and replacement on dialysis. The third study compared blood pressure differences during dialysis between the peripheral and central measurement points.

Physically, things are going great for George – the battery of tests, that showed the impacts of the meningococcal infection having been contained, proved to be true over time. So the visible damage to his skin, most obvious on his shins, is now fading. With a bit of hair growth from adolescence, the scarring will not be noticeable, even to a self-conscious teenager. The damage that can't be seen, where bleeding took place deep in the body or in delicate organs, has had no lasting effect, so hearing, sight and balance are all back to normal.

Best of all, George is back – the real George. He is bogged down in the joys of GCSEs, which will determine what future career options are open to him. He is desperate to go skiing next winter and keeps dropping the idea into conversation, as conniving teenagers do.

George has asked what does it take to be a Hells Angel?

THE END[82]

---

[82] At the time of publication, the wrangling over availability & pricing of Bexsero has been resolved and a price agreed. But Bexsero is not widely available. It is still true that time lost is lives lost.

No changes to the laws surrounding organ donation have been made. Doctors are planning to offer organs from 'high-risk' donors such as cancer victims and drug addicts to seriously ill patients because of a desperate shortage of healthy donors.

Acknowledgements

The phrase 'the author would like to acknowledge' does not come anywhere close to the depth of gratitude we have for the healthcare staff who have done so much for George and us. Being a superb professional at your job is one thing, but to do it with human warmth and compassion is truly special and that is what helped us most.

I apologise unreservedly, as I have not listed everyone who has cared for George. The prompt action of the team in the Emergency Department at Kingston Hospital undoubtedly saved George's life. The PICU team at St George's Hospital cared for us all with the greatest of skill in our darkest times. We were welcomed by the team at the Evelina Hospital into a unique & special family. We count our blessings to this day.

Out of professional courtesy, I have changed the names of many people below. Unfortunately, it makes a nonsense of thanking people publically. It is our sincere and personal gratitude that matters for those who know who you are.

George's PICU Nurses

Georgina, Claire, Sophie, Beth, Rowena, Holly and Izzy.

Evelina Nurses

Mel, Tinu, Becca, Georgina, Georgie (Blonde one, Bubbly one), Katie (Little), Kay, Emily, Rachel, Esther, Lauren, Aaron, Sheila and Carmen.

Michelle – transplant co-ordinator.

Roisin – transplant specialist.

Doctors

Katherine (GP), Jonathan (PICU)

Stewart, Bahdri, Allyn (ECH Renal Unit)

Mac (Surgeon).

Caroline, Dean, Amy (Beach Ward)

Barbara, Paul, Laura (Talking Doctors and Psychologists)

Inger (Plastic Surgeon)

The description of disease and its treatment are as accurate as I could make them. I would be ashamed of any errors in such a sensitive area, so if there are any, then the shame is all mine due to a lack of understanding or listening. Anyone seeking more information on meningitis should go to the MRF website or Meningitis Now website. Similarly the National Kidney Federation website is a source of expertise on anything to do with dialysis and transplantation.

Our trusted friends who offered their help unconditionally, cooked for us when the complaints over my cooking were loud, and showed their true and treasured friendship in many ways.

Sarah T., Sarah B., Sally, Grainne and Diana were my sounding-board to review this book in its early rough drafts. Sam Jordison from Galley Beggar Press was a superb editor who truly empathised with the story George had to tell. As a first-time writer I was – and still am – very needy, to have a fragile confidence nurtured. I needed people I trusted to tell me what worked and what does not, and put it in words that did not leave me a wimpy wreck.

Gail and Tim, who shared the same experience as us, with Gail as Tim's donor. Their dilemma was what to tell us and what to leave out. They got it just right.

My Mum and Dad, Jean and Dave, and mother-in-law Margaret, have been brilliant. They have always been supportive in many ways; for good advice, sometimes just listening and being there. I think they have built a special bond with George.

My biggest thanks go to my wife Siobhan, who in reality is my co-author. I say this as we lived every moment together, so I had the luxury of discussing every element of judgment, appropriateness, and accurate recall of events. I understood how it felt for another person whose emotional depth is far greater than mine.

Author Q&A

What is *Better Angels* about?

Better Angels is about a teenage boy of fourteen years old who contracts a life threatening infection, his fight to return to normality and deal with the impacts that will persist for the rest of his life. George is your average teenager, leading a normal life. He and his family have to cope with a switch from normality to near-death in the space of five hours. We see George find a maturity that he is forced to take on, and his parents search for positives at the bleakest of times. Few parents can claim to understand teenagers, but telling the story with George's voice may show some of the dilemmas they face. The cliché that *'ordinary people do extraordinary things'* is borne out in the people that rally to help George. These better angels gave rise to the title of the book and it is their story, their compassion and selflessness that inspires. Despite the gruelling subject matter, I hope readers will be uplifted by this story.

What inspired you to write *Better Angels*?

The story is a very personal one. It happened to us and we wanted to tell it. My worry was that it was too personal and it would have limited resonance for others. But the more we talked, we realised that it is a universal story — hero overcomes adversity, initially alone, but then with a cast of others on his journey to find himself.

My reasons for wanting to write Better Angels changed over time. To begin, with my motives were simple and uncomplicated.

1.   **To tell the full story**. The meningitis charities do a phenomenal job of fund raising, research, lobbying and publicising the impacts of the disease. Despite this, unless you have experienced it directly, or know someone who

knows someone, then it is one of life's worries that you switch off from. The Patient Stories on the charities' websites are harrowing – if you want to end in tears on a rainy afternoon, go there and read a selection. George is blessed compared to some – and we say that in the full knowledge now of what could have been. But those powerful real-life stories are a fraction of what happens, and fail to explain the life-long impacts. We so wanted to convey what it felt like to have your world blown apart, to cope with the aftermath and find a path forward with the help and support of so many others.

2. **To tell it from George's viewpoint**. I wanted to give George a voice and tell the story from what it was like for him as a young adult. Was he the same person afterwards, would he lead a normal life, what psychological time bombs were ticking away unseen?

But the more the story developed in its re-telling, the more opinionated I became. Not to claim that I could be a righter-of-wrongs, but I at least wanted to highlight some areas where we could be better. Perhaps a little of this campaigning zeal comes across!

3. **To tell a good news NHS story for a change.** The NHS is a political issue in the UK. There tend to be handful of template NHS stories reported in the press – elderly relative let down by NHS so Party A are to blame, new funding for NHS so Party B takes the credit, new miracle cure discovered, standards falling as doctors/nurses are overworked and underpaid. I wanted to give our experience of the people that looked after us. *Better Angels* is the story of some truly inspiring and selfless human beings who do this as their job but give all of themselves.

4. **To rattle some cages and debunk some myths**. In the UK, 600 people contract meningitis B each year and one in ten die, while one in twenty suffer a life-long disability.

Yet 50% of those presenting with the infection are sent home by their GP with their symptoms dismissed as a self-limiting cold. In Jan 2013, just three months before George fell ill, the first vaccine for Meningitis B, Bexsero was licensed, but by a cruel quirk of fate, only as paid-for-medicine and not freely available on the NHS. So in a different circumstance George could have avoided the infection, and also the 60 people who died in 2013 would still be here. Even now, the awareness of the availability of the vaccine is low and a national vaccination program is slow off the blocks. I think what I would do now if I were a parent with under-twos? I would want to know now and not find out through experience.

5. **To make us all challenge our views on kidney donation**. Other than carry a Donor Card since my student days, I have never given organ donation a second thought. I had no experience of waiting lists, knew of no-one in UK needing a transplant, had no ethical view that had taken consideration beyond ten seconds. I was staggered that, for kidneys alone, we could rid ourselves of the waiting list and meet demand within two years – all by a change in attitude.

About halfway through writing the book, I had a bit of an epiphany. *'What use is this book? How can it help others?'* So with a bit more understanding from retrospection, I refreshed my view.

6. **To make the book *useful.***All of us have experienced illness to different degrees already, or unfortunately, will do in the future. A miserable but realistic statement. There are no right answers or optimal behaviours for coping with such eventualities. Our experience – which I hope comes through – was that sometimes we coped well but at others we floundered, overcome with stress, confusion, fear or simply just not knowing what to do. I hope the reader will judge us, *'yes, that was all you could do'* or even, *'perhaps if you had taken*

a step back ...' and that will be useful learning and possibly preparation. It is ok for the wheels to fall off, it is no failing to struggle and there are no right answers, or even any answers, sometimes. We never had counselling as parents – maybe this story would make others consider if this was wise.

My last reason for writing this story is unashamedly a very selfish and personal one. George is my hero and as a proud dad, I want people to know why he is so special. It is rare that we truly say what we think of others. I can think of a handful of instances in life where we actually do in full public honesty – perhaps a Best Man's Speech, a Lifetime Award or, grimly, an Obituary. This is my one attempt to open my heart, tell him he has my respect and admiration, and for George to hear it.

Is *Better Angels* a true story?

Yes – I suspect you won't believe me but the Hells Angels did visit George, Spiderman and Superman really do clean the windows at the Evelina, and my wife Siobhan is always right.

There are a handful of changes to the timeline and sequence of events, just to make the story flow better. The participants of some conversations may have been altered, but the content is the same. I only used the first names of all the healthcare professionals out of courtesy, but I am sure they will recognise themselves and allow me some latitude with representing their thoughts and words.

The story is essentially a novel that is based on the retelling of a true story. A dramatisation of real life, if you like. It is a true story, so I can't deviate too far, but I did allow myself to extrapolate, provided it was not too far. As an example, in early drafts, I did have Siobhan winning the award for Inspirational Mother of the Year, thinking it made for a better ending. On reflection I took it out and reverted to the truth, that Siobhan was one of ten shortlisted and a runner-up. It was a step too far to change the truth. It would have been disrespectful to the judges and, most importantly, to the fully-deserving actual winner. Also, I'd lost sight of the fact that the 'gong' was irrelevant compared to the important story – the human element.

Where did the title *Better Angels* come from?

The title *Better Angels* comes from Richard Nixon's Inaugural Speech in 1969, quoted on page 5. I loved the sentiment that in troubled times, there are better angels who are among us or within us. We just need to look for them.

'Tricky Dicky' may seem an odd choice to put up there as a paragon of wisdom. He is hardly in the league of Nelson Mandela, Pope Francis et al. Despite this, Nixon did articulate his ideals and vision, but perhaps, like other complex and flawed characters, he failed to live up to them in life. When he looked back on his life and what historians would remember him for, there are no doubt many things Nixon would want to do differently. As parents, we felt the same in dealing with situations we had never faced before, and hope never to again.

Did your professional background help in the writing of *Better Angels*?

Not really. I suppose working in drug research and being familiar with how healthcare professionals operate meant that it was an environment I was comfortable in. So I was very willing to seek advice, and having ready access to experts was helpful. Unlike, perhaps, my parents' generation, who put doctors on pedestals, the majority of us today have access to web-based information sources. So we are better at asking questions, working through the treatment options and so are fully involved in medical decisions. Despite this, I can picture a cartoon of a doctor looking over his spectacles at a chippy patient and uttering the put-down: *'Yes madam, we both have access to the World Wide Web but only one of us has a Medical Degree.'*

How did you decide what information was crucial to include in *Better Angels*?

I really struggled with this. My tendency is to chuck everything in and let the reader wade through it all. Fortunately, I had a group of friends willing to review early drafts and cut out all the stuff that did not add to the core of the story. They are all still friends, but I have many scars.

Do you believe all children should be vaccinated for meningitis B?

Yes, absolutely.

What is your favourite line/paragraph in the book?

The last-but-one line – "Just being with you guys." There is nothing intellectual or deep here, just a simple top-of-head response from George about what matters most to him. To play armchair philosopher for a second, what else in life is there other than to take pleasure from being with the people you love?

Have you been a writer all your life?

I wish!

No, this is my first real attempt at writing a novel. I have always written a lot, but nothing that anyone would willingly read or get enjoyment from! I was nicknamed Tolkien by a previous boss for my ability to make business reports into *Lord of the Rings* tomes of unrelenting detail. Several rounds of brutal editing beat this out of me. I like reading books written by journalists – they have a clear, punchy style with no frivolity in how they communicate. So that became the style I wanted to have – so do not expect any poetry from me, ever.

I have always had the ambition to write a book, but doubted my capabilities. I have started several times, if you can call buying a bound journal and a new pen and filling a dozen pages a start. But it never went anywhere and I gave up. In truth, I never found a story I felt strongly enough about to persevere, to learn, to rewrite, to seek help and to get to The End. This mattered to me and I had to finish it.

I loved writing this book. A fair chunk of it was written sitting on Beach Ward with George during his five-hour dialysis sessions. I want to write another, but not sure on what yet...

A Note on the Author

Ian Birks has worked in the pharmaceutical industry for 25 years and has just finished a six-month sabbatical. He returned to work in January 2015. He lives with his family in South-West London.